Bow Porcelain

circa 1748~1774

Bow Porcelain Figures

circa 1748~1774

PETER BRADSHAW

BARRIE & JENKINS

LONDON

TO MY WIFE, MARY

First published in Great Britain in 1992 by
Barrie & Jenkins Ltd
20 Vauxhall Bridge Road
London SW1V 2SA

Copyright © Peter Bradshaw 1992

A catalogue record for this book is available from the British Library.

ISBN 0-7126-5402-X

Designed by David Fordham

Typeset by Servis Filmsetting Ltd, Manchester

Printed and bound in Singapore by Kyodo Printing

(*Page 1*) (B59) *Standing Turk* 8in
(20.3cm) c.1755
(*Page 2*) (C65) *Fortune Telling Group*,
after Watteau 10¾in (27.3cm) c.1765

CONTENTS

IN DECEMBER 1744 THOMAS FRYE AND EDWARD HEYLYN, later named as two of the four proprietors of the Bow manufactory, registered a patent for a non-phosphatic soft-paste porcelain. However, no items made from this formula have been identified and, indeed, it is unlikely any could successfully have been fired. Nevertheless, a profusion of table wares are reported to have been made at the newly established Bow factory in the fourth edition of Daniel Defoe's *Tour of Great Britain*, published in June 1748, and this information must have been gathered no later than the first quarter of that year. All of the supposedly earliest wares and sherds are constructed from a phosphatic paste that was not patented by Frye until November 1749. Some 40 per cent of bone ash was incorporated into the mix, which greatly enhanced stability during the biscuit firing and gave rise to a semi-translucent, milky-white and very strong ceramic. Bone ash was included in the body at Chelsea c.1757 and at Derby c.1770. By the turn of the century, it was incorporated into a hard-paste formula to create bone china which, with only minor modifications, remains the standard British porcelain mix to the present day. Thus, although the Bow proprietors were by no means the first to make soft-paste porcelain successfully in England, they were undoubtedly at the spearhead of ceramic research and development.

Bow, unlike its contemporary competitors on the mainland of Europe, received neither royal patronage nor government subsidy, and depended for survival upon commercial success. A sound financial base was established from the manufacture of inexpensive table wares mostly decorated with blue designs painted underglaze. Thomas Frye was later able to diversify production and issued white-sprigged, enamelled and transfer-printed wares of fine quality. Despite the risks attendant when figures were passed through the kiln, over 300 items, comprising either single models, sets or groups, were issued in little more than a quarter of a century. Many have considerable artistic merit, yet they fail to receive adequate mention in standard textbooks. Publications relating to soft-paste English figures by William King (*English Porcelain Figures of the 18th Century*, 1925), Frank Stoner (*Chelsea, Bow and Derby Porcelain Figures*, 1955), Arthur Lane (*English Porcelain Figures of the 18th Century*, 1961) and the present author (*18th Century English Porcelain Figures, 1745–1795*, 1981), illustrate fewer than 60 examples. Others concerned only with products of the Bow factory, by Frank Hurlbutt (*Bow Porcelain*, 1926) and Elizabeth Adams and David Redstone (*Bow Porcelain*, 1981, 1991) provide less generous coverage. It is true that Anton Gabszewicz (*Bow Porcelain – the Collection formed by Geoffrey Freeman*, 1982) includes photographs of some 120 models, but by his terms of reference these all relate to a single private collection, so that many rare examples are excluded and the text is necessarily rather brief.

It is to be hoped the present work will fill some of the gaps. After historical and technical introductions in Parts I and II, roughly 450 different models are described in Part III, of which about 235 are illustrated. These are presented in three chapters that correspond approximately to the periods of manufacture 1748–53, 1754–64 and 1765–74. The paucity of documentary material invalidates any attempt to draw sharp divisions between them and, when the earliest example of a model is very rare or has failed to survive, the date of first issue may be fixed too late. Further, many models continued to be made over a number of years, and contemporary examples were often mounted upon differently styled bases. Animal models are notoriously difficult to date, especially when they are left uncoloured. Here the vast majority of white ones have been tentatively allocated to the first phase of production, 1748–53, with full realisation that some may not have been created until a few years afterwards. Human models in the style of the *Muses modeller* are also included in the first period. Others, either lavishly enamelled in the late Bow palette, mounted upon elaborately sculpted bases or bearing the device of an anchor and dagger in red enamel, have been ascribed to c.1765–74, whereas the remainder by exclusion fall into the middle period, 1754–64. Differences of opinion will inevitably arise as to whether a particular model was first issued just before or after one of these date margins.

Minor differences in the size of otherwise similar figures may be due to the design of their bases, the presence or absence of bocage, or the attachment of fitments like candle-tulips or sconces. Models cast from replacement moulds may be up to one-sixth smaller than their originals, owing to shrinkage of soft paste by approximately this amount during biscuiting. When this process is repeated more than once, semi-miniature models are thereby created. Conversely, it was occasionally the practice, when a mould was beyond its useful life, to fashion a fresh master model that was larger than its precursor.

Among the most attractive Bow models are those depicting characters from the *Commedia dell'Arte* (Italian Comedy), which are reviewed in Appendix A. Others are drawn from classical mythology and are summarised in Appendix B. Some of the contemporary garments portrayed on Bow figures are described in Appendix C. The vexatious matters of reproductions, forgeries and fakes receive attention in Appendix D whilst damage and restoration are considered in Appendix E.

PETER BRADSHAW

ACKNOWLEDGEMENTS

I WISH TO THANK GEOFFREY GODDEN, who made various amendments to my manuscript and offered some valued suggestions, all of which have been incorporated. I am indebted to Peter and Shirley Neve, who photographed several items in private collections; David Thorn, who afforded me access to both his stock and private collection; Mrs Elizabeth Adams, Robert Devereux, John and Diana Mould, Mrs Margaret Newton, George Savage and Dr Bernard Watney.

I ALSO EXPRESS MY THANKS TO THE FOLLOWING DEALERS:
Hoff Antiques Ltd, 66a Kensington Church Street, London; Morris and Pamela Rowan, late of Aldbury Antiques, Blockley, near Moreton-in-Marsh; Simon Spero, 109 Kensington Church Street, London; David Thorn, 2 Fore Street, Budleigh Salterton, Devon; J. Thornton, Thornton's of Harrogate, 1 Montpellier Gardens, Harrogate; Sheila Davis of Venner's Antiques, 7 New Cavendish Street, London; Elizabeth Wise and Stafford Lorie, 27 Holland Street, London.

THE FOLLOWING KINDLY SUPPLIED PHOTOGRAPHS:
The Trustees of the British Museum, and Hugh Tait and Miss Aileen Dawson; The Honourable Simon Howard of Castle Howard; The Syndics of the Fitzwilliam Museum, Cambridge, and Miss Julia Poole; The George Gardiner Museum of Ceramic Art, Toronto, and Ms Meredith Chilton, Curator; The Trustees of the Cecil Higgins Art Gallery, Bedford, and Miss Helina Grubert, Curator and Miss Jennie Clarke; The Metropolitan Museum of Art, New York, and Ms Jessie MacNab; The Museum of Fine Arts, Boston, Massachusetts, and Ms Janice Sorkow, Assistant Curator and Miss Karen Otis; The National Museum of Ireland, Dublin, and Miss Mairead Dunlevy; The Geoffrey Freeman Collection of Bow Porcelain, on loan to Pallant House Gallery, Chichester, Mrs Norah Freeman and David Coke, Curator; Temple Newsam House, Leeds, Leeds Borough Council and Ms Sarah Nichols; The W. H. Williamson Bequest at Tullie House, Carlisle, on temporary loan to Hanley Museum, Stoke-on-Trent; The collection of Lord Bearsted at Upton House, near Banbury; J. Finlinson of the National Trust and Miss K. Willis of the Severn Regional Office; The Governors of the Victoria & Albert Museum, London, and D. M. Archer, Keeper of Ceramics and Ms Isobel Sinden; Williams College Museum of Art, Williamstown, Massachusetts, and Ms Marion Goethals; Christie Manson & Woods, St James's, London, and Anton Gabszewicz; Phillips Son & Neal, New Bond Street, London, and John Sandon; Sotheby Parke Bernet, New Bond Street, London, and Peter Williams.

NOTE
The author has devised a numbering system for all models and groups, for ease of identification. The letter A, B or C preceding the number denotes the probable first issue of the model, during the first, second or third phase of production respectively.

Plate numbers in arabic numerals refer to the models illustrated in black and white in the relevant section. Roman numerals (Col. Plate I, etc.) refer to the colour plate section between pages 128 and 129. Figure numbers refer to illustrations that appear in the body of the text and support points made therein.

PART I

HISTORY OF THE BOW PORCELAIN MANUFACTORY

1 PROPRIETORS OF THE BOW MANUFACTORY

RECORDS OF THE SUN INSURANCE COMPANY for July 1749, discovered by Mrs Elizabeth Adams,[1] name the four proprietors of the Bow manufactory as Edward Heylyn, Thomas Frye, John Weatherby and John Crowther. The omission of George Arnold came as something of a surprise but it would seem he was no more than a financial sponsor, whilst the inclusion of Weatherby and Crowther was also unexpected, for hitherto it had always been supposed they were concerned only with the wholesale trade.

George Arnold (1691–1751), son of William Arnold, a cloth merchant of Exeter, was apprenticed in that trade to John Heron of London in 1711; in 1718 he obtained the Freedom of the Haberdashers Company and served as their Master in 1735/6. He was a member of the Board of Governors and subsequently President of St Thomas's Hospital. In 1749 he was elected Alderman for the Cheap Ward, when he resided in Rood Lane in Cheapside and conducted a thriving trade there as a linen draper. His cousin, George Yeo,[2] lived in Virginia in the American Colonies, and nominated George one of two Trustees to manage his estate in his will. Later, it will be shown, a potter named André Duché claimed to have discovered a china clay in the Virginian interior called Unaker, which was one of the constituents of the Bow soft-paste porcelain patented in 1744. It would seem likely that Yeo effected the introduction of Duché to Arnold. In 1744 Arnold and Heylyn purchased buildings and land, under the jurisdiction of the Courts Baron of the Manor of Stepney,[3] located upon the west, or Middlesex, side of the river Lea. This was probably the venue where initial experimental trials were conducted into the formation of a frit porcelain, and where commercial manufacture was first established. Support for this contention is found in a passage in the fourth edition of Samuel Richardson's *Daniel Defoe's Tour of Great Britain*, published in June 1748.[4] This describes the scene as the traveller approaches Bow Bridge from the south-west: 'The first village we come to is Bow: where a large Manufactory of Porcelain is lately set up. They have already made quantities of Teacups, Saucers &c. which by some skilled persons are said to be little inferior to those imported from abroad.' The data required for this entry must have been gathered not later than the first quarter of 1748, or possibly the last quarter of 1747, by which time the Bow factory must have been operational. The absence in the Bow Parish Register of any mention of a 'Potter' until 1748 may simply reflect the earlier practice of omitting to record the occupation of the father in baptismal and burial entries.[5]

In 1750, Arnold and Heylyn acquired additional land on the Middlesex site, which may have been used as an annexe to the main factory, by now transferred across to the Essex side of the river Lea. The Poor Law Account Book for West Ham at this time refers to the new factory as 'Alderman Arnold & Co.' but by the following year this was amended to 'Mssrs. Porcelain Company', and subsequently appears as 'Frye and Company'.[6] On 25 June 1751 the *London Daily Advertiser* announced the sudden death of 'William Arnold Esq., Alderman of Cheap Ward, President of St Thomas's Hospital, one of the Principal Proprietors of the Porcelain Manufactory at Bow'. Here the Christian name of his brother, who survived George to become President of Hoare's Bank, was written in error.[7]

Edward Heylyn (1695–1765) was the son of John Heylyn,[8] who was twice Master of the Saddlers Company, in 1711 and 1722. Edward became a Member of the same Worshipful Company in 1718, and in 1731 was nominated a Freeman of the city of Bristol by the Mayor, where his brother Henry was in business as an importer of copper ore. His twin sons were packers in London, and his younger brother John was sometime Chaplain to King George II, a Prebendary of St Paul's Cathedral and subsequently of Westminster Abbey. The Bow Memorandum Book associates Heylyn's name with a consignment of fire-bricks for a glasshouse, but this is likely to have been the one owned by Weatherby and Crowther. There is no hard evidence to connect Edward Heylyn either with Lowdin's Glasshouse in Bristol, or with the enigmatic Limehouse porcelain manufactory. Despite having been declared bankrupt along with Robert Rogers in August 1737 at Bristol, he was a signatory to the first Bow patent of 1744. Likewise, he remained a proprietor of the porcelain factory, despite further declarations of bankruptcy in London, until 1757, after which he retired to the Isle of Man, presumably to escape from his creditors, and died there eight years later.

Thomas Frye (1710–62) was born in or near Dublin but little else is known about his early life; in particular where and from whom he obtained his artistic training. He was a portrait painter of moderate distinction, a fine miniaturist, and like so many of his fellow countrymen including Houston, McArdell and Spencer, a mezzotint engraver.[9] His etchings portray, among others, George II, Queen Charlotte, David Garrick and Captain Cook. His engraving of Paolo Veronese's 'Queen of Sheba' shows attendant handmaidens clad in head-dresses of most unusual forms, which reappear upon the heads of a pair of Bow model *Sphinxes* (A7), implying that craftsmen in the figure department may at times have based their work upon Frye's etchings. He arrived in around 1732 in the City of London, and around 1734 moved to West Ham, probably, as Dr Watney has suggested,[10] to engrave copper plates for the calico-printing industry. One such establishment, owned by Richard Emery,[11] was situated on the south side of Queen Matilda's Causeway, almost opposite the china works. William Pether (1731–1821), whose name and the year 1754 are inscribed upon a Bow creamer in the British Museum, was a pupil engraver of Frye's, who subsequently shared a studio with him. In 1756, he was awarded a prize by the Royal Society of Arts for 'the most ingenious and best fancy designs composed of fruit, foliage, and birds, proper for weavers, embroiderers, or calico printers, by a boy under seventeen'.

It is difficult to ascertain why a successful painter and engraver became associated with a porcelain manufactory. However, in 1736, Thomas Sherman, a late Master of the Saddlers Company, commissioned Frye to paint the portrait of Frederick Prince of Wales, who had accepted the position of Perpetual Master. Sherman was an uncle of Edward Heylyn, and probably introduced his nephew to the artist. Heylyn, together with Weatherby and Crowther (see below), were at that time attempting to make soft-paste porcelain, most likely at a glasshouse in East Smithfield. Sherman also knew Hillary Torriano,[12] whose miniature Frye painted in 1737. His father, Nathaniel Torriano, was a supercargo in the East India Company, and may have shown him examples of oriental porcelain that kindled his interest in ceramics. Later, Frye became acquainted with John Brooks, an Irish engraver, who between c.1750 and 1756 worked for Alderman Stephen Theodore Janssen at York House, Battersea, from whom he must have learned much about opacification of glazes with tin oxide, transfer printing, and enamelling on copper.

Although the portraits of Frederick and his spouse, the Princess Augusta, were destroyed in 1940 by enemy action, a portrait of Dr Jeremy Bentham survives which confirms Frye's ability as a painter. It is clear that his artistic direction of the Bow factory was largely responsible for its success. In November 1749, he registered a patent for a phosphatic paste, omitting from it the name of Heylyn. This prompted Hugh Tait to suppose a rift between the two men.[13] Further, payments made by Heylyn in 1752 and 1753 for property in Bromley St Leonards, recorded in the Poor Law Books and Land Tax, led him to believe Heylyn had established a small rival porcelain factory there that failed in around 1754. However, throughout this time, Heylyn continued to be named as a proprietor of the Bow works in the insurance policies, while in a list of Liverymen of the City of London, his address is given as 'The China House at Bow'. In 1759, owing to poor health, Frye took a convalescent holiday in Wales, and after he returned to London took no further part in the Bow factory. He died in the spring of 1762 from pulmonary tuberculosis, and his obituary was carried 3/6 April in the *Public Advertiser*: 'He was the inventor and first Manufacturer of PORCELAIN in England: to bring which to Perfection he spent fifteen years amongst the furnaces, till his constitution was near destroyed.'

Frye's wife Sarah bore him five children, two of whom died in infancy. A son, Thomas, was baptised on 20 December 1731 at St Olave's Church, Old Jewry, and is said to have become a wastrel. Two daughters, Sarah and Mary, both worked for a short time as enamellers at Bow and both married china painters. Sarah wed Ralph Wilcox, and shortly afterwards left Bow for Worcester, subsequently helping to decorate the 'Frog Service' for Josiah Wedgwood. Mary was rumoured 'to have married indiscretely'.

John Weatherby (d.1762) was a Staffordshire man, the first of his family to be connected with ceramics. His uncle, Benjamin, had been a brewer and corn factor who resided on Tower Hill until his death in 1708.[14] John initially dwelt at St Botolph's in Algate, and later in Sharp's Buildings in Rosemary Street. In 1744 he moved to St Catherine's-by-the-Tower where, since 1725, he had conducted a wholesale pottery trade in partnership with John Crowther. They also owned both a Glasshouse and Warehouse in Green Yard, East Smithfield.[15] Correspondence between the two men and John Wedgwood,[16] relating to spurious claims made by Thomas Briand that he could make porcelain, indicate they were associated with Frye in the Bow venture from at least as early as 1748, while in 1749 they were named as proprietors of the manufactory. In October 1762 the *London Chronicle* announced: 'Mr. John Weatherby, one of the Proprietors of the Bow China Warehouse, died at his home on Tower Hill.'

On 1 February 1764, William Weatherby, possibly a nephew or cousin of the late proprietor, took out insurance with the Sun Company to cover 'His House in his own occupation, near Mill Bridge' and stock therein for £1,050.[17] In an earlier policy of 24 July 1759, he had been entitled 'Dealer in China, Glass and Earthenware'. Benjamin Weatherby, the eldest son of the proprietor, was first mentioned in the Sun Company records in December 1752, when he and his partner, Timothy Pitman, were described as 'Glass and Chinamen of Half Moon Street, on the south side of the Strand'.[18] Elizabeth Adams has gleaned from subsequent insurances with the Sun Company that, by March 1759, Benjamin was trading on his own as a 'Merchant of St. Catherine's Cloysters near the Tower', but by February 1760 he was gazetted bankrupt. On 28 April 1766, he was able to establish a partnership with John Higgons trading as 'Dealers in Glass, China and Earthenware', from premises at Mill Bridge, formerly occupied by John

Weatherby, when buildings and stock were valued at £1,300. In 1771 Higgons died, and his widow shortly after remarried. Disputes between Weatherby and the executors arose that remained unresolved and the business declined, failed and was liquidated in 1775. Whether Benjamin Weatherby played any significant role in the management of the Bow porcelain factory remains uncertain. His name was included in the London Account Book of James Giles, alongside those of some important figures in the ceramic industry such as William Duesbury, Phillip Christian and Thomas Turner.

John Crowther (d.1790) was the son of Ralph Crowther, of Butley in Cheshire.[19] His close business associations with Weatherby have already been noted. It appears that he resided at St Catherine's-by-the-Tower only between 1758 and 1763. He was a member of the Skinners Company, and in 1759/60 served as Master. In February 1764 he was declared bankrupt and, on 12 March that year, the *Public Advertiser* carried the notice:[20]

> To Be Sold by Auction, on Wednesday next and the following day, at the Large Exhibition Room in Spring Gardens. The Remaining Part of the Large Stock in Trade of JOHN CROWTHER, a bankrupt, near Stratford, and the Bow Warehouse in Cornhill: consisting of the Finest Porcelain, chosen out of the said Collection, in Curious Figures, Girandoles and Branches for Chimney Pieces, Compotiers, Leaves &c., Fine Deserts of Old Partridge and Wheatsheaf Patterns . . .

Between 7 May 1764 and 15 January 1765, notices appeared sporadically in the *General Advertiser*, informing debtors where and how to settle their accounts with the executors, and by what means proven creditors should apply for dividends.[21]

It has been suggested that Crowther's bankruptcy involved only the glasshouse and warehouse at East Smithfield, and that the Cornhill warehouse for the Bow porcelain factory escaped sequestration. On 5 November 1764, the *General Advertiser* announced: 'Notice of removal of the Bow China Warehouse from Cornhill to St. Mildred's Court, opposite the Mansion House'.[22] The choice of the new venue must surely have been made by the proprietor's son, the Reverend John Crowther, who had been ordained in 1759 and became the rector of St Mildred's Church, Bread Street. The young cleric officiated at the wedding of his sister Joyce, reputed to have been a great beauty, to Sir James Lake. Since the happy event took place after the bankruptcy of the bride's father had been gazetted, the Baronet, in the delightful phrase coined by Frank Hurlbutt, 'accepted her ungilded'![23]

Perhaps the first omen of impending disaster came in August 1767, when the first of a series of notices appeared in the *General Advertiser*, announcing first the closure of the warehouse at St Mildred's Court, and ending with the advertisement of the sale of the factory stock and equipment in 1774. Crowther was admitted to Morden College, Blackheath, a refuge for distressed merchants, where in 1790 he died.

2 BOW PATENTS

IN 1736, ROGER LACEY, who was the Agent for the Chirokee Indians, persuaded a potter named André Duché to settle in Savannah, Georgia.[1] Duché (1704–78) conducted research into the manufacture of porcelain after the manner of the Chinese, and in 1738 claimed to have been successful in this quest. However, he steadfastly refused to disclose his secrets or to submit samples of his wares to the Trustees of Georgia. His application for a grant to enable him to cross the Atlantic to appear in person before that authority was denied, but after many vicissitudes, including his arrest and imprisonment, he made the journey at his own expense and arrived in London in May 1743.

William Cookworthy, who in 1768 became proprietor of the Plymouth porcelain factory, probably met Duché, for on 10 May 1745 he wrote in a letter to his friend, Richard Hingstone, a surgeon of Penryn:[2]

> I had lately with me the person who discovered the china-earth. He had with him several samples of china ware, which I think equal to the Asiatic. It was found on the back of Virginia, where he was in quest of mines; and having read Du Halde [*Description de l'empire de Chine*, 1735], he discovered both the petunze and kaolin. It is the latter earth which he says is essential to the success of the manufacture. He has gone for a cargo of it, having bought from the Indians the whole country where it rises. They can import it for £13 per ton, and by that means afford their china as cheap as common stoneware; but they intend only to go about 30 per cent. under the [East India] Company.

Cookworthy had, by this time, located ample sources of china clay on Tregonning Hill in Cornwall and was then engaged in a search for china stone. He does not appear to have had further dealings with Duché.

Records of cargoes brought to the Port of London for the year 1743/4 include: 'Earth, unrated, 20 tones – value £5: imported into London from Carolina'.[3] This may have been acquired by Frye and Heylyn in view of the wording of their first patent registered on 6 December 1744:[4]

> Edward Heylin, in the parish of Bow, in Middlesex, merchant, and Thomas Frye, of the parish of West Ham, in Essex. A New Method of manufacturing a certain kind of mineral, whereby a ware might be made of the same nature or kind, and equal to, if not exceeding in goodness and beauty, china or porcelain imported from abroad. The material is an earth, the product of the Chirokee nation in America, called by the natives UNAKER. A glass is formed in the usual way with one part of either 'pot-ash, fern-ash, pearl-ash, kelp or any other vegetable lixiviall salt', and one part of 'sand, flints, pebbles or any other stones of the vitrefying kind', and reduced to an impalpable powder, and mixed in different proportions, according to the nature of the ware to be made, with 'unaker', from which sand and mica have been removed by washing. They are then kneaded

together, thrown or moulded, and put in a kiln burned with wood, called biscuiting, then painted and glazed with unaker and the glass above described . . .

The lack of more precise measurements suggests that the mix was experimental, and many have passed the opinion that soft-paste porcelain could not have been created using this formula. The purpose of the patent may have been to forestall any claim made by Duché to have exclusive rights to use unaker and to manufacture a frit porcelain, when it was realised that Nicholas Sprimont of Chelsea and William Steers of Pomona were likely to become competitors. Certainly no sherds have been recovered from the Bow factory site fashioned from non-phosphatic porcelain.

Whether or not unaker continued to be employed at Bow after the initial period of trial and error remains an open question. Hugh Tait[5] pointed out that it constituted an especially fine china clay, and the cost of transportation might not have been great if it was carried as ballast in ships returning from the New World. By the year 1762, Duché was back in America, and in 1778 he died in Philadelphia, when his estate was valued at £2,516 12s 4d, excluding his town house in the city and lands in Virginia. Such wealth may very well have been derived by the sale of unaker, but the names of possible purchasers have never been identified.

On 17 November 1749, a second Bow patent was registered in the name of Thomas Frye only:[6]

For a New Method of making a certain ware, which is not inferior to in beauty and fineness, and is rather superior in strength than earthenware that is brought from the East Indies, and is commonly known by the name of China, Japan, or Porcelain Ware. Animals, vegetables and fossils, by calcining, grinding and washing are said to produce an insoluble matter named *Virgin Earth*, but some greater quantities than others as all animal substances, all fossils of the calcareous kind, as chalk, limestone &c., take therefore any of these classes, calcine it, grind and wash it in many waters; these ashes are mixed in certain proportions with flints, white pebble or clear sand, and with water, made into balls, highly burned and ground fine, and mixed with a proportion of pipe-clay; it is then thrown on a wheel, and when finish'd, dried, burnt, and painted with smalt and saffer, when it is ready to be glazed, made by making a glass with saltpetre, red lead, and sand flint, or other white stones, grinding up well and mixing it with a certain proportion of white lead, adding a little smalt to clear the colour . . .

It is probable that the second formula, or one very much like it, was employed at Bow for a considerable time prior to registration of the patent in November 1749, and may have been used for the first wares to have been successfully fired. The inclusion of bone ash imparted a milky opalescence to the porcelain and also greatly enhanced stability of the paste in the biscuit firing. It was incorporated into the mix both at Chelsea and Lowestoft c.1757 and at Derby in 1770 and may be detected on chemical analysis by the phosphoric acid test.

3 BOW INSURANCES

THE PRECISE SITE ON THE MIDDLESEX SIDE OF THE RIVER LEA where the Bow manufactory was first established is unknown, but at some time between January 1748 and July 1749, operations were transferred to the Essex side of the river. The works were situated upon the north aspect of Queen Matilda's Causeway (now Stratford High Street), about 250 yards east of Bow Bridge, from which it was separated by a terraced row of tenements. The chief building was based on one in Canton, owned by the East India Company, and Bow proprietors advertised their factory as the 'New Canton'; a title inscribed on several cylindrical ink-wells, some of which carry the date 1750. Behind and to the north-west lay Bow Back river, where a wharf was built, providing access to the waters of the Lea and thence to the Thames.

The discovery of the Bow insurances by Elizabeth Adams not only established the identities of the proprietors, but supplied details of buildings, equipment and stock, which reflect the expansion and later retrenchment of the business.[1] The first policy with the Sun Assurance Company is dated July 1749, only four months prior to registration of the second Bow patent; subsequent policies issued by the same company are dated November 1750, July 1763 and January 1766, while in December 1755 another was taken out with the Royal Exchange Company[2]. A summary of their contents is shown in Table 1.

The policy of 1749 mentions the 'Long Workshop', described by Thomas Craft (see Chapter 7), and an 'Elaboratory' which was most probably an experimental laboratory that was closed when the formulae for paste and glaze were finalised. The vulnerability to fire of buildings housing kilns may account for their high valuation. Additions mentioned in 1750 include both a second kilnhouse and millhouse, two drying houses and one sliphouse, together with a warehouse containing £2,000 worth of stock. The 1755 policy shows cover for a 'New brick building', and valuation of stabling rose fourfold from £25 to £100. The omission of 'Millhouse' and 'Warehouse and workshop' may be because such details lay outside the specifications drawn up by the Royal Exchange Company. Stock was revalued at £3,000 and transferred to the Cornhill warehouse.

Table 1. Contents and valuations of the Bow insurance policies.

Item	1749	1750	1755	1763	1766
Mr Frye's house	£ 300	£ 300	£ 300		
Household effects	£ 200	£ 200			
Mr Crowther's house				£ 150	£ 120
Household effects					£ 400

Item	1749	1750	1755	1763	1766
House elaboratory & warehouse/timber	£ 100				
Utensils & stock therein	£ 600				
Long workshop/brick	£1200	£1200	£ 800	£ 600	£ 300
Utensils & stock therein	£ 300	£ 600	£ 400	£ 150	£ 200
1 millhouse & workhouse	£ 300				
2 millhouses		£ 100		£ 100	£ 50
Utensils & stock therein	£ 300	£ 300		£ 100	£ 150
Warehouse & workshop		£ 200		£ 175	£ 50
Utensils & stock therein		£2000		£ 200	£ 50
Kilnhouse brick/timber	£ 600				
2 kilnhouses		£1000	£2000	£ 400	£ 300
Utensils & stock therein	£ 100	£ 200	£ 700	£ 200	£ 300
Warehouse & stock		£ 150	£1200	£ 300	
2 drying & 1 sliphouse		£ 225	£ 400	£ 200	
Stables		£ 25	£ 100	£ 25	£ 30
New brick building			£ 150		
Utensils therein			£ 300		
Enamelling kiln house & utensils therein				£ 150	
Dipping house, stock & utensils therein				£ 150	£ 150
Engine house, stock & utensils therein					£ 100
Cornhill warehouse stock			£3000	£2000	
Mildred's Court stock					£1000
Totals:	£4000	£6500	£8650	£4900	£3400

Business evidently entered a decline at some time between 1755 and 1763, and it is tempting to relate this to the departure in 1759 of Thomas Frye. By 1763, the overall sum insured was £4,900, which was only £900 more than it had been in 1749, and by 1766, it fell further to £3,400. Over this whole period the cover for the Long Workshop was reduced from £1,200 to £300, which would seem to be a greater amount than could be attributed only to dilapidations of a brick structure. Nevertheless, in 1763 both an enamelling house and a dipping house receive mention for the first time and, in 1766, also an engine house. Presumably activities proper for these new buildings had formerly been conducted elsewhere in the factory complex. Valuation of stock fell, first to £2,000 and, after removal to St Mildred's Court, to £1,000.

Elizabeth Adams found that the physical condition of policies issued after 1766 was too poor to allow meaningful appraisal, and this left a hiatus that included the last years of the factory's existence. Fortunately, Nancy Valpy has been able to shed light upon this twilight area by her discovery of notices and advertisements in contemporary English newspapers, which are summarised in Chapter 5.

4 EXCAVATIONS ON THE BOW SITE

GEORGE HIGGINS IN 1868

DURING THE ERECTION OF THE BELL & BLACK MATCH FACTORY in 1868 upon the south side of Stratford High Street, George Higgins noticed that children were playing with fragments of old porcelain in the area. He and his sister gathered as many sherds as they were able while access to the site remained. Most of the items were recovered from what was supposed to have constituted the factory waste heap, and from a trench eight to ten feet deep leading to a sewer. Some were presented to Lady Charlotte Schreiber, and the residuum to the Victoria & Albert Museum. They were described in the *Art Journal* of 1869,[1] and the findings summarised in 1926 by Frank Hurlbutt.[2]

A quantity of bricks cemented together, with vitrification of their inner surfaces, represented remnants of a kiln. A cylindrical saggar, 10in (25.4cm) in diameter and 8½in (21.6cm) tall, was perforated by three lines of holes into which clay pegs fitted, and was designed to house plates, separated by the pegs, during their biscuit firing. There were also pitcher moulds for casting sprigged roses, prunus and hawthorn ornamentation, conical spurs, and dumps of animal bones, china clay, calcined flints and quartz. Most porcelain sherds were biscuit fragments of useful wares decorated in blue with landscapes, birds, flowers and figures, but the remnants of two enamelled plates were included. Items relating to figures were:

> Two biscuit seated *Pug Dogs* (A75), wearing studded collars to which roses were attached.
> Biscuit head of a *Turk* (A62) wearing a plumed tall head-dress.
> Two tureen handles taking the forms of female heads.

MAJOR AUBREY TOPPIN IN 1921

DURING THE DEMOLITION of the Iron Foundry of Wilmer & Sons on the north side of Stratford High Street that commenced on 21 July 1921, a second and more thorough excavation was made by Major Aubrey Toppin.[3] A large number of sherds were recovered, including moulded knife-handles and an assortment of sprigged, blue and white, enamelled and transfer-printed service wares. The following items related to figures:

Shield matching that held by *Minerva* (B28).
Base of the model of *Liberty* (A53, Plate 46).
Portions of a *Huntsman* and *Lady Falconer* (B110, Plate 153).
Mould for a triangle held by a lady *Triangle Player* (B103, Plate 147).

DR DAVID REDSTONE IN 1969

A THIRD EXCAVATION was conducted upon what appears to have been the extreme south-west portion of the factory site by Dr David Redstone.[4] Exploration of an area of about 254 square feet and approximately 4 feet deep was effected. This bore evidence of earlier disturbance, both in the late eighteenth and early nineteenth centuries. Most of the sherds were blue decorated biscuit fragments, but there were also pitcher moulds, cockspurs and ceramic props with pointed ends, used to support projecting limbs of figures during their biscuit firing. Only one object related to any model:

The biscuit torso of a *Pugilist* (C58, Plate 227).[5]

5 CONTEMPORARY NEWSPAPER REFERENCES

NOTICES AND ADVERTISEMENTS RELATING TO PORCELAIN factories from eighteenth-century English newspapers have been published by J. E. Nightingale,[1] A. J. B. Kiddell,[2] and latterly by Nancy Valpy in a series of communications extracted from other papers in the British Library of the American Congress.[3]

Possibly the earliest reference to Bow was published on 26 August 1748 in the *Daily Advertiser*: 'BOW CHINA. A Great Variety of useful and ornamental China to be sold at Mr. Mitchell's Toyshop, at the Dial and King's Arms in Cornhill, near the Royal Exchange'. A further announcement in the same newspaper in December 1749 reads: 'Bow China . . . for ready money only, by Mr. Mears, Flanders-Lace Merchant, at his Lace Chamber, at the sign of the Brussels Lace Lappits, near Mercer's Chaple in Cheapside . . .' Again, on 9 January 1750, an advertisement discovered by A. J. P. Kiddell reads: 'Bow China, to be sold by John Sotro, Goldsmith and Toyman, at the Golden Heron, on the North Side of St. Paul's Church Yard, at the same price as at the Manufactory, for the sake of ready money only . . .' Later, in October of that year, Mr Sotro signed over his effects to 'Mr. Weatherby, of Tower Hill, Glass-Man and Mr. Samuel Taylor'.

On 5 March 1753, *Aris's Birmingham Gazette* announced:

BOW CHINA WARE. Was opened on Wednesday the 7th February, near the Royal Exchange in Cornhill, with a Back Door facing the Bank, in Threadneedle-street, for the Convenience of all Customers both in Town and Country; where all Sorts of China will continue to be sold in the same Manner as formerly at Bow, with Allowance made to wholesale dealers.

Similar notices appeared in the *Daily Advertiser*, *Norwich Mercury* and *Derby Mercury*. In July 1754, the *Daily Advertiser* bore an advertisement:

Painters, particularly Enamellers upon China Ware, may meet with Encouragement suitable to their Merit, and Constant Employment, by applying to the Compting-House at the China Manufactory, near Bow. Likewise Persons that can undertake to press and repair Figures in Clay may, by applying as aforesaid, meet with Employment . . .

On 5 November 1753, *Aris's Birmingham Gazette* bore a similar notice with the addendum: 'NB. – At the same House, a Person is wanted who can model small Figures in Clay neatly'.

On 24 March 1757, there appeared in the *Public Advertiser:*

To be Sold by Auction by MR COCK & COMPANY, at their New Auction Rooms in Spring Gardens, leading into St. James's Park . . . the very Extensive and Valuable Products of the Bow Porcelain Manufactory, consisting of many compleat and useful Services, and an Abundance of curious and ornamental Pieces . . .

Either some lots failed to find a buyer, or the proprietors attempted to sell off seconds, because on 13 April of that year an advertisement read: 'To be sold cheap, at Mr. Hughe's Iron-monger in Pall Mall, several Lots of Bow China, particularly fine etc.' Ten days later there appeared: 'Sale by Auction by COCK & Co. Some lots were not cleared in the Bow China Sale, which finished on Saturday the 17th inst . . .'

The *Daily Advertiser* of 27 and 29 August 1757 announced to the public the opening of a second Bow China Warehouse 'on the Upper Terrace St. James's

Street'. It would seem, however, that the volume of business was insufficient to maintain the two. On 27 February 1758, the *Public Advertiser* carried the notice:

> To be Sold by Auction by Mr. Lambe, at his House in Pall Mall . . . A Large and Valuable Collection of Fine Porcelain or China, from the Manufactory at Bow; consisting of Perfume Pots, Beautiful Groups of Figures, Jars, Beakers, Birds, Beasts &c. Services of Dishes, Plates, Sauceboats, compleat Tea and Coffee Equipages, a Large Assortment of the most useful Pieces, both blue and white and enamelled . . . Some Part of this Porcelain is very little inferior to the fine old brown Edge Japan, and wants no other recommendation than its own beauty . . .

Shortly afterwards in the same newspaper there was a notice: 'For Sale. All the Intire Stock of their Warehouse, on the Terraces in St. James's Street . . .', to which was appended: 'The [Bow] proprietors having quitted the same . . . There is a large quantity of Chelsea Manufactory among the stock.'

We learn from the *Daily Advertiser* of 24 and 26 January 1759:

> Whereas the late Partnership between John Weatherby, John Crowther, Thomas Quinton and Richard Windel, at Green Yard Glasshouse, was dissolved on 14 October last, that Branch of the Business is now carried on by J. Weatherby, J. Crowther and James Abernethy, at their Warehouse in St Katherines.

Other advertisements seeking recruitment of skilled craftsmen for the Bow manufactory appeared sporadically in the *Daily Advertiser*. Thus, on 26 January 1759, a notice reads: 'AT BOW CHINA WAREHOUSE in Cornhill are sold all Sorts of Goods of the Manufactory, wholesale and retail, with Great Improvements. Encouragement will be given to good Blue and Enamel Painters . . .' Again, on 28 January 1763: 'Blue China or Pot Painters are wanted at the China Manufactory at Bow. None need apply but what are very good Hands.'

Mention has been made in Chapter 1 of Frye's obituary notice in the *Public Advertiser*. The *Gentleman's Magazine* did not record this until 1764. The *London Evening Post* of 3/6 April 1762 published theirs without delay: 'Last Saturday night at about ten o'clock, died the very ingenious and celebrated Painter, Mr. Thomas Frye; a man universally beloved, and who must be regretted by every person who has the least taste for the polite arts . . .' The demise of John Weatherby that same year has already been noted. A natural disaster, resulting in one death, reported in the *Gentleman's Magazine* of October 1762,[4] must have contributed to the declining fortunes of the porcelain factory: 'The China Works at Bow were overflowed in such manner that the current rushed through the great arch [the main entrance] in like manner as the tide runs through the arches of London Bridge.' A rise in the water-level of the Bow Back River seems to have been responsible for an incident when a gentleman who was passing was said to have been trapped in his coach and drowned.

The illegible state of the later Bow insurances in the records of the Sun Company leave us in considerable doubt concerning the last few years of the Bow factory. On 3 November 1764, the *Gazetteer and New Daily Advertiser* announced closure of the Bow Warehouse in Cornhill and transfer of the stock to Mildred's Court, on the south side of St Paul's Church Yard. This event was evidently related to the bankruptcy of John Crowther. However, the manufactory was far from moribund, for on 15 April 1772, the *General Evening Post* carried the advertisement: 'WANTED, at the Bow Manufactory, some Blue Painters, sober, industrious and good workmen. Also two India Figure Painters on Enamel, that will meet with Constant Employment. The Goods made at the above Manufactory continue to be sold at the Warehouse, No. 28, St. Paul's Church Yard.'

Unmistakable signs of impending disaster began to appear the following year. On 17 August 1773, it was announced in the *General Evening Post*: 'To be Sold cheap, all the Stock of the Bow Warehouse, No. 28, St. Paul's Church Yard; the Proprietor intending for the future to serve his Customers from the Factory.' On 6/7 and 9/12 March 1774 the same newspaper carried the notice:

> The Sale of All Fixtures and Utensils in Trade of the Bow China Manufactory, near Bow Bridge, Essex; consisting of a Mill-House, Mill-Work, a Turret Clock, a large Parcel of Moulds, a Cart Horse, Boarding-Racks etc. . . . Catalogues then to be had at the Queen's Head at Bow . . .

Evidently the projected auction was postponed, but it must have been held prior to 14 April 1774, when the *General Evening Post* announced:

> To be lett, near Bow Bridge, Essex, a large and spacious Piece of Ground, late Part of the Bow China Works, measuring in Depth from the Road to the River 300 feet, and in Width 100 feet, with a convenient Dock, and a large Space of Warf, next adjoining to a navigable Branch of the River Lea, with some Buildings on the Premises . . .

There followed on 9/12 May, in the same organ:

> To be Sold by Auction of Mr. HARDING, by Order of the Trustees of Mr. JOHN CROWTHER, at his late Bow China Warehouse, in St. Paul's Church Yard, on Wednesday 11 inst. and the following day. Stock in Trade consisting of all Sorts of Services of Plates and Dishes etc. To which is added, by Permission, Part of the Stock of the Country Shopkeeper . . .

John Crowther's creditors later met in the Nag's Head Tavern, Leadenhall Street, where they received their Dividends.

Llewellynn Jewitt wrote: 'The Bow factory failed c.1775 when Crowther sold his entire concern, works, moulds, tools &c. to Mr. Duesbury . . . Mr. Duesbury, as he did with those of Chelsea, removed moulds, models and implements &c. to

Derby and Bow was brought to a close.'[5] This statement evidently was based on the testimony of Samuel Keys, cited by William Chaffers, that: 'Bow closed at about this time [1775] and Mr. Duesbury had several beautiful figures and ornaments from thence.'[6] Duesbury had, by 1774, attained the summit of a highly successful business career, so would scarcely have wanted to purchase the ailing Bow establishment, and there is no hard evidence to suggest that he did. No models or groups issued between 1770 and 1848 by the Derby factory can be traced back to Bow prototypes, apart from a few animals and a pair of musicians during the Bloor period, and all of these examples derive from Meissen originals.[7] When in 1848 the Derby factory failed, many master models, moulds and clay squeezes held in stock were acquired by Alderman William Taylor Copeland. This material was transferred to his works at Stoke-on-Trent, although some of it fell into the canal whilst being unloaded from a barge and was lost. It remains in a building at Copeland's to this day, and was examined during the late 1920s by the brothers William and Frank Stoner.[8] More recently a second survey, albeit not yet completed, has been undertaken by Pamela Rowan.[9] None of those concerned have identified either models or moulds ascribed to Bow, although there are several from Chelsea.

6 JOHN BOWCOCK AND THE BOWCOCK PAPERS

JOHN BOWCOCK HAD SERVED AS A PURSER in the Royal Navy prior to his appointment to the Bow factory in around 1753, and had seen action in the War of the Austrian Succession. His mother sold stockings from her shop in Halifax, Yorkshire, and his brother William was a portrait painter who lived in Chester. He married Anne Wilkinson in 1749, who may have been the daughter of the famous potter of Wapping. She died from bubonic plague while her husband was abroad in 1760, which caused dire distress to her family, since it had been rumoured that she had been buried while yet alive.[1] In his time at Bow, John Bowcock acted as factory clerk, accountant, secretary, travelling representative and, when the need arose, took on the task of auctioneer.

The Bowcock Papers consist of letters, books and documents which were once the property of John Bowcock. A portion of them is now in the Department of Medieval and Later Antiquities of the British Museum.[2] They consist of letters written when he served in the Navy; personal notes pertaining to his family tree; sketches made by his sister Bridget; and also the Factory Memorandum Book for the year 1758, with sundry bills covering the period between 16 March 1757 to 18 June 1760, from Richard Dyer, enameller, at Mr Bolton's, near the church at Lambeth.

The remainder of the Bowcock Papers, once the property of Lady Charlotte Schreiber, have been lost, but their contents were summarised in the *Art Journal* of 1869,[3] and subsequently by William Chaffers.[4] These include four books, two comprising sketches of subjects such as plants, trees and festoons of flowers by the French artist De La Cour; another comprising coloured engravings of foreign nationals, gallants, ladies and pastoral folk, by Martin Engelbrecht of Nuremberg; the last by Edwards and Darley, published in 1754, comprising drawings of interiors of buildings, pagodas, bridges, birds and insects. Far more important was the Account Book, which is said to have shown a rise in the annual cash flow from £6,573 0s 8d in 1750/1 to £11,228 15s 2d in 1755 which, when corrected for credit outstanding, amounted to £18,115 8s 9d. Further, the average weekly takings at Cornhill came to £120.

The Memorandum Book shows that the following models were available in 1756:

Chinese Heads	New Shepherds and Shepherdesses
Cooks, pairs	Men with salt boxes, white
Cupids and Boys	Paris Cries
Fluter and Companion	Woman with Chickens [not known]
Harlequin and Columbine	Bucks and Does, pairs
Pierrot	Goats
Gentleman and Lady	Squirrels
Turks, pairs	Swans [not known]
Dutch Dancers, pairs	

The following models were available in 1758:

Boys riding Lion and Leopard	Musicians, Italian
Dianas	Piper and Companion
Gardeners, large	Seasons, small
Grape-cutting Boys	Turk, salts
Minervas	Bucks

It is evident that some otherwise identical models were issued contemporaneously upon differently styled bases, i.e. 'with, or without, Plint[h]s'. Some entries relate to the reduction of cost for damage or return of the item: '29 Jan. 1756 Mr. Fogg, a sprig'd sallad vassel 12s; 1 pair sprig'd boats 6s; 16 cooks 2s each unabated; a swan and 2 Harlequins returned 7s.' On 8 May 1756: 'Mrs. Whitfield to have 1p. white biscuit candlesticks', shows that even at this early date some items were issued without glaze. Sprigged decoration is mentioned on 27 March 1756: 'What's to be done with white bud sprigs?'

Some memoranda relate to the day to day business: on 7 May 1756, 'Quy. whether Windsor bricks were received at the glasshouse which is charged to the porcelain company?' Presumably similar bricks were used at both establishments. There are also records of problems arising over personal accounts: on 30 August 1756, 'paid Mr. Heylyn's draft on Mr. Crowther for £13 and charged Mr. Crowther's cash acct. with it. Quy. [query] How is Mr. Heylyn made Dr. to J.C. creditor?' Sometimes Bowcock proffered advice to his employers: on 27 March 1756, 'Mrs. Anne Howard has it greatly in her power to serve the factory. I hope they [the plates she had ordered] will be very neat and charged reasonable; I have not told her a price.' Several of the patterns executed on useful wares both in underglaze blue and in enamel are listed including *Partridge* [Quail], *Dragon*, *Image*, and *Wheatsheaf* [Banded Hedge], as well as *Cock Plates*, after Japanese originals. Nappy plates were those whose rims had been reduced, or napped.

Some of the more important clients are named, including the Duke of Argyll, the Duchesses of Leeds and Portland, Lord Southwell, and the Ladies Cavendish and Stairs. Less exalted folk were Colonel Griffin of Brooke Street, Mrs Anne Howard, Mrs McNally, Mr Coleman and Mrs Whitfield. A number of dealers who conducted business with the factory are also named, and Elizabeth Adams has been able to add their domiciles:[5]

Baxter, Dudley	6 Bedford Row
Bernadeau, James	Russel Court, Drury Lane
Fogg, Robert	Opposite Pall Mall, St James's
Hunter, William	Queen Street, Mayfair
Kentish, John [Toyman]	Lombard Street
Morgan, Thomas	St James's
Taylor, John	Pall Mall, St James's
Vanderkiste, Joseph	The Strand (later Southwark)
Vere, Charles	Fleet Street
White, Richard	New Bond Street

During the first eight months of 1758, Bowcock was in Ireland, mostly Dublin, where he formed liaisons with potential customers, received consignments of porcelain and glass, and established agencies. After his return to London, on 9 February 1759, he went to see Sheridan in *Hamlet*. On 19 April, he recorded 'Lady Freik showed me two tureens she had brought from France.' He travelled to Nottingham in August, where he mounted the rostrum as auctioneer, but on 24

September was back in the metropolis to hear the Reverend John Crowther preach his first sermon. On 16 October 1759, he 'bought a China figure for Mrs. McNally', later treating her to wine and escorting her to the theatre. On 27 November he 'observed in the burning of biscuit ware that dishes and plates should be burnt in new cases, and only one in each, as when two are burnt in one, it is certain one is always bad.'

THE BOWCOCK BOWL

THE BOWCOCK BOWL is 8in (20.3cm) in diameter and stands upon a tall foot-rim; it is decorated underglaze in blue and, beneath the base, is inscribed 'John & Anne Bowcock 1759'. The interior is painted with a scene depicting Bowcock disembarking from a ship in the company of sailors bearing staves, and the rim is decorated with a diaper pattern. The exterior is covered by a powder-blue ground, broken by four reserves containing chinoiseries and in one of these the monogram IB is evident.[6]

The purpose of the presentation is uncertain. It may have commemorated the conclusion of a successful business trip to Ireland, or Bowcock's tenth year of marriage, or possibly his promotion following the retirement in that year of Thomas Frye. Little is known of his last few years, except that he died from tetanus (lockjaw) in 1765. The bowl evidently passed to his brother William and, via his descendants, to a Mrs MacIntire, whose daughter wrote of her heirloom in a letter dated 21 August 1922: 'John and Anne Bowcock were uncle and aunt to my grandfather; they were Liverpool people, John being a sea captain. The bowl was made for them, I am told, at Shaw's potteries, Liverpool. It was presented to him after one of his voyages . . .'[7]

The Bowl found its way into the Rimmer collection, and for a while was erroneously ascribed to Liverpool, until it was purchased by Ernest Allman, who established its association with John Bowcock, and hence its Bow manufacture. It is now in the British Museum.

7 THOMAS CRAFT AND THE BOW ENAMELLERS

A. J. TOPPIN SUGGESTED THAT THOMAS CRAFT may have worked in the Battersea enamel atelier at York House between August 1753 and November 1755. He drew this conclusion after finding in the parish records baptismal entries of three children, of whom only one survived named Ann, born to Thomas and Ann Craft, between those dates.[1] However, the name of Thomas Craft is included in the Bow parish registers in March 1756, and his wife, Elizabeth, who died in April 1758, was buried in the churchyard there. Unless Craft was married twice and both his wives died young the entries must refer to two different persons. However this may be, Craft was a painter of porcelain who was employed at Bow between about 1756 and 1770.

In 1851, a Bow porcelain bowl came to light in a cardboard box in the British Museum which was 8½in (21.8cm) in diameter and 3¾in (9.9cm) tall.[2] Enamelled both inside and out with festoons and detached sprays of flowers, it bears a floral monogram T.C. together with gilt embellishments. Upon the undersurface of the box lid, the following message is penned in ink:[3]

> This bowl, was made at the Bow Manufactory, at Stratford-le-Bow, in the County of Essex, about the year 1760, – and painted there by Thomas Craft, my Cypher is in the Bottom; – it is painted in what we used to call the old Japan taste, a taste at the time much esteemed by the then Duke of Argyle; there is near 2 penny-worth weight of Gold [3g], about 15s; I had it in hand at different times about three months, about 2 weeks twice was bestowed on it, it could not have been manufactured, &c., for less than £4, there is not it's similitude; I took it in a Box to Kentish Town and had it burned in Mr. Gyles's Kiln, cost me 3s, it was cracked the first time of using it; Miss. Nancy Sha, a Daughter of the late Sir Patrick Blake was christened with it, I never used it but in particular respect to my Company, and I desire my Legatee (as mentioned in my Will) may do the same; – Perhaps it may be thought I have said too much about this trifling Toy; – A reflection steals in my Mind, that this Bowl may meet with the same fate that the Manufactory where it was made has done; and like the famous cities of Troy and Carthage &c. and similar to Shakespeare's Cloud-cap't Towers &c. – The above Manufactory was carried on many years under the firm of Mssrs Crowther and Weatherby, whose names were known almost over the World; – they employed about 300 Persons; about 90 Painters (of whom I was one), and about 200 Turners &c. were employed under one Roof; the model of the Building was taken from that at Canton in China; – the whole was heated by 2 Stoves, on the outside of the Building, and conveyed through Flews or Pipes, and warmed the whole, sometimes to an intense heat, unbearable in Winter; now it bears a miserable aspect, being a Manufactory for Turpentine, and small Tenaments, – like Shakesperes Baseless Fabric of a Vision &c.; – Mr. Weatherby has been dead many years – Mr. Crowther is in Morden College, Blackheath, and I am the only Person, of all those employed there, who Annually visit him.
>
> T. Craft, 1790.

A. J. Toppin ascertained that Sir Patrick Blake lived with a mulatto woman, named Peggy Sha, who bore him a daughter in about 1770 called Nancy.[4] It was customary, in those days, for the family and close friends to sit around a table and toast the new-born baby, brought for them to see, with hot punch. Possibly on this, or some earlier occasion, the temperature of the punch cracked the bowl. Elizabeth Adams discovered that a James Parsons took out insurance with the Sun Company in January 1780 for his Tar and Turpentine Works, located on the site of the Bow Long Workshop.[5] She also found that, following Craft's departure around 1770 from the porcelain factory, he established his own calico printing business, insured for £1,800, including £1,275 for stock, also with the Sun Company.[6]

Mention of Frye's daughters, Sarah and Mary, who worked for a while at Bow as painters, has earlier been made. Little is known about other members of the enamelling staff, but some of their names have been listed by Elizabeth Adams:[7]

Angel, John Phillip	Bow Parish Register, July 1751
Barber, Lewis	Apprenticed Painter to Heylyn, later at Worcester
Barrs, Francis	Land Tax, 1760
Bonner, John	Bow Parish Register, June 1750
Gadd, William	Bow Parish Register, May 1760
Gazeley, John	Bow Parish Register, November 1747
	In 1761 said by Bowcock to have been overpaid
Lanauze, John de	Name coupled with 'Mary Bromley' on a Bow Mug, dated 1776, in British Museum
Mason, ?	According to William Chaffers worked at Chelsea and Bow
Redgrave, James	Land Tax, 1747. Later at Lowestoft
Welch, James	Bow Parish Register, August 1754
Weyman, Charles	Cited as an ex-Bow painter in *Norwich Mercury*.

Dates in the above list are those when the name first appeared.

8 MODELLERS AND OTHER CRAFTSMEN AT BOW

LITTLE IS KNOWN OF THE CRAFTSMEN who worked in the Figure Department at Bow. The name of a Staffordshire potter, William Bullock was entered into the Bow Parish Register in April 1749.[1] Earlier, on 26 January 1741/2, he had married Elizabeth Barker, of Fenton, at Stoke-on-Trent, where the birth, baptism and subsequent death eight months later of their first-born child Lydia are recorded.

This tragedy probably prompted their move to London, but in June 1749 the Bow Parish Register recorded the death of their second child, Letitia, who lived for only two days. They must have returned to Stoke a few months later, where in November 1750 and in June 1753 their two sons, William and John, were born, and survived to attain adulthood. In June 1758 and again in April 1761, John Baddely made two large payments to Bullock for 'Modells supplied', so it is reasonably certain his trade was that of modeller. Examples of his work whilst at Bow have not been identified, but are likely to have been executed in a primitive style and to show many technical faults. Another modeller, George Mosers, has been mentioned, although nothing is known about him.

Some Bow models issued between c.1748 and 1753 display many unusual sculptural qualities described later and which in muted form remain identifiable until c.1760. The unknown craftsman has come to be known as the Muses Modeller, from the set of models representing the nine Muses that he created. Some, but by no means all, of these models are marked with an impressed T or T° beneath their bases, and a similar device may also be found on a few models issued by Dr Wall's Worcester, Cookworthy's Plymouth, and Champion's Bristol manufactories. Some of these other examples lack sophistication, and display a number of different modelling styles unlikely to represent the hand of a single modeller. The possible significance of these incised marks has been discussed by Geoffrey Godden who ascribes the T° to a modeller named John Toulouse.[2] Henry Sandon has presented evidence to support the contention that there was a family of modellers named Toulouse who most probably came to England from France, which would explain the widespread use of the mark on models executed in different styles.[3] The name of Charles Toulouse occurs in the Bow parish register in October 1750.[4]

Others have elected to relate the T and T° marks to the modeller called 'Tebo' or 'Thiebaud', who is alleged to have been first a repairer, and later, despite the possession of only modest talent, a modeller. Certainly a man of that name was employed by Josiah Wedgwood between November 1774 and October 1775, for Wedgwood, in a letter to his partner, Nicholas Bentley, complained bitterly of Tebo's poor workmanship as a modeller, and the disruptive influence he exerted over other employees.[5] Later, Tebo was employed on his own account making porcelain portrait plaques in Dublin. There is no evidence to support the belief that he ever worked at Bow.

It is necessary to refute any assertions that the impressed B mark signifies the work of the sculptor John Bacon.[6] This mark appears in some examples beneath the bases of Bow Cooks (B69) which, according to the Memorandum Book, were available in January 1756, at a time when Bacon was 15 years old, and had not yet completed his apprenticeship to Nicholas Crisp at the Vauxhall manufactory.

The name of William Ball appears in the Bow Parish Register in December 1746 before his residence in Limehouse was recorded in March 1747.[7] It is possible that as an expert potter his skills were sought prior to the employment of the phosphatic paste. Assuredly he was no ordinary employee, for he owned property in Bromley-le-Bow, rated at £8 per annum, and in 1745 and 1746 paid £1 12s 0d in Land Tax.

According to Simeon Shaw,[8] a number of Staffordshire workmen came to London in 1747, to assist in the establishment of the Chelsea porcelain manufactory. They included three, named Samuel Parr (Turner), Richard Meir (Fireman) and Thomas Lawton (Slip-maker), who subsequently moved to Bow. Elizabeth Adams found the following people named in the Bow Parish Register, who were probably employees at the Bow manufactory.[9] The dates appended relate to the earliest entry in the register:

Harrison, Robert	November 1760
Harrison, Thomas	August 1755
Phenix, Robert	January 1749/50
Smith, John	April 1748
Smith, Joseph	December 1748
Stevenson, John	June 1750

9   INDEPENDENT PORCELAIN DECORATORS

ENAMEL COLOURS DO NOT APPEAR TO HAVE BEEN EMPLOYED for the decoration of Bow figures before c.1751, although a number of models that are now white were once coloured with unfired pigments embellished with gold leaf attached with size. Probably the bulk, if not all, of this work was executed outside the factory by independent porcelain decorators, who after that time also used enamels.

THOMAS HUGHES, FATHER AND SON

OUR KNOWLEDGE OF the Hughes family stems mainly from the researches of Major Tapp.[1] Thomas Hughes (père) was born at Bermondsey in 1686, the son of Herbert Hughes, watchmaker. After serving an apprenticeship in his father's trade to Thomas Carter of St James's, Clerkenwell, he obtained his Freedom in 1707 and became Assistant Clockmaker (1735), Rentner Warden (1740) and Master (1742), and in 1752/3 retired to St Pancras where, in 1758, he died. His son, also named Thomas, was baptised on 28 October 1718 at St Botolph's Church in the Aldgate, and followed in his father's footsteps, obtaining his Freedom (1742), becoming Rentner Warden (1763), and Master (1765). Members of the Guild of Clockmakers often learned skills of enamelling clock dials, gilding spandrels and so on, and in the Hughes' case employed their techniques in the decoration of porcelain from Chelsea, Bow, Derby and Longton Hall. They were probably the first in England to undertake this task.

Rate Books of Clerkenwell from the period 1746–7 include the names of George Holmes and Constantine Smith, while John Gabriel is mentioned in 1749, and James Bouskell is recorded in 1753 as being bound to Thomas Hughes 'Chany Painter'. It seems that the Hughes family established a training school for porcelain decorators, where their pupils included possibly William Duesbury, William Complin, John Copeland and Moses Webster. A Chinese saucer painted with a copy of a Hancock print[2] is the only known signed example of their work. John and Thomas Hughes, who were possibly cousins, ran a retail business in Market Lane between 1750 and 1754, and later on the north side of Pall Mall from 1754 to 1765. One of their advertisements of 5 March 1755 reads 'China Flowers and Figures for Sale', which may well have been supplied after decoration by their uncle.

NICHOLAS CRISP

NICHOLAS CRISP WAS BORN in 1704, the son of Thomas Crisp, citizen and draper.[3] Apprenticed haberdasher in 1725, he obtained his Freedom in 1737 and, in 1740, became proprietor of a jewellery business in the Cornhill. He joined John Saunders in 1752 at a small porcelain factory in Vauxhall, that failed c.1761. Nancy Valpy discovered a receipt book, once the property of Samuel Martin, containing the entry: '3 May 1755. Pd. Mr. Crisp of Bow Church Yard for four small figures of Vauxhall China – a guinea and a half'.[4] Recent excavations of the Vauxhall site have unearthed sherds matching wares formerly ascribed to William Ball's Liverpool manufactory.[5] No models have so far been recovered, but there are strong reasons for supposing that some late Longton Hall figures were enamelled at Vauxhall, and possibly others from Bow.

JOHN BOLTON

JOHN BOLTON WAS A MASTER POTTER employed by Crisp at Vauxhall, but in 1755 he was enticed away from his position by William Kempson and Michael Alcock, to help them establish a small pottery in Kentish Town.[6] This venture failed in January 1756, when Bolton set up a porcelain decorating atelier, near Lambeth Church. The Bowcock Papers contain a number of bills from Richard Dyer, at Mr Bolton's, covering the period from 5 May to 2 August of that year. It is not known whether Dyer was himself an enameller, or worked in some other capacity.

Dr Bernard Watney described a style of painting floral sprays common to dry-edge Derby, Girl-in-a-Swing and some other porcelains which he tentatively ascribed to Bolton, although nothing of this kind has been reported upon Bow figures.[7] Accounts from Richard Dyer mention the following Bow models:[8]

Item				Total	No.
5 May 1760					
6 pairs Italian Musicians	@	3s 0d	—	18s 0d	(B2)
2 sets small Seasons	@	1s 0d	—	8s 0d	(B46)
4 Dianas	@	1s 6d	—	6s 0d	(B19)
4 Grape-cutting Boys	@	1s 6d	—	6s 0d	(B46)
21 May 1760					
3 Fostinas	@	3s 6d	—	10s 6d	(B22)
2 pairs Turks	@	1s 3d	—	5s 0d	(B59)
18 June 1760					
3 pairs Turk Salts	@	1s 6d	—	9s 0d	(B60)
19 July 1760					
4 Slave Candlesticks	@	1s 6d	—	12s 0d	(C33)
6 New Dancers	@	1s 3d	—	7s 6d	(B108 or B9)
4 New Dancers with plints	@	1s 6d	—	6s 0d	(C50)
12 Nuns and Fryers	@	10d	—	10s 0d	(B34–40)
12 Boys, no plints	@	5d	—	5s 0d	(B129)
6 Boys, with plints	@	6d	—	3s 0d	(B129)
28 July 1760					
8 Pipers and Companions	@	1s 0d	—	8s 0d	(B115 and B6)
2 August 1760					
2 Minervas	@	6s 0d	—	12s 0d	(B28)
6 large Gardeners	@	1s 6d	—	9s 0d	(C30)
1 pair double Birds	@	2s 0d	—	4s 0d	(B158)
Boys on Lion and Leopard	@	1s 0d	—	2s 0d	(B132)

WILLIAM DUESBURY

WILLIAM DUESBURY WAS BORN at Longton in Staffordshire, the son of a leather trader from Cannock, also named William. He may have learned his trade as a porcelain decorator from Thomas Hughes of Clerkenwell, but then established his own atelier in London. His London Account Book, covering the period November 1751 to August 1753, written in several different hands and using phonetic spelling, survives.[9] He may, of course, have commenced practising his art before the autumn of 1751, but by October 1754 he was at Longton Hall, and early in 1756 he became manager and proprietor of the Derby porcelain manufactory. Most of his work was executed in unfired pigments, but he also employed 'Henamel' for which he charged almost three times as much. Entries relate to porcelain from 'Bogh', 'Chelsay', 'Darby' and 'Staffartshire'. He also mended broken porcelain and created metal mounts. Only a few entries refer specifically to Bow figures:

2 Large groups of Bogh Birds	@	2s od	—	4s od
2 pairs Bogh Sesons	@	3s od	—	12s od
1 Large group Bogh Figars				4s od
6 Bogh Doggs	@	1s od	—	6s od
1 pair small figars Bogh				2s 6d
Mr. Woodward and Mrs. Clive	@	3s od		6s od

Undesignated models that are likely to have been from Bow include 'Junoes and Jupiteors', 'Gouts' (Goats), 'Ships' (Sheep), 'Howls' (Owls), 'Phesans' (Pheasants), and the most amusing of all, 'Hostorridge jepand for Coll. Oyron' (Ostrich japanned for Col. Orion). Some believe Duesbury used an enamel palette in which puce, lemon-yellow and yellowish-green predominate, and that he painted rather dense, compact floral sprays of no great artistic merit. He may have made some of the brass fitments with large porcelain flower-heads attached, but cannot have created those on Bow figures after c.1754.

JAMES GILES

JAMES GILES WAS BORN in 1726, the son of a jeweller of the same name and, in 1733, he was apprenticed in this trade to John Arthur of St Martin-in-the-Fields, obtaining his Freedom in 1740. During the early 1750s, he turned his hand towards the enamel decoration of Worcester porcelain, but by 1756 had moved to London. He established his own atelier in Kentish Town, where he decorated both porcelain and glass.[10] He was described in *Mortimer's Directory* of 1763 as: 'A China and Enamel Painter, Berwick Street, Soho. This ingenious Artist copies patterns of any China with the utmost exactness, both with respect to design and colours.' In 1776, Giles opened a warehouse in Cockspur Street, but soon afterwards encountered financial difficulties, and was constrained to accept loans from William Duesbury, who took over the venture when Giles was gazetted bankrupt in 1780.

It would seem that Giles employed several different artists in his studio who produced the following decoration:[11] 'Dishevelled Birds', by the so-called Wet Brush Painter; landscapes executed in green and black enamels; Teniers-like figures in the manner of Antoine Watteau; sliced fruit and flower painting; family crests and armorial bearings. Clearly, with the exception of painted floral sprays, it is not possible to relate this work to porcelain models. Dr Watney has described a style of painting floral sprays in a rather bright palette, which he suggested might stem from the hand of Giles,[12] but although sometimes present on dry-edge Derby and Chaffers's Liverpool figures and wares, it has not been recognised on Bow models.

W. B. Honey drew attention to the alteration in both the enamel palette and the style of decoration that was evident on Bow models after c.1762/3.[13] This, he suggested, might be explained if they were decorated outside the factory by Giles, and the red anchor and dagger mark placed on many examples might have been the device Giles employed.

PART II

TECHNICAL CONSIDERATIONS AND MARKS

10 MANUFACTURING AND DECORATING PROCESSES

THE FORMATION OF SOFT-PASTE PORCELAIN

THE INGREDIENTS REQUIRED FOR THE FORMATION of soft-paste porcelain are china clay, sand, an alkaline flux and water. Bow most probably used Unaker, a white china clay imported from Virginia, until c.1748/9, when it is likely that ball clay, obtained either from Poole in Dorset or Teignmouth in Devon, was substituted. The plasticity of the mix depends upon the proportion of clay included, and is reflected by the aluminium content. A highly plastic paste is said to be fat and one lacking this property is described as short. The *pâte tendre* of Sèvres was so short that before it could be thrown or moulded, it had to be blended with soft-soap. Sand is likely to have been brought from King's Lynn, and the amount incorporated is proportionate to the silica content. When china clay, sand and water are formed into a paste and heated, no significant chemical reaction ensues unless an alkaline flux is added. This was supplied as pearl-ash and potash, obtained from incinerated vegetable and marine life respectively. Unfortunately, when the mixture is heated after the flux is added, a troublesome effervescence takes place, causing the salts to crystallise out and the mass to crumble. This hazard was averted by first transforming the silica into an alkaline silicate by a process known as fritting. Lime (calcium oxide), obtained either from granite or white stones burned in a lime-kiln, was mixed with the sand and raked over the floor of a hot oven until all effervescence ceased and the sand, so treated, was used to create the raw soft paste.

Various devices were employed to enhance stability of the soft paste during its first firing in the biscuit kiln. Some factories included ground up fragments of

35

pottery or even Oriental porcelain, collectively known as grog. At Bow, calcined cattle bones (bones reduced to a calx, or ash, by heat) were preferred, and must have been readily available from slaughter houses in east London. This ingredient was called, somewhat mysteriously, 'Virgin Earth', and the content is reflected by the phosphoric acid level. The quantity can be calculated as being about 40 per cent of the mix. Analyses of the Bow porcelain body by different researchers have been presented by Elizabeth Adams and, with one set of figures at variance with the rest removed, are as follows:[1]

Na_2O	1.0–1.4%
MgO	0.6–0.8%
Al_2O_3	4.8–8.4%
SiO_2	38.9–49.1%
P_2O_5	16.4–20.1%
K_2O	0.9–1.4%
CaO	24.5–29.1%
PbO	0.44–1.75%

The low level of lead oxide precludes inclusion of fragments of lead glass, or cullet, as employed in the early pastes of Chelsea, Girl-in-a-Swing and Derby manufactories. Overall the above results are in accord with the view expressed by Josiah Wedgwood, that the Bow paste contained four parts of bone ash, four parts Lynn sand, a quarter part either alabaster or gypsum plaster, and a quarter part blue ball clay. A phosphatic paste was adopted c.1757 at Chelsea and Lowestoft, and c.1770 at Derby.

The Bristol factory of Benjamin Lund incorporated soap rock c.1749 into their porcelain mix. Soap rock was adopted by Worcester c.1751, and subsequently by her daughter establishments. This ingredient has many of the properties of petuntse employed by the Chinese in their hard paste, and enabled those English factories using it to create a durable porcelain far stronger than that of Bow.

THE FORMATION OF A LEAD GLAZE

THE BOW GLAZE was formed from saltpetre (potassium nitrate), red lead (lead oxide), silica and water. The murky colour was cleared by the addition of white lead (lead carbonate). The early Bow glaze has a warm tone, although sometimes it has a greyish hue, but after c.1760 it was deliberately blued with smalt, doubtless in an attempt to simulate the cold glitter of Meissen feldspathic glaze. Cobalt ore was fritted with sand to form zaffre, of which a small quantity was fused with potash to form a dark-blue glass. This was poured in a molten state into cold water, which caused it to fragment into minute particles, in which the intensity of the blue was greatly reduced and which constituted smalt.

MODELLING IN WAX OR CLAY

IT IS EXTREMELY difficult to model in raw soft paste, owing to the physical properties of the material. A master model was therefore fashioned in wax or clay, from which moulds were taken. Rarely, some other medium was preferred, and it is possible that Franz Anton Bustelli, the talented *Modellmeister* of Nymphenburg, may have elected to carve his work in lime-wood. Until c.1753, craftsmen at Bow were still learning how best to handle the unfamiliar materials and, mindful of the risk of damage to such delicate items as models during each passage through the kiln, were reluctant to use enamel colours for their decoration. Accordingly, all features had to be represented in the round after the manner of sculpture, and any additional embellishment required was provided by incised designs or sprigging. Facial features and furrows in garments were usually exaggerated to allow for their subsequent coverage by a thick lead glaze. It was also necessary to avoid portraying figures in poses which entailed the angular projection of an unsupported limb or trailing drapery, for neither would have been likely to survive the biscuit kiln intact. Models were placed beside or before substantial vertical supports, often thinly disguised as tree-stumps, to minimise the risk of collapse.

In May 1751, Nicholas Sprimont, proprietor of the Chelsea factory, persuaded his patron, Sir Everard Fawkener, to write to the British ambassador in Dresden, asking him to purchase Meissen porcelain that he might copy. The diplomat in question was Sir Charles Hanbury Williams, who had already formed a collection that included 166 *Porzellanfiguren*, which was stored in Holland House during his sojourn abroad. This he lent to Sprimont in order to 'save him unnecessary expense'[2] and, by the spring of 1752, Chelsea copies of the *Puppen* began to appear, based on prototypes first issued five to eight years earlier in the baroque taste. However, by c.1755 the time interval had shortened to twelve months, and models in the ensuing rococo style were copied. Apart from a copy of a Meissen *Negress* made in 1750, Bow craftsmen evidently did not obtain Meissen *Puppen* until c.1753. The source of these, together with those obtained by Derby, remains undetermined, although both factories often issued versions of the same subjects.[3] It was, of course, impossible in soft paste to recreate the devilry and *élan* of the hard-paste originals.

THE FORMATION OF MOULDS

THE WAX OR CLAY master model was dissected into portions, each one of which could be cast without becoming locked into its mould. In this process, V-shaped incisions were employed to facilitate reassembly. A single mould usually sufficed for the torso, together with one leg and often the base as well, whilst the other limbs and head each had one of their own. A wooden box, called a coffin, was packed tight with sand and a central excavation scooped out. The cavity was half filled with plaster of Paris, into which the part of the model to be moulded was pressed, leaving its upper surface exposed. Small terracotta or metal balls were likewise pressed into the surrounds of the plaster surface which, when removed, left hemispherical indentations known as natches. The upper leaf of the mould was made by completing the coverage with more plaster of Paris, which entered the natches to form male/female connections, ensuring correct alignment when the two leaves were taken apart and put together again. The complex configuration of some model parts necessitated formation of a third leaf, by cutting away a segment of the dried plaster, forming natches, and pouring into the gap more plaster. Adherence between model parts and the leaves, and between leaves, was prevented by coverage with soft-soap. This process was repeated for each portion of the figure including large accessories. Sprigging of leaves and flower petals was cast in pitcher-moulds, and complex blossoms were assembled in rest-moulds. Small flat items were stamped out of a sheet of semi-solid paste with a metal die, after the manner in which a pastry chef decorated a pie-crust. The mould for a musical triangle, held by a female *Musician* (B103, Plate 147) was recovered from the Bow factory site.[4]

Small porcelain factories lacking a modeller of their own, like the Liverpool establishment of Richard Chaffers,[5] took moulds from bronzes, terracottas or their competitors' models, and one Bow model of *Arlecchino* (B1, Plate 69) seems to have been taken from a mould formed directly from the Meissen prototype.

Casting the Models

BEFORE CASTING A fresh model, it was customary to take clay squeezes from the moulds, which were assembled and lightly fired, both to provide guidance to the repairer and to facilitate the replacement of moulds past their useful life. Two distinct methods of casting were available.

Press-moulding was routinely employed at Bow, Lowestoft, Worcester and most Continental factories. A sheet of semi-solid paste was rolled out and portions of it pressed manually into component leaves of every mould. The paired leaves were then bound tightly together with twine, contained in grooves that had been previously cut into their external surfaces. A handful of figures were cast solid at Bow prior to c.1755,[6] but nearly all have a central cavity at least within the main section of the model. Models so cast have thick walls and are accordingly heavy in the hand. When it is possible to see their interior it is rough and bears the marks of tools or of the potter's fingers.

Slip-casting was introduced c.1740 by Staffordshire potters for salt-glazed stoneware, and was subsequently employed at most ceramic establishments not mentioned above, and on the mainland of Europe. Dr Redstone noted slip-casting was used at Bow for service wares, alongside press-moulding for figures.[7] All the component leaves of the mould were keyed together, inverted, and liquid slip run into the interior via a wide aperture in the base. A desiccated crust forms adjacent to the plaster of Paris, which includes the area around the ventilation hole, the thickness of which depends upon the time elapsing before the excess of slip is poured off. Models so cast have relatively thin walls and are light in weight, and their interior surface is smooth, mirroring the external contours.

ASSEMBLY OF THE CASTINGS

CASTINGS WERE LEFT in their moulds until they formed a leathery state when, owing to shrinkage by desiccation, they could readily be removed without risk of damage. They were assembled by a craftsman called a repairer who luted them together using liquid slip as a cement. Features lacking crispness were sharpened up with a knife, junctions between castings were smoothed over with a wet brush, and any proud mould marks evident were fettled (cut away). Sprigged ornament was removed from its pitcher-mould and applied while still moist and pliable. The repairer was sometimes responsible for modifying the design of the base and, on press-moulded figures, he attached, trimmed and vented a base plate. Finally, he added any incised or impressed marks that might be required.

BISCUIT FIRING

ASSEMBLED MODELS WERE placed in earthenware cases, or saggars, suitably vented to afford an even distribution of heat, and to protect them from smoke and debris from the furnace. Saggar floors were liberally sprinkled with fine sand, to reduce the risk of items adhering to the casing. Projecting parts were supported with ceramic struts, pointed at both ends, which had coefficients of expansion and contraction similar to those of the model, thereby avoiding any distortion during firing. Saggars were stacked upon shelves in the kiln, all doors and ports sealed, and the wood-fired furnace ignited. The temperature in the kiln chamber was slowly raised to between 1000 and 1150 °C, estimated by inspection of the colour of the flames viewed through ports. Firemen were, or so it was said, immediately recognisable by the loss of their eyebrows and hair; many of them became unruly from drunkenness after consuming huge quantities of ale to combat the dehydration from working long hours in an intense heat. The kiln was struck between 12 and 24 hours and allowed to cool very slowly, for any sudden drop of temperature might turn a whole batch into wasters.

Unequal shrinkage of paste led to surface tearing or to full thickness fire-cracks, while failure to eliminate air bubbles from the paste gave rise to pitting of the body when they burst through to the surface. Despite all precautions, sagging out of alignment and smoke-staining were fairly common prior to c.1755. The early paste is either compact and creamy or granular and greyish in hue. During the last decade of production the body lacks translucency due to underfiring.

BISCUIT MODELS

FIRED BUT UNGLAZED models are said to be in Biscuit, and if left in this state every blemish remains overt. Biscuit models were introduced c.1751 at Vincennes by Jean-Jacques Bachelier and were acclaimed by the Marquise de Pompadour. This lead by the acknowledged arbiter of elegance and good taste ensured that thereafter in France, as far as figures were concerned, biscuit was *de rigueur*. In England during the 1750s and 1760s, biscuit was eschewed by a society that took delight in the satirical and brilliantly enamelled *Porzellanfiguren* created at Meissen. Nevertheless, a few early English biscuit models were made. One example of the Bow portrait figure of Kitty Clive as *Mrs Riot* lacks an arm and may be no more than a waster,[8] but a biscuit version of the companion model of Henry Woodward as the *Fine Gentleman* is in fair condition,[9] whilst a *Huntsman and Lady* from Bow,[10] a pair of *Street Vendors* from Derby[11] and a *Pheasant* from Longton Hall[12] are also known.

UNDERGLAZE COLOURS

COLOURS APPLIED TO the surface of biscuit models later to be glazed had to be capable of withstanding the temperature of the glost kiln without degradation, and only cobalt and manganese possessed this quality. Underglaze blue was used on Bow figures after c.1762 to replace the earlier blue enamel. Manganese was used on a few early models made at Chelsea, Derby and Longton Hall, but this practice was abandoned when enamel colours became more plentiful.

GLAZING

THE POROUS NATURE of fired soft paste necessitated coverage with a glass, or glaze, to enable hollow wares to retain liquids. Glaze also facilitated fixation of enamel colours to the surface. The biscuit model was inverted and dipped into a vat of glaze; if any aperture pierced the back of the figure, the glaze gained access to the central cavity through it and, when returned again to the upright position, escaped through the ventilation hole. The glazed model was placed upon either cockspurs or cones on the sanded floors of the saggars, and reheated to a temperature of about 1000 °C for a few hours in the glost kiln. When the batch was unloaded, spurs and cones were removed and the undersurface was ground to ensure level and secure stance.

Blemishes of the glaze include dark brown spots with raised black centres, called sanding, smoke-staining, pin holes due to rupture of air bubbles, dry patches where an area of glaze has failed to adhere to the body, and crazing that resembles fissures in ice.

ENAMEL DECORATION

ENAMELS ARE DERIVED from the oxides of heavy metals which, during the eighteenth century, were laboriously prepared by hand with a pestle and mortar. Cobalt gives an intense blue; manganese, if applied thickly, provides vermilion or, used sparingly, gives a streaky pink; copper results in a bluish-green or turquoise, arsenic an opaque white; lead and tin are the bases for a spectrum of yellows; whilst iron can be manipulated to yield red or black. Trichloride of gold produces a range of colours from yellow through purple to rose-pink, depending upon the temperature at which it is fired. Enamels at Bow were more thickly applied than at Derby but were less generously used than at Chelsea.

Enamels are applied over the glaze and matured in a muffle-kiln. In their raw state they do not have their final mature colours, which posed a problem for the enamellers. Nowadays vegetable dyes, approximately matching the colour of the mature enamel, and which burn off in the kiln, provide guidance to painters on porcelain. During the eighteenth century, instead, artists kept their enamels in numbered bottles and referred to fired specimens bearing corresponding numbers on a porcelain plaque. To add to the difficulties, some colours only mature at a temperature at which others become debased. In modern times this is overcome by multiple passages through the kiln at progressively lower temperatures but, in the eighteenth century, most often a single firing had to suffice. The inclusion of alkaline flux reduced the heat required from 900 °C to around 700 °C, but this still melted the surface glaze, into which the enamels sank and where, after cooling, they were fixed. The lack of intensity of colour on soft-paste porcelain, which often has a blotchy uneven texture, contrasts with the brilliance and glossy qualities of decoration on hard-paste porcelain, where the enamels remain upon the surface of the feldspathic glaze, since it does not melt below their maturation temperatures.

The maturation and eventual hue of enamels depends also upon the relative acidity:alkalinity (the Ph) of the materials and the oxygen content of the kiln chamber. An oxidising kiln contains oxygen in atmospheric proportions whereas a reducing kiln, created by throwing damp wood into the furnace, is oxygen deficient. The tale is told how, during the reign of the Chinese emperor Kangxi (1622–1722) the superintendent of the Imperial Kilns had repeatedly failed to recreate the much admired Ming copper-red. In despair he threw himself into the flames as a sacrifice to the kiln gods and, when the batch was unloaded, the wares were resplendent in an immaculate copper-red. *Flambé* colours require a reducing kiln and incineration of the corpse had effected the requisite adjustment!

41

TECHNICAL CONSIDERATIONS AND MARKS

GILDING

HONEY GILDING WAS employed by all English manufactories prior to c.1795. Bow gilders first prepared the ground with a fired chocolate enamel, but after c.1754 this practice seems to have been abandoned. Powdered gold leaf was mixed with honey and the sticky mass blended with lavender oil to render it workable. This was brushed on the ground and fired at 650 °C for a few hours, to provide a brown colour which, after burnishing with an agate, gave a sumptuous gold. Early Bow examples have badly rubbed gold probably lacking adequate fixation, while during the last decade the gilding has a coppery appearance, suggesting that impure gold may have been purchased for reasons of economy.

Mercury Gilding was used by the Romans to embellish small metal objects but they took care to ensure that the noxious fumes generated were blown away by the wind. Later Benvenuto Cellini (1500–71) described the process in his *Treatise on Goldsmiths' Work*, while Denis Diderot (1713–84) illustrated a goldsmith's workshop in his *Encyclopédie*. Mercury gilding was widely employed in France from about the middle of the reign of Louis XIV on bronze doré mounts for furniture. The virtual inevitability of mercury poisoning in craftsmen long employed in the industry was recognised and they were paid exceptionally high wages to compensate them for the loss of teeth, ill health and often premature death. Strangely enough, mercury gilding was evidently not used by English porcelain factories until c.1795 so that it is not a feature of Bow products. However, it has been used for restoration or replacement of missing parts of Bow figures and may also appear on reproductions, forgeries and fakes.

An amalgam of mercury and gold is formed, known as Gold-Water, to which is added fat dissolved in alcohol to enable the mixture to be applied with a brush. The mercury vaporises in the kiln to leave a brilliant, though rather pale, gold precipitate.

11 BOW MARKS

PROBABLY LESS THAN FIVE PER CENT OF BOW MODELS issued before c.1762 bear marks and it is clear no standard factory device was adopted. Date marks include 1750 incised beneath the bases of at least one example of Kitty Clive as *Mrs Riot*

(A1, Plate 1), Henry Woodward as the *Fine Gentleman* (A2, Plate 2) and a *Negress* standing before a basket (A58, Plate 49). Further, the monogram IB and the year 1757 within an oval are pencilled upon the mouthpiece of bagpipes held by a *Shepherd Bagpiper* (B117, Plate 160).

Incised repairers' marks all appear beneath the bases except for the letter W which is present upon the upper surface. They include:

Mark	Symbol	Model	No.	Reference
☿	Mercury	Actor in Turkish costume	A5	Schreiber[1] No. 51
☿	Mercury	Recumbent Pug Dogs	A72	Schreiber No. 4
♂	Mars	Flemish Woman with a Crib	A40	Freeman[2] Pl. 192
♂	Mars	Lion and Lioness (white)	A66	British Museum
♀	Venus	Unknown to author on a model		
W		Huntsman in a peaked cap	B110	Freeman pl. 211
AF		Boy seated with Grapes	B74	V. & A. C.1314–1924
✳		Henry Woodward	A2	Freeman pl. 187

Impressed marks include the T and T° which have earlier been discussed. The so-called Ladder Mark appears to have been made by serrated jaws of an instrument used to lift the unfired model gripping the base-plate on either side with one blade positioned through the ventilation hole.

Mark	Model	No.	Reference
B	Male and Female Cooks	B69	Schreiber No. 46
D	Unknown to author on a model		Cited by Lane[3] p. 92
H	Huntsman and Lady Companion	B111	Private Collection
T	The muse Urania	A33	Private Collection
	Marquis of Granby	B124	Schreiber No. 54a
	Major General James Wolfe	B128	Schreiber No. 54
	Tea Party Group	B127	Freeman pl. 232
T°	Seated pair of Musicians	B104	Freeman pl. 233

Mark	Model	No.	Reference
T°	Dutch Dancers (candlesticks)	B107	Stoner[4] pl. 83
⚓	An Actor unknown to author		Cited by Chaffers[5] p. 285
⬤▭⬤	Boy Shepherd Piper	B155	V. & A. C.232–1926

Pseudo-Chinese ideograms pencilled underglaze in blue may be found on blue and white service wares, particularly when decorated with chinoiseries, but are unknown on models. Other marks pencilled in blue are:

Mark	Model	No.	Reference
B	Huntsman and Lady Companion	B111	Private Collection
G	Peacock in a bocage		Cited by Chaffers p. 286
I	Boys with drum and fife	C42	Schreiber No. 86
•	Male Idyllic Musician	B103	Hurlbutt[6] pl. 62
T F	Female Idyllic Musician	B103	Hurlbutt pl. 62
⊏	Group of Idyllic Musicians	C45	Untermyer[7] fig. 246
c	Ceres emblematic of Earth	C24	King[8] fig. 13
✗	Winter from the Adolescent Seasons	B47	Hurlbutt pl. 49

In addition the upper case letter E mark, pencilled in red, may be found upon the early group:

E	Ki Mao Sao	A22	Freeman pl. 136

After c.1762 rather more than half the models are marked with the device of an anchor and dagger pencilled overglaze in red enamel. This has many variations but usually there is neither cable nor ring and the crown is U-shaped. Rarely it may be painted either in brown or gilt whilst in some examples another mark is drawn in underglaze blue (Fig. 1):

Red Enamel	Blue Enamel	Model	No.	Reference
⚓ †	+	The Blown Kiss	C64	Untermyer fig. 256
† ⚓	╱	Winter from the Rustic Seasons	C27	Hurlbutt pl. 52
⚓ †	C	A Boy Singer	C43	Hurlbutt pl. 46a
	†	Male New Dancer	C49	Hurlbutt pl. 45
⚓ †	G	Female New Dancer	C49	Hurlbutt pl. 45
⚓ †	X	Pugilist	C58	Freeman pl. 235
⚓ †	Brown	Arlecchino	B1	Hurlbutt pl. 43a
⚓ †	Gold	Columbina dancing	C1	Untermyer fig. 249

It will be evident that otherwise similar models may either bear different marks or alternatively be unmarked, and it is clear no regular plan was enforced.

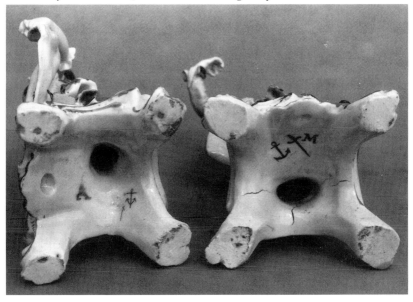

Fig. 1 (C44) Glazed concave undersurfaces of a pair of *Dancers*, with red anchor and dagger marks, accompanied by the letters 'A' and 'M' in underglaze blue.

45

PART III

BOW PORCELAIN MODELS

12 BOW PORCELAIN MODELS C.1748–53

MODELLING

EARLY BOW MODELS MAY BE CONSTRUCTED either from a compact paste clad in a greyish glaze or have a granular body that has a creamy appearance. Three examples incised 1750 display a modelling competence that bespeaks previous experience although this may have been obtained elsewhere. If, indeed, any figures were issued before this date they would presumably be less sophisticated, marred by numerous blemishes and, like the earliest table wares, be covered in a glaze which has a faint mushroom tinge. Prior to 1752/3 only a single Meissen *Puppen*, a *Negress* (A61, Plate 52) was copied and it would seem craftsmen in the figure department were largely unaware of the techniques evolved by J. J. Kändler and the manner in which his *Porzellanfiguren* were presented. This ignorance, coupled with a reluctance to use enamel colour on models, led to the representation of all features in the round as obtains in conventional sculpture. Human subjects each have a rather small head, receding forehead and chin, heavy-lidded prominent eyes, aquiline nose and moulded lips often framing a half-open mouth. Arms often appear to be too long and, when the legs are draped, the deeply furrowed folds are frequently at variance with correct anatomical considerations. Garments are usually embellished by sprigging, incised designs, or by the attachment of frills, ruffles and flounces whilst ear-rings and beaded necklaces may provide personal adornment. Models lack both the noble physiognomy of Chelsea and the crisp potting of Derby counterparts.

These traits are shared among most Bow figures of the period and are exemplified by a set of nine *Muses* (A25–33, Plates 22–7, Col. Plate I); their

46

Fig. 2 (B112) The back of a *Huntsman*, showing the supporting tree-stump left uncoloured, and a triangular aperture.

Fig. 3 (B112) The back of the companion *Lady*, showing the incorporation of additional support into the skirt. Red anchor and dagger marks.

unknown craftsman has, accordingly, been called the 'Muses Modeller'. After c.1753 his style becomes muted but remains discernible until c.1760. Most early examples are robustly sculpted yet primitive, although a few are more sophisticated. The wide spectrum of achievement may either reflect the hand of more than one craftsman or, alternatively, the work of one modeller whose expertise was salted by experience.[1] There is, indeed, a small coterie of figures, including *Ki Mao Sao* (A22, Plates 19 and 20), *Liberty and Matrimony* (A53, Plate 46) and a *Thames Waterman* (A44, Plate 37) that exist in rather crude white as well as more accomplished coloured versions. Further, one might expect a greater degree of excellence in models copied from three-dimensional sources than in those adapted from prints, water-colour sketches or engravings. In general this does obtain but there are a few notable exceptions that include fine portrait figures of *Kitty Clive* (A1, Plate 1) and *Henry Woodward* (A2, Plate 2) both of which were based on two-dimensional sources. Copies of Meissen *Porzellanfiguren* began to appear at Bow c.1753 incorporating many of the technical and stylistic innovations earlier introduced by Kändler. Craftsmen were assisted also by a greater readiness to employ enamel colours which allowed a general tidying-up and simplification of the modelling that is described in Chapter 13.

BASES

BEFORE c.1751 bases were plain white squares or rectangles, occasionally provided with detachable plinths moulded with swags and trophies in high relief. Upper surfaces of rare coloured examples were washed over with lime-green streaked with brown, or a greyish-blue. Within a year or two, white mound or pad bases were introduced, sparsely sprigged with enamelled leaves and flowers in the baroque manner. The first manifestations of the rococo appeared at Bow c.1753/4 as rather clumsy moulded scrolls picked out in a dark purplish-grey, arranged in a manner revealing an incomplete understanding of the new style. Undersurfaces were ground flat but often residual traces of glaze remain in shallow indentations. Ventilation holes vary considerably in both shape and size (Figs 4 and 5): some are oval, measuring up to 3in (7.6cm) in their long diameter; others are round and under 1in (2.5cm) across; rarely there are two apertures and in a very few instances the inferior surface is left open. Ceramic props behind figures may be disguised as a tree-stump (Fig. 2), an architectural plinth, a rocky mound or even a stack of books, but in some models of women they are incorporated into their skirts (Fig. 3).

DECORATION

MENTION HAS EARLIER been made of the decoration of figures in cold pigments, most of which seems to have been effected by men like William Duesbury outside

48

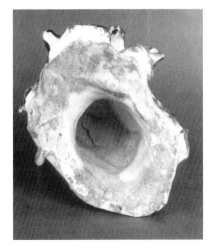

Fig. 4 (A30) Flat ground undersurface of *Polyhymnia*, showing a large oval ventilation hole.

Fig. 5 (A33) Flat ground undersurface of *Urania*, showing a ventilation hole of intermediate size.

the factory. His London Account Book[2] shows that he also employed enamel colours but no examples of this work have been firmly identified. Some have ascribed to him decoration, which includes compact floral sprays, upon the model of Kitty Clive as Mrs Riot, in the collection of Lord Bearsted at Upton House.[3] However, very similar sprays appear on another model of the actress in Geoffrey Godden's collection, associated with gilding laid upon a chocolate enamel ground.[4] This form of honey-gilding is now universally accepted as having been accomplished in the Bow factory.

The early palette embraces lime-green, primrose-yellow, a dry orange-red, yellow-green, light blue, lilac, bluish-grey, and both a dark brown and black which have a purplish cast. Flesh tints, often omitted, are a pale buff heightened by a faint orange blush. The hair, frequently arranged either in a bun, ringlets or plaits, is depicted with fine strands of dark brown and black. Eyebrows are steeply arched and pencilled in dark brown, a colour also employed for eyelashes, eyelids and comma-shaped nostrils that may often lack precision in execution. Pupils are purplish-black, set in irises of brown or grey whilst orange-red lips frequently look smudged. Garments are covered with pale washes of often discordant colour between large passages of white that may be painted with floral sprays portraying red and blue rather full-blown blossoms with yellow centres and small yellow-green leaves. Occasionally stylised stems, leaves and florets are represented in either a red or puce monochrome. The simulation of moss upon some bases is effected by placement of a lime-green wash upon an area stippled with a sharp tool.

Surprisingly, perhaps, many early models have sparse gilding laid upon a chocolate ground of enamel that is restricted to the edges of garments, and accessories such as crowns or musical instruments. Between c.1754 and 1756 gilding was rarely used on models.

THE MODELS

UNDOUBTEDLY THE BEST known of the early models are those of *Kitty Clive as Mrs Riot* (A1, Plate 1) and *Henry Woodward as the Fine Gentleman* (A2, Plate 2), from Garrick's farce *Lethe*. The play opened in 1740 at Drury Lane but Mrs Clive did not join the cast until 1749. The scenario relates to fashionable characters from contemporary London who pour out their woes to *Old Aesop* as they cross the river Styx, hoping thereby to gain access to the waters of Lethe and obtain oblivion. The Bow Kitty Clive, like her Derby sister,[5] was adapted from Charles Mosley's engraving of a water-colour sketch by Thomas Worlidge,[6] portraying her wearing a mob-cap, blouse and hooped skirt, standing with a spaniel under her arm. Garrick wrote:

> She lies abed all morning, rattles about all day, sits up all night; she goes every-where and sees everything; she knows everybody and loves nobody; ridicules her friends, coquets with her lovers, sets 'em together by their ears, tells fibs, makes mischief, buys china, cheats at cards, keeps a pet dog and hates parsons . . .

Mrs Clive, née Rafter (1711–85), was born in Kilkenny and made her stage debut at Drury Lane in 1728. After the failure of her marriage she became friendly with Horace Walpole and, during her retirement, resided in a cottage on his Strawberry Hill estate. An inventory of the contents of the Great House made in 1761 mentions: 'Mrs. Clive, the excellent comedian, in the character of the Fine Lady in Lethe; in water-colour by Worlidge'. Her epitaph composed by Walpole reads:

> Here lived the laughter-loving dame,
> A matchless actress, Clive her name.
> The Comic Muse with her retired
> And shed a tear when she expir'd.

Henry Woodward (1717–77) inspired the companion model, adapted from James McArdell's mezzotint after Francis Hayman[7] portraying him attired in a huge tricorn hat, long foppish waistcoat, jacket, breeches, hose and buckled shoes; he stands feet apart, with both hands thrust into his pockets and, in some versions, bears a rapier in a sword-belt. Garrick wrote of him:

Faith, my existance is merely supported by amusements. I dress, visit, study, taste, write sonnets; by birth, travel, education and natural abilities I am entitled to lead the fashion. I am the principal connoisseur at all auctions, the chief arbiter at assemblies, professional critic at the theatre and a Fine Gentleman everywhere . . .

One model of Woodward[8] and another of Kitty Clive[9] are incised 1750 beneath their bases.

A model of *Sir John Falstaff* (A3, Plate 3), from Shakespeare's *Henry IV* and *Henry V*, shows the corpulent wine-bibbing knight attired in a plumed hat, doublet, baggy breeches and top-boots, holding a sabre and a studded oval shield. Traditionally based on James McArdell's engraving of James Quinn (Fig. 6),[10] Aubrey Toppin suggested the source was, instead, an etching by Truchy,[11] while Arthur Lane favoured an earlier engraving by Grignion which, if correct, is more likely to portray Garrick than Quinn in the role,[12] thus differing from the Derby version.[13] Another model of an *Actor* (A4, Plate 4) has been erroneously identified as Garrick who played Archer alongside John Weston as Scrubb, in George Farquhar's comedy *The Beaux' Stratagem*. The work is remembered for the lines: 'No woman can be a beauty without a fortune', and 'There is no scandal like rags nor crime so shameful as poverty'. Although the play opened in 1707, Garrick did not take the part until 1767, many years after the first issue of the model. A pair, *Actor and Actress in Turkish costumes* (A5, Plate 5) may, possibly, represent

Fig. 6 Engraving by Truchy, after Francis Hayman, of James Quinn as *Falstaff* in Vauxhall Gardens.

dramatis personae from Christopher Marlowe's *Tamburlaine the Great*, for a revival of the work was staged in 1740 at Drury Lane when James Quinn took over the role of Bajazet, at short notice, to rave reviews.

A pair of *Sphinxes* (A6, Plate 6) on rococo-styled bases resembling ormolu mounts, each with the head and breasts of a woman, are said to have been adapted from Sir Arthur Pond's portrait of c.1741 of Margaret Woffington (1717–60).[14] The actress was born in Dublin the daughter of a journeyman bricklayer, and was reared by her widowed mother in penurious circumstances. She was taught as a child to sing and dance by Madame Violante[15] and made her stage debut in her Lilliputian Theatre, later receiving instruction from Charles Coffee, an author and composer of operettas, besides Francis Elrington and Colly Cibber. She rose to fame in the breeches role Sir Harry Wildair from George Farquhar's farce *The Constant Couple*, which prompted the doggerel:

> The excellent Peg who showed such leg
> When lately she dressed in Men's clothes –
> A creature uncommon who's both man and woman
> And the chief of the Belles and the Beaux!

After this triumph she was invited to Drury Lane by John Rich where subsequently she appeared in the company of most of the great thespians of her day. A talented actress and a beautiful woman, she became notorious for many torrid love affairs and, between 1742 and 1744, lived openly with David Garrick whose repeated offers of marriage she declined. On one occasion, after playing another breeches role, she entered the Greenroom and exclaimed to Kitty Clive, 'By God, Madam, half the audience thinks me to be a man!' This was too much for the comedienne, who retorted, 'By God, Madam, the other half know you to be a woman!' In 1757 whilst reciting a prologue on stage she collapsed and was never again able to return to the theatre; she died after a long illness three years later at the age of only forty-three.

There are enamelled examples of the Sphinxes in the Museum of Fine Arts, Boston, which seem to portray two young women bearing a family likeness so that it is possible they represent the Gunning sisters, two Irish beauties who came to England from Dublin to become the toast of London in 1740. Earlier they had been invited to the Viceroy's Ball in Dublin Castle, when Peg Woffington, knowing they had nothing suitable to wear, allowed them to select gowns from her own wardrobe. Although the actress was herself *persona non grata* in that exalted company, paradoxically her dresses were most welcome! Maria Gunning (1733–60) wed the Earl of Coventry, whilst her sister Elizabeth (1734–90) married the Duke of Hamilton and, after his death, the Duke of Argyll. Their portraits were painted by Francis Cotes[16] and oval plaques in the Victoria & Albert Museum are believed to have been based on engravings made by John Brooks.[17]

The colourful costumes worn by members of the *Commedia dell'Arte*, together with their histrionic gestures and poses, rendered them ideal subjects for modellers and examples in red Böttger stoneware were issued as early as 1715 at Meissen. The first porcelain versions were probably adapted from etchings made before 1729 by J. B. Probst after Schübler, published in Augsburg. After c.1736 J. J. Kändler created a host of *Porzellanfiguren* of Comedy characters, some of which found echoes at Bow, namely *Arlecchino* (A7, Plate 7) standing in cap, mask and motley; *Columbina* (A8) wearing a brimmed hat, blouse and skirt, dancing; and *Pulcinella* (A11, Plate 9) attired in a conical cap, blouse and baggy trousers.[18] A *Fruitress* (A9) standing with a tray of fruit, holding up a bunch of grapes, was probably intended to represent Columbina in disguise.

In 1743/4 Kändler and Peter Reinicke created a set of 36 Comedy figures to commemorate the marriage of Johann Adolf II, Duke of Weissenfels, shortly before his death, to a princess of the House of Coburg-Gotha. Inspiration came from engravings made by François Joullain in Luigi Riccoboni's *Histoire du théâtre italien*, published in Paris in 1728. These, in turn, were derived from etchings by Giacomo Calotto, and loosely based on the works of Charles-Antoine Coypel (1661–1722), Claude Gillot (1673–1722) and others. Most Bow Comedy models echo those in the Weissenfels series but only one, *Scapino* (A12, Plate 10), was issued before 1754. He stands bearded and laughing but holds a mask in place of a cap in the Meissen version.[19]

After c.1740 Kändler made several Italian Comedy groups including the *Indiscreet Arlecchino*[20] copied at Bow (A13, Plate 11). Here, the recumbent Zanni lifts the hem of Columbina's skirt to inspect her ankles, as she sits upon the knee of a love-sick Mezzetino. Meanwhile paintings and chalk sketches by Antoine Watteau (1684–1721) endowed the Commedia with fresh elegance and charm. Many of his *œuvres* were engraved by different artists and published in 1737 as a folio entitled *Recueil de Julienne*. Two plates by C. N. Cochin[21] prompted Bow groups. 'Belles, n'écoutez rien' inspired the *Italian Lovers* (A15, Plate 13) in which Arlecchino sits beside Columbina, his left arm encircling her waist, his right hand upraised. 'Pour garder l'honneur d'une belle', prompted the *Italian Musicians* (A14, Plate 12) in which Scaramuzzi sits holding a musical score and singing, with Isabella on his left side playing a guitar. A Meissen version, adapted from 'La Sérénade italienne' reverses both the positions and the roles of the two characters.[22] A third Bow group depicting *Pedrolino and Isabella as Lovers* (A10, Plate 8) may have been loosely based upon 'Le Conteur', which survives only as a preliminary chalk drawing by Watteau and in a transposed engraving by Cochin.[23]

During the eighteenth century almost all gentlemen of quality made the 'Grand Tour' before either taking up public office or settling down to manage their estates. Familiar with Latin and Greek, they were conversant with classical mythology, at least as it was presented in Ovid's *Metamorphoses*. Bow, like other contemporary factories, created a veritable pantheon of porcelain divinities, few of which have Meissen prototypes. Paired models of *Juno* and *Jupiter* (A19 and A20, Plate 17) stand in mirror poses holding sceptres, respectively beside an eagle or a peacock; both are bareheaded and barefoot and are clad in simple robes. *Neptune* (A34) is crowned but scantily draped and stands barefoot holding a trident. All three models are solid cast and are known both in white, when traces of unfired pigments and gold leaf may be attached, and in possibly later enamelled examples.

Their sources of inspiration are undetermined, unlike the model of *Apollo* (A16, Plate 14), crowned with laurels and with his eyes turned towards the firmament for inspiration as he plays his lyre, which has affinities with an earlier Meissen figure by J. F. Eberlein.[24] The nature of these and other Olympians and their deeds are summarised in Appendix B.

Aubrey Toppin[25] first drew our attention to seven of the nine *Muses* and, since Thalia has been located in the Museum of Fine Arts, Boston, only Calliope remains missing. They are ugly wenches who sit or stand 6–7in (15.2–17.8cm) in height. *Urania* (A33, Plate 27, Col. Plate I) stoops over a celestial globe with a pair of dividers in her left hand; in some examples her right hand is lacking and the wrist-stump glazed over. *Terpsichore* (A31) seemingly dances with her right arm elevated but only her left leg is sculpted in front of a supporting plinth. *Clio* (A26, Plate 22) leans forward over an open tome, quill in hand. She was adapted from the frontispiece in *The Works of L'Abbé de St. Real*, c.1700, engraved by D. Coster,[26] but the sources of the other Muses are unknown. Their misspelled titles sometimes scratched upon their bases or supporting props may be derived from captions beneath French prints. Thus, *Erato* (A27, Plate 23) seated with flowers in her lap presenting a longbow to Cupid, is inscribed 'Eraton for Love'; *Clio* is labelled 'Clion', whilst *Euterpe* (A28, Plate 24) seated holding a recorder amidst musical trophies is inscribed 'Euterpe for the musical instruments'. *Polyhymnia* (A30, Plate 25, Col. Plate I), entitled 'Polimne', is seated holding a chaplet over an obelisk to which she points with her right forefinger. She alone has wings which, together with the military trophies at her feet, have led to her being identified as 'Winged Victory'. *Thalia* (A32, Plate 26) stands robed and bareheaded holding the mask of 'Comedy', whilst *Melpomene* (A29) in a crown of gold holds a dagger and a chalice in either hand. Some have detected in this model a resemblance to later figures of *Juno* (B23, Plate 82) and *Ceres* (B41, Plate 95) and have noted that the style in which Melpomene is modelled differs from that of the other Muses.[27] Many were issued in white but those decorated within the factory have orange-red smudged-looking lips, steeply arched dark brown eyebrows and a pale complexion that reminded Arthur Lane of 'An over-emphatic maquillage'.[28] The enameller certainly had a liking for ringlets of dark brown hair, also evident upon figures in two contemporary groups of the *Italian Musicians* (A14, Plate 12) and *Two Lovers with a Bird-cage* (A54, Plate 47). The example of Clio illustrated by Aubrey Toppin has

'A History of Wales' inscribed upon the exposed title page, which may possibly be the concealed signature of James Welch, an enameller mentioned in the Bow Parish Register in August 1754.

Minerva (A24, Plate 21), clad in crested helmet, cuirass, thonged skirt and sandals, stands left hand on hip, leaning upon a shield bearing upon its centre the head of Medusa. *Hope* (A18, Plate 16) is portrayed as a lady wearing a veil and a long robe, standing beside an architectural plinth, leaning upon an anchor. Most examples lack a left hand owing to unequal shrinkage between the figure and the anchor shaft and, when this obtains, the wrist-stump is glazed over, showing that at this early date even the loss of a hand did not constitute a waster. The companion model has hitherto been identified as *Justice* (A21, Plate 18) who stands before a stack of tomes, wearing a helmet and gown, holding a sword and scales in either hand. However, these accoutrements are invariably either lacking or severely damaged and Dr Bernard Watney has suggested she may represent *Faith*. The source of these two 'Virtues' remains undetermined, but *Charity* (A17, Plate 15) follows J. F. Eberlein's group that depicts a woman supporting a babe upon her left arm, and offering an apple to a child standing at her right side.[29] It may possibly have been based on a transposed and simplified adaptation of Alessandro Algardi's bronze, an example of which may be seen in the National Museum of Scotland. *Mercury* (A23) wears a round helmet, cloak and winged sandals and stands before a tree-stump holding the caduceus, after an original by J. F. Eberlein.[30]

Assuredly the most ambitious early Bow group is that which portrays the goddess *Ki Mao Sao* (A22, Plates 19 and 20), seated upon a low plinth inscribed with pseudo-Chinese ideograms, flanked by two kneeling Chinamen, based on Michel Aubert's engraving, after Watteau, of 'Idole de la Déesse Ki Mao Sao dans le Royaume de Mang au Pays des Laos' (Fig. 7).[31] The painting was one of thirty chinoiseries executed c.1709 for adornment of La Muette that were later destroyed. Fortunately they were engraved by Aubert, Boucher and Jeurat who advertised their work in the *Mercure de France* in 1731.[32] Other engravings by P. Aveline after Boucher's 'Décoration chinoise'[33] prompted Bow groups emblematic of the Elements, of which only two survive: *Fire* (A59) is shown as a Chinaman standing beside a brick stove pouring tea from a pot into a cup held by a seated companion. The same design was employed to decorate a silver kettle by Nicholas Sprimont.[34] *Air* (A59, Plate 50) is portrayed by a Chinese woman leaning upon a cage, holding aloft a bird, with a seated Chinaman with a second bird, beside a flying fish. Both serve to remind us that a fine engraving may be too detailed to allow successful translation into porcelain.

Busts of a *Mongolian Prince and Princess* (A60, Plate 51) have almond eyes, and wear fantastic head-dresses embellished with beads which in a coloured example are blue. Minor variations of the man's beard and moustache and decorative details are known and despite their unknown source, they have been called the 'Rumanian

Fig. 7 Déesse Ki Mao Sao dans le Royaume de Mang au pays des Laos, engraved by Michel Aubert, after Watteau.

Ambassador and his Wife'. An entry in the Bow Memorandum Book of April 1756 reads: 'Think of the Chinese head for Mr. Weatherby',[35] but the style of their execution favours an earlier date of issue. Bellamy Gardner discovered a pair of carved rococo wall-brackets with similar heads.[36] A pair of *Sphinxes* (A37), after J. F. Blondel c.1738, are mounted upon wedge-shaped rectangular bases and have the head and breasts of an unidentified woman.[37] A charming group of *Two Putti playing with a Dolphin* (A35, Plate 28) echoes one copied at Vincennes from a bronze fountain at Versailles;[3] it prompted also a Longton Hall replica[39] and a Chelsea version[40] in which an ugly fish replaces the dolphin. A *Naked Boy* (A36, Plate 29), with head turned to the left, semi-reclining and with his left hand elevated, recalls early Chelsea models of children based on terracottas made by François Duquesnoy (1597–1643).

A rare *Shoeblack Group* (A55) portrays a bareheaded gallant taking a pinch of snuff as he stands, one foot upon a stool, before a squatting boy in a brimmed hat. A primitive group of a *Lady with a Page* (A52, Plate 45) shows her attired like *Mrs Riot* (A1, Plate 1), taking peaches from a tray proffered by the attendant. A *Lady playing a Lyre* (A50, Plate 43), wears seventeenth-century dress, ear-rings and a necklace and may either represent an actress in period costume, or have been adapted from an old engraving; the model is mounted on a deeply scrolled base rarely encountered on a Bow model until after c.1758. The *Lady Tatting* (A51, Plate 44), echoes Eberlein's portrait model of Barbara Uttman, the famous Dresden court lace-maker,[41] seated with a bobbin in either hand, but the strange semi-cylindrical object in her lap is replaced by a conventional cushion.

A *Sailor* (A43, Plate 35) clad in hat, scarf, jacket and trousers, standing left hand on hip, has mistakenly been called 'Tom Bowling', a jack tar in a sea shanty written by Charles Dibden (1754–1814) long after issue of the model: 'Faithful, below he did his duty, but now he's gone aloft . . .' The companion *Lass* in bonnet, bodice and skirt holds out a long apron. A *Thames Waterman* (A44, Plate 37) stands wearing a peaked cap, jacket and breeches, his left arm abducted, and a badge upon his shoulder. This may bear the device of a fouled anchor, or the armorial bearings of Thomas Doggett, awarded to the winner of a race rowed annually from London Bridge to the Old Swan at Chelsea, inaugurated by the comedian to commemorate the accession of George I. A *Huntsman and Lady* (A46, Plates 38 and 39) sit in mirror poses holding a gun and with a dog beside them; both white-glazed and biscuit[42] versions are known. *A Huntsman Toper* (A56, Plate 48) reclines upon a steep mound, holding a flask and a goblet and surrounded by trophies of the chase.

Two rather similar groups are in the genre of Boucher. One shows a *Gallant and Fishergirl* (A48, Plate 41) in which the bareheaded man with hand on heart turns towards a maid seated beside him who wears a brimmed hat and has a fishing net across her lap. The other portrays a *Gallant and Lady* (A47, Plate 40) showing the man kneeling before a seated lady attired in a riding habit. The beautiful *Gipsy Fortune Telling* group (A49, Plate 42) was adapted from P. Aveline's engraving after Boucher[43] of 'La Bonne Aventure', depicting a gipsy clad in a laurel chaplet, wide-sleeved robe and boots, reading the palm of a young lady, beneath a tree. Other engravings by Nicolas de Larmessin after Nicolas Lancret prompted the exquisite group *Two Lovers with a Bird-cage* (A54, Plate 47) as well as a pair of Meissen models emblematic of *Liberty and Matrimony*[44] copied at Bow (A53, Plate 46). Here, a bareheaded gallant stands holding aloft a bird, a gun at his side and a ram and dog at his feet, while his sour-faced female companion holds open the gate of an empty cage. The Freudian innuendo is abundantly clear.

In 1737 Edmé Bouchardon made 60 red chalk drawings of hawkers, itinerant musicians and beggars then extant in the streets of Paris. These were engraved by Anne-Claude-Philippe de Tubières, comte de Caylus[45] and between 1738 and 1747 appeared in five sets, each of twelve etchings, comprising a folio entitled *Études prises dans le bas peuple ou les cris de Paris*. Between c.1740 and 1748 Kändler and his associates at Meissen created a series of robustly sculptured models loosely based on these engravings. They were decorated in strong red, deep yellow, dark green, dark blue and black enamels, and mounted on mounds sparsely sprigged with leaves and flowers. Bow copies include the *Map Seller* (A42) which, like the Meissen version[46], wears a brimmed hat, carries a rucksack on his back and holds an open and a rolled chart. Bouchardon had portrayed him bareheaded, grasping a single large rolled map with both hands. Larger models of *Fruit Sellers* (A41, Plates 33 and 34) however, more faithfully follow the engravings[47] and smaller figures of a *Beggar and Peasant Woman* (A39, Plate 30) carrying a basket of vegetables do likewise. The *Hurdy-gurdy Man*, paired by a *Flemish Woman* (A40, Plates 31 and 32) who holds a crib in which a baby sleeps, are more in the genre of David Teniers (*fils*) than of Bouchardon.

Water-colour sketches by Christophe Huet c.1752–5 prompted a second Meissen series of 'Paris Cries'. These are more slender and less dramatically posed, decorated in cool pale yellows, greens, pinks and mauves, and are mounted upon scrolled bases. They seem to portray members of the aristocracy in masquerade, rather than honest working folk, for many wear tie-wigs, clothes with gold buttons and shoe-buckles to match. The *Absinthe Seller* (A38) was the only Bow model based on these issued prior to 1754, carrying a lantern and with a tray of bottles suspended by a strap about his neck. The Meissen original[48] was adapted to provide a *Night Watchman*,[49] subsequently copied at Chelsea, and a Derby vender also exists.[50]

A white model of a *Negress* (A61, Plate 52) wearing only a cloth head-dress and loin-cloth, incised 1750 beneath the base, stands before a covered basket. She provides a contrast with the sophisticated modelling and brilliant enamel colouring of Kändler's original.[51] A *Turk* (A62), after J. F. Eberlein's prototype,[52] wears a tall plumed hat and kneels before a sucrier.

Paired groups of *Ewe and Lamb* (A63, Plate 53) and *Goat and Kid* (A65, Plate 54), are common to Derby[53] and echo Meissen.[54] The *Medici Lions* (A70, Plate 58), once kings of the Bow pride, have been reassigned to Chelsea, owing to their non-phosphatic body and peach fluorescence under the mercury lamp.[55] They are based on Famminio Vacca's marbles of c.1594, which once stood outside the Villa Medici in Rome until moved to the foot of a stairway leading up to the Loggia dei Lanzi, in Florence. A small seated *Lion and Lioness* (A66, Plate 29), each with one paw upon a tree-stump, were probably adapted from one of a Meissen pair in which the support is absent.[56] A large standing *Lion* (A67, Plate 55) also has one front leg supported and lacks a mate. A pair of recumbent *Lions* (A68, Plate 56) have their heads turned in mirror poses, while prowling *Lions* (A69, Plate 57) with mouths half open, possibly reflect larger work by Kändler.[57] They give added meaning to the invocation of St Peter: 'Brethren: Be sober, be vigilant; because your adversary the devil, as a roaring lion, walketh about, seeking whom he may devour.'[58] Equally fierce is a toothsome *Fox* (A64) with its belly supported by a branched tree-stump.

In 1736 Pope Clement XII excommunicated all Catholics who remained Freemasons, but allowed men and women of his flock to join a superficially similar organisation, the *Moporden* (Order of the Pug). The Pug Dog became the coveted emblem of an aristocratic secret society and, in response to the demands of the nobility, many porcelain replicas of this creature were created at the Meissen factory. Some, like the pet of Count Heinrich von Brühl,[59] were single models but most were issued as pairs, seated, standing or begging,[60] many with cropped ears,[61] others incorporated beside Brethren and Dames in *Masonic Groups*.[62] Bow versions depict *Pug Dogs* scratching (A71, Plate 59), recumbent with heads rotated (A72, Plate 60), lying upon tasselled cushions (A72, Plate 60), seated wearing studded collars (A75) or standing (A74, Plate 62). Similar models appeared at Chelsea,[63] Derby,[64] Longton Hall,[65] Lowestoft,[66] and in Staffordshire earthenware.[67] A fine *Retriever Barking* (A76, Plate 63), which in some versions has one front paw upon a dead game bird, completes the Bow kennel.

The early Bow aviary is small. A *Crane* (A77) taperstick, known also at Chelsea,[68] was probably copied from imported *blanc de chine* models made at Dehua (Tê-hua) in China.[69] It may have been the 'Hostorridge crame candles', mentioned in Duesbury's London Account Book. A *Pheasant* (A79, Plate 65) on a rocky mount, its tail and breast supported by props, recalls another item described as 'Enameld Fesan', not to be confused with 'Chelsay phesan' in the same ledger. A pair of *Herons* (A78, Plate 64) with bulging eyes and bedraggled plumage, are modelled directly from a solid bolus of soft paste and must number amongst the first models to have been made at the factory. Yet more endearing is a *Tawny Owl* (A80, Plate 66) despite its proud mould marks. Both white and coloured versions are known, the latter sometimes with three claws on one leg and four upon the other[70] boldly painted with firm strokes of red, brown, purple and yellow. Some have preferred to date this model to c.1755.

There remain a pair of *Caryatid Candlesticks* (A82, Plate 68) composed of youths in classical robes standing with baskets upon their heads, shown by Arthur Lane to have been based on seventeenth-century bronze fire-dogs.[71] Lastly a *Sucrier supported by Putti* (A83) was made up from the basket taken from the *Negress* (A61, Plate 52) and the Putti from the group of *Two Putti playing with a Dolphin* (A35, Plate 28).

I

2

3

1 (A1) White glazed model of *Kitty Clive as Mrs Riot* 9in (22.9cm) c.1750

2 (A2) Companion model of *Henry Woodward as the Fine Gentleman*.

3 (A3) *Actor*, possibly David Garrick, as *Sir John Falstaff* 7in (17.8cm) c.1752

4 (A4) *Actor*, possibly David Garrick 7in (17.8cm) c.1752

4

5

6

7

8

9

5 (A5) *Actor and Actress in Turkish costumes* 8¼in (21cm) c.1752–3

6 (A6) Pair of *Sphinxes*, supposedly in the likeness of Margaret Woffington 4¾in (12.1cm) c.1752

7 (A7) *Arlecchino* (Harlequin), wearing a plumed hat, mask and motley 5¼in (13.3cm) c.1752

8 (A10) White group of *Pedrolino and Isabella* as lovers 4½in (11.4cm) c.1751

9 (A11) *Pulcinella* (Punch) 6in (15.2cm) c.1752–3

10

12

11

10 (A12) *Scapino* (Scapin) 5in (12.7cm) c.1753

11 (A13) A group known as the *Indiscreet Arlecchino* 7in (17.8cm) c.1753–4

12 (A14) *The Italian Musicians* 6¾in (17.1cm) c.1752–3

13 (A15) *The Italian Lovers* 6¾in (17.1cm) c.1752–3

14 *Left*, (A31) *Terpsichore* 6¾in (17cm); *Right*, (A16) *Apollo* 6¼in (15.9cm). Both c.1751–2

13

14

15

16

17

15 (A17) *Charity* 9¾in (24.8cm) c.1753

16 (A18) *Hope* 8¾in (22.2cm) c.1750

17 *Left to right*, (A19) *Juno* beside a peacock 5½in (14cm); (A33) *Urania* 6¾in (17.1cm); (A20) *Jupiter* beside an eagle 6in (15.2cm). All c.1751–2

18 (A21) Traditionally *Justice*, but possibly *Faith*, holding a chalice and dagger after the manner of Melpomene 8in (20.3cm) c.1751–2

66

18

19

19 (A22) White glazed group of *Ki Mao Sao* 6¾in (17cm) c.1751–2

20 (A22) Enamelled version of *Ki Mao Sao* c.1752–3

21 (A24) *Minerva* 6¾in (17.1cm) c.1752–3

22 (A26) *Clio* 6¼in (15.2cm) c.1751–2

23 (A27) *Erato* with Cupid 6¼in (15.2cm) c.1752

20

C.1748–53

21

22

23

24

25

24 (A28) *Euterpe* 6in (15.2cm) c.1751–2

25 (A30) *Polyhymnia* 7in (17.8cm) c.1751–2

26 (A32) *Thalia* 6½in (16.5cm) c.1751–2

27 (A33) *Urania* 6¼in (16.5cm) c.1751–2

28 (A35) White group of *Two Putti playing with a Dolphin* 7in (17.8cm) c.1752

26

27

29 *Clockwise from left,*
(A46) White glazed
Huntsman 5½in (14cm)
(*see Plates* **38** *and* **39**
for biscuit pair);
(B80) *Pilgrim* 6½in
(16.5cm) c.1760;
(A36) *Naked Boy* with
head turned, semi-
reclining with left arm
raised 4¼in (11cm);
(A66) White pair of
seated *Lions*, each with
its left front paw upon
a tree-stump 4½in
(11.5cm). All c.1752–3

28

29

30

30

31

32

33   34

30 (A39) *Beggar* and companion *Peasant Woman* 6¾in (17.1cm) c.1752

31 (A40) Enamelled *Hurdy-gurdy Man* 6½in (16.5cm) c.1752–3

32 (A40) White companion model of a *Flemish Woman* holding a crib, ibid.

33 (A41) White model of a male *Fruit Seller* 8¾in (22.2cm) c.1752

34 (A41) Enamelled companion *Fruitress*, ibid.

35 (A43) White model of a *Sailor* 5½in (14cm) c.1753

35

36

37

36 (A43) Enamelled version of the companion *Lass* to *Sailor* (Plate **35**) 5½in (14cm) c.1753

37 (A44) White model of a *Thames Waterman* 7in (17.8cm) c.1753–4

38 (A46) Biscuit model of a seated *Huntsman*, lacking his gun 5in (12.7cm) c.1752–3

39 (A46) Companion biscuit model of *Lady*, ibid.

40 (A47) White group showing a *Gallant and Lady* 7in (17.8cm) c.1750–1

41 (A48) White group showing a *Gallant and Fishergirl* 7½in (19.1cm) c.1750–1

38

39

40

41

42

42 (A49) *Gipsy Fortune Telling* group, after Boucher 6¾in (17.1cm) c.1752–3

43 (A50) *Lady in seventeenth-century attire playing a Lyre* 6½in (16.5cm) c.1753–4

44 (A51) Seated *Lady Tatting* 5¼in (13.3cm) c.1753–4

45 (A52) White group showing a *Lady with a Page* 7in (17.8cm) c.1752

43

44

45

46

47

46 (A53) White models emblematic of *Liberty and Matrimony* 9¾in (24.8cm) c.1753

47 (A54) Group of *Two Lovers with a Bird-Cage* 7½in (19.1cm) c.1752–3

48

49

48 (A56) White model of a
Huntsman Toper 4¾in
(12.1cm) c.1752

49 (A58) *Flower Girl*,
emblematic of Spring 6¾in
(17.1cm) c.1752

50 (A59) *White chinoiserie
group*, emblematic of Air
7¾in (19.7cm) c.1750

50

51

52

51 (A60) White bustos of a *Mongolian Prince and Princess* 10½in (26.7cm) c.1753–5

52 (A61) White model of a *Negress* 8¾in (19.1cm) incised 1751

53 (A63) White group of *Ewe and Lamb* 4⅓in (11cm) c.1752

54 (A65) Companion group of *Goat and Kid*, idem.

53

54

55

55 (A67) *Lion* standing with one paw upon a tree-stump w.9in (24cm) c.1752

56 (A68) Recumbent *Lion and Lioness* w.4½in (11.4cm) c.1753

56

57

57 (A69) Pair of *Lion and Lioness*, prowling w.9in (22.9cm)
c.1752-3

58 (A70) *The Medici Lion*, one of a pair w.10in (25.4cm)
c.1752. *Now ascribed to Chelsea.*

58

59   60

59 (A71) *Pug Dog* scratching 3¾in (9.5cm) c.1750

60 (A72) *Pug Dog* reclining, one of a pair w.3½in (8.9cm)
c.1750

61

61 (A73) *Pug Dog* reclining upon a tasselled cushion, one of a
pair w.4¾in (12.1cm) c.1752

62 (A74) *Standing Pug Dog*, one of a pair
2¾in (7cm) c.1753

62

63

63 (A76) *Retriever* with a game-bird, barking w.3½in (9cm)
c.1752

64

65

66

67

64 (A78) Pair of *Herons*, solid cast w.6¾in (17.1cm) c.1748-50

65 (A79) *Pheasant* on a rocky mound w.6¾in (17.1cm) c.1750-2

66 (A80) *Tawny Owl* 8¼in (21cm) c.1752-4

67 (A81) *Group of two Birds*, possibly Finches, in foliage, watched by a Dog 6½in (16cm) c.1754

68 (A82) *Caryatid Candlestick*, one of a pair 17¾in (37.8cm) c.1753

68

BOW PORCELAIN MODELS C.1748-53

THEATRICAL

A1   *Kitty Clive as Mrs Riot*, 9in (22.9cm). She stands wearing a mob-cap, bodice with pagoda-sleeves and a hooped-skirt, holding a lap-dog. Victoria & Albert Museum, Lane pl. 37; National Museum of Ireland; G. Godden, Adams and Redstone col. pl. H. *See Plate 1.*

A2   *Henry Woodward as the Fine Gentleman*, 9in (22.9cm). He wears a foppish tricorn hat, waistcoat, jacket, breeches and buckled shoes, and stands with hands thrust into his pockets. References as A1. Version wearing a sword-belt and rapier, with large buttons, in a tie-wig *en queue*, Bow Special Ex. Cat. no. 42a. *See Plate 2.*

A3   Probably *David Garrick as Sir John Falstaff*, 7in (17.8cm). He wears a brimmed hat decorated with plumes, doublet, jerkin, breeches and top-boots, and stands bearing a cutlass and an oval shield. Victoria & Albert Museum, Hughes pl. 8; *Trans. E.C.C.*, 1948, Vol. 2, no. 10, pl. CId. *See Plate 3.*

A4   Unknown *Actor*, possibly *David Garrick*, 7in (17.8cm). He stands with his hat under his left arm. Cecil Higgins Museum; Sotheby's 25.8.39, lot 203. *See Plate 4.*

A5   *Actor and Actress in Turkish costumes*, 8¼in (21cm). Possibly characters from *Tamburlaine the Great*, the man wears a turban and carries a scimitar, while the lady has a tall head-dress. Savage pls 34a–b; Christie's 13.2.84, lot 173 (coloured). *See Plate 5.*

A6   *Sphinxes* (pair), 4¾in (12.1cm). Each supposedly with the head and breasts of Peg Woffington, mounted on rococo-styled bases. Schreiber pl. 9, no. 143 (new no. 6); Savage pl. 39; Museum of Fine Arts, Boston, (coloured versions). *See Plate 6.*

ITALIAN COMEDY

A7   *Arlecchino (Harlequin)*, 5¼in (13.3cm). He wears a hat, mask and motley and stands with his right hand raised to his chin, mounted on a square base. *Apollo*, 1963, Vol. 78, fig. 12; Cecil Higgins Museum. *See Plate 7.*

A8   *Columbina (Columbine)*, 5in (12.7cm). Clad in a brimmed hat, bodice and skirt, she dances holding slapsticks. Private collection.

A9   *Columbina as a Fruitress*, 4¾in (12.1cm). Attired as A8, she holds up a bunch of grapes in her left hand and has a tray of fruit suspended by a strap from her neck. Mounted on a square base. *Country Life*, June 1970, 1138, fig. 9.

A10   *Pedrolino and Isabella (Pierrot)* (group), 4½in (11.4cm). She wears a round hat and sits playing a hurdy-gurdy, whilst Pedrolino clad in a brimmed hat and loose garments on her right has both arms about her. Freeman pl. 194. *See Plate 8.*

A11   *Pulcinella (Punch)*, 6in (15.2cm). The hunchback wears a conical cap, blouse and baggy trousers and leans against a tree-stump, on a square base. *Apollo*, Vol. 71, 271, fig. 12; George R. Gardiner Museum of Ceramic Art, Toronto, cat. p. 65. *See Plate 9.*

A12   *Scapino (Scapin)*, 5in (12.7cm). Bearded and laughing, he leans against a tree-stump, his right hand concealed in his cloak, holding in his dependent left a mask. *Antique Dealer & Collector's Guide*, Vol. 18, No. 3, pl. 13, fig. 1. Simon Spero late stock. *See Plate 10.*

A13 *Indiscreet Arlecchino* (group), 7in (17.8cm). A recumbent clown lifts the hem of Columbina's skirt as she sits upon the knee of Mezzetino (Mezetin). *E.C.C.* 1948 Ex. Cat. pl. 36, no. 166; Poole, Fitzwilliam Museum, no. H.1. *See Plate 11.*

A14 *Italian Musicians* (group), 6¾in (17.1cm). Scaramuzzi sits holding a song-sheet singing, beside Isabella playing a guitar. Untermyer pl. 90, fig. 240. See also C.11. *See Plate 12.*

A15 *Italian Lovers* (group), 7¼in (18.4cm). Arlecchino sits beside Columbina, his left arm encircling her waist, his right elevated. *Trans. E.C.C.,* 1948, Vol. 2, No. 10, pl. CIIId; Museum of Fine Arts, Boston. *See Plate 13.*

MYTHOLOGICAL AND RELIGIOUS

A16 *Apollo*, 6in (15.3cm). He stands clad in a laurel chaplet and robe playing a lyre. Christie's 9.10.89, lot 217. *See Plate 14.*

A17 *Charity* (group), 9¾in (24.8cm). A woman standing clad in a veil and robe, supporting a baby on her left arm, proffering an apple to a child at her side. Lane pl. 42; Bradshaw pl. 57. *See Plate 15.*

A18 *Hope*, 8¾ (22.2cm). A woman standing clad in a veil and robe, leaning upon an anchor. Bradshaw pl. 58; Sotheby's 7.5.68, lot 121; *E.C.C.* 1977 Ex. Cat. pl. 137 (coloured). *See Plate 16.*

A19 *Juno*, 5½in (14cm). She stands bareheaded and barefoot, a sceptre in her right hand, beside a peacock. Freeman pl. 199; Savage pl. 46a; Albert Amor Bow Ex. Cat. no. 68. *See Plate 17.*

A20 *Jupiter*, 6in (15.2cm). He stands bareheaded and barefoot, a sceptre in his left hand, beside an eagle. References as A19. *See Plate 17.*

A21 *Justice*, 8in (20.3cm). She stands before a stack of tomes, clad in helmet and robe gathered by a sash, a short sword in her right hand and scales in her left. *E.C.C.* 1977 Ex. Cat. pl. 137 (coloured); Museum of Fine Arts, Boston. A strange version in a private collection shows her with a dagger and chalice, one in either hand, in the manner of Melpomene. *See Plate 18.*

A22 *Ki Mao Sao* (group), 6¾in (17.1cm). The Chinese goddess, clad in a tunic and trousers, sits upon a low shaped plinth, with both arms extended, flanked by two kneeling Chinamen. *E.C.C.* 1977 Ex. Cat. pl. 136; Hampshire County Museum, Adams and Redstone pl. 71. *See Plates 19 and 20.*

A23 *Mercury*, 7in (17.8cm). He stands clad in helmet, winged sandals, tunic and cloak, holding the caduceus. Savage pl. 65.

A24 *Minerva*, 6¾in (17.1cm). She wears a plumed helmet, cuirass, thonged skirt and sandals, and stands left hand on hip leaning with her right on a shield bearing Medusa's head. Lane pl. 41b. *See Plate 21.*

The following Nine Muses, A25 to A33, are illustrated excepting Calliope and Thalia, *Burl. Mag.*, Vol. LIV, 1929, pls Ia–c and IIa–d.

A25   *Calliope.* Example unknown to author.

A26   *Clio*, 6¼in (15.9cm). She stoops over an open tome, quill in hand, clad in a laurel chaplet and robe. Adams and Redstone pl. 65; Castle Howard. *See Plate 22.*

A27   *Erato*, 6½in (16.5cm). Bareheaded in a long robe, she sits with flowers in her lap, presenting a longbow to Cupid. Victoria & Albert Museum, Adams and Redstone pl. 65. *See Plate 23.*

A28   *Euterpe*, 6in (15.2cm). Bareheaded, she sits holding a recorder in her left hand, amid musical trophies. Victoria & Albert Museum, Adams and Redstone pl. 66; Freeman pl. 198; David Thorn collection (as illustrated). *See Plate 24.*

A29   *Melpomene*, 6in (15.2cm). Crowned, she stands leaning against a column, holding a dagger and chalice. *Burl. Mag.* (see above).

A30   *Polyhymnia*, 7in (17.8cm). The winged muse wears a laurel chaplet and holds a second wreath over an obelisk to which she points, with military trophies at her feet. Adams and Redstone pl. 64; *E.C.C.* 1948 Ex. Cat. pl. 36. *See Plate 25, Col. Plate I.*

A31   *Terpsichore*, 6¾in (17.1cm). Clad in a tunic, she dances barefoot with right arm upraised. Salisbury and South Wiltshire Museum, Adams and Redstone pl. 63; Museum of Fine Arts, Boston.

A32   *Thalia*, 5¾in (14.6cm). She stands bareheaded, clad in a long robe, the mask of 'Comedy' in her dependent right hand. Museum of Fine Arts, Boston. *See Plate 26.*

A33   *Urania*, 6½in (16.5cm). Clad in a veil and robe, she stoops over a celestial globe upon a plinth, a pair of dividers in her left hand. Christie's 1.6.87, lot 230; Freeman col. pl. VIII; author's collection. *See Plates 17 and 27, Col. Plate I.*

A34   *Neptune*, 6in (15.2cm). Crowned and scantily draped, he stands holding a trident. B. & T. Thorn, late stock.

A35   *Two Putti playing with a Dolphin* (group), 7in (17.8cm). Freeman pl. 185; Fitzwilliam Museum (as illustrated). *See Plate 28.*

A36   *Naked Boy*, 4¼in (10.8cm) wide. He reclines leaning upon his right hand, his left upraised and his head turned to the left, mounted on a rectangular base. Christie's 25.11.91, lot 103. *See Plate 29.*

A37   *Sphinxes* (pair), 4¾in (12.1cm). Each with head and breasts of an unidentified woman, after J. F. Blondel, mounted upon rectangular wedge-shaped bases. *E.C.C.* 1948 Ex. Cat. pl. 36, no. 37; Sotheby's 5.10.75, lot 109.

PEASANTS, ARTISANS AND SAILORS

A38   *Absinthe Seller*, 7½in (19.1cm). He stands with right foot advanced and head turned to the left, wearing a tricorn hat, jacket and breeches, a lantern in his right hand and supporting with his left a deep rectangular tray of bottles. Sotheby's 3.12.68, lot 147.

A39   *Beggar and Peasant Woman* (pair), 6¾in (17.1cm). The man wears a brimmed hat, shirt, short trousers with hose rolled down, and holds a bowl; his companion in a head-scarf, dress and apron, grasps a basket of vegetables with both hands. Savage pls 49a–b; Bradshaw pl. 59. *See Plate 30.*

A40   *Hurdy-gurdy Man and Flemish Woman* (pair), 6½in (16.5cm). The stocky male stands clad in tricorn hat, coat, waistcoat and breeches with a hurdy-gurdy; the woman in linen cap, dress and apron, holds a crib in which a baby sleeps. Adams and Redstone pl. 126; Freeman pl. 92. *See Plates 31 and 32.*

A41   *Fruit Sellers* (pair), 8¾in (22.2cm). The man wears a wide-brimmed hat and stands with a basket of fruit over his right arm, proffering an apple; the woman wears a linen cap, dress and apron in which she secures fruit with both hands. Stoner pl. 69 (pair); Sotheby's 16.6.87, lot 372 (female); Christie's 15.2.88, lot 240 (male). *See Plates 33 and 34.*

A42   *Map* (or *Print*) *Seller*, 5¾in (14.6cm). He stands clad in a brimmed hat, a pack upon his back, holding an open and a rolled map. Sotheby's 30.5.67, lot 147.

A43   *Sailor and Lass* (pair), 5½in (14cm). He wears a tricorn hat, scarf, open jacket and trousers, and stands left hand on hip with his right outstretched; his companion in a head-scarf, dress and long apron that she holds in her left hand. Lane pl. 40; Savage pl. 61b; Sotheby's 23.2.88, lot 622 (male); Christie's 13.2.84, lot 140 (male). *See Plates 35 and 36.*

A44   *Thames Waterman*, 7in (17.8cm). He stands with his left arm abducted, wearing a peaked cap, jacket and breeches with a badge bearing Doggett's arms on his shoulder. Christie's 10.10.88, lot 271; Adams and Redstone pl. 272. Another version with the device of a fouled anchor, Lane pl. 41a. *See Plate 37.*

A45   *Vintner*, 6¼in (15.9cm). He wears a wide-brimmed hat and stands cross-legged beside a hod of grapes, leaning his right elbow upon a tree-stump. Lane pl. 40b.

GALLANTS, SPORTSMEN AND LADIES

A46   *Huntsman and Lady* (pair), 5in (12.7cm). The man wears a tricorn hat, the lady a brimmed hat, and both sit in hunting costume leaning upon tree-stumps, beside a dog holding a gun. Freeman pl. 193; *Trans. E.C.C.*, 1969, Vol. 7, pls 129b–c (biscuit versions). *See Plates 29, 38 and 39.*

A47   *Gallant and Lady* (group), 7in (17.8cm). A bareheaded gallant, clad in coat, breeches and gaiters, kneels with one hand upon his heart before a seated lady wearing a riding habit. National Museum of Ireland. *See Plate 40.*

A48   *Gallant and Fishergirl* (group), 7½in (19.1cm). A bareheaded beau sits beside a fishergirl on his left, to whom he turns with hand on heart. Bow Special Ex. Cat. fig. 15. *See Plate 41.*

A49   *Gipsy Fortune Telling* (group), 6¾in (17.1cm). A gipsy clad in a laurel chaplet, wide-sleeved robe and boots, examines the palm of a young lady beneath a tree. Freeman pl. 196; Adams and Redstone pl. 70; Hurlbutt pl. 42; King fig. 2. *See Plate 42.*

A50   *Lady Playing a lyre*, 6¾in (17.1cm). She sits bareheaded wearing ear-rings, necklace and seventeenth-century attire, playing a lyre, mounted on a deeply scrolled base. *Apollo*, 1960, Vol. 71, p. 96, figs ix and x. Museum of Fine Arts, Boston. *See Plate 43.*

A51   *Lady Tatting*, 5¼in (13.3cm). She sits, bareheaded, tatting a pillow on her lap, a bobbin in either hand. Temple Newsam House, Leeds. *See Plate 44.*

A52   *Lady with a Page* (group), 7in (17.8cm). A lady wearing a mob-cap, jacket and hooped skirt accepts peaches proffered on a tray by a page. Victoria & Albert Museum, W. B. Honey pl. 14a. *See Plate 45.*

A53   *Liberty and Matrimony* (pair), 9¾in (24.8cm). A bareheaded beau stands holding aloft a bird, with a gun at his side and a dog and a ram at his feet; the companion lady wearing a hat and dress holds open the gate of an empty bird-cage. Hurlbutt pl. 39; Bow Special Ex. Cat. figs 95–6; Katz collection, Lane pls 44–5. *See Plate 46.*

A54   *Two Lovers with a Bird-cage* (group), 7½in (19.1cm). A man clad in a brimmed hat, jacket and breeches sits with his right arm about the shoulders of a bareheaded lady, a bird-cage balanced upon his knee. Victoria & Albert Museum, Lane pl. 38. *See Plate 47.*

A55   *Shoeblack* (group), 5¾in (14.6cm). A bareheaded gallant stands taking a pinch of snuff, his right foot upon a stool, with a boy in a wide-brimmed hat polishing his shoe. *Trans. E.P.C.*, 1928, no. 1, pl. xix.

A56   *Toper, Huntsman*, 4¾in (12.1cm). A huntsman reclines upon a steep mound, holding a flask and goblet, with trophies of the chase about him. Freeman pl. 190. *See Plate 48.*

A57   *Women as Flower Seller*, 7in (17.8cm). She sits wearing a brimmed hat with a tall crown and dress, supporting a basket of flowers with her right hand and holding a posy aloft in her left. *Trans. E.C.C.*, 1989, Vol. 13, pt. 3, 193.

A58   *Women as Flower Girl*, emblematic of Spring, 6¾in (17.1cm). She stands clad in a floral diadem, blouse and skirt, with flowers in her apron, left hand upon her heart and right extended. Christie's 12.2.90, lot 182. *See Plate 49.*

FOREIGN PERSONS

A59   *Chinoiserie Groups* (pair), 7¾in (19.7cm). *Air* as a Chinese lady leaning upon a bird-cage, holding aloft a bird, beside a seated Chinaman who holds a second bird and has a flying-fish at his side. *See Plate 50.* British Museum (as illustrated). *Fire* as a Chinaman standing while pouring tea into a cup held by a reclining companion, beside a brick stove. Untermyer pl. 74, fig. 139, both Elements in coloured versions.

A60   *Mongolian Prince and Princess* (pair of busts), 10½in (26.7cm). The prince with beard and moustache, and his spouse, both wearing fantastic beaded head-dresses. King fig. 4; Adams and Redstone pl. 69; Untermyer pl. 79, fig. 242, coloured versions. *See Plate 51.*

A61   *Negress*, 8½in (21.6cm). She wears a cloth head-dress and loin-cloth and stands before a covered basket. Adams and Redstone pl. 61; Bow Special Ex. Cat. fig. 6; Museum of Fine Arts, Boston. *See Plate 52.*

A62   *Turk*, 4¾in (12.1cm). He wears a tall plumed hat and robe and kneels before a sucrier. Sotheby's 27.2.68, lot 169.

ANIMALS

A63 *Ewe and Lamb* (group), 4¼in (11cm) long. The lamb lies against the flank of a recumbent ewe. Savage pl. 46; Hurlbutt pl. 1; Freeman pl. 252; Christie's 20.10.88, lot 195. *See Plate 53.*

A64 *Fox*, 5¾in (14.6cm) long. It stands with half-open mouth and tail drooped, its belly supported by tree-stumps. – *Connoisseur*, 1970, Vol. 175, 'Some Rare White English Porcelain in the Dudley Deleringne Collection', no. 3; *Trans. E.C.C.*, 1969, Vol. 7, pt. 1, pl. 2b.

A65 *Goat and Kid* (group), 4¼in (11cm) long. A recumbent goat suckles her kid. Savage pl. 46; Christie's 20.10.88, lot 195. *See Plate 54.*

A66 *Lion and Lioness* (pair), 4in (10.2cm) long. Each seated with one paw upon a tree-stump. Savage pl. 47a; Freeman pl. 248. *See Plate 29.*

A67 *Lion*, 9½in (24cm) long. Standing with one paw upon a tree-stump. Christie's 25.11.91, lot 99. *See Plate 55.*

A68 *Lion and Lioness* (pair), 4½in (11.4cm) long. Recumbent with heads turned in mirror poses. Savage pl. 47b. *See Plate 56.*

A69 *Lion and Lioness* (pair), 9in (22.9cm) long. Prowling with half-open jaws. Freeman pl. 251; Schreiber pl. 9, no. 145 (new no. 5). *See Plate 57.*

A70 *Medici Lions* (pair), 10in (25.4cm) long. They stand with one paw upon an orb. Bradshaw pl. 40 (one only). Now allocated to Chelsea. *See Plate 58.*

A71 *Pug Dog*, 3¾in (9.2cm) long. Seated scratching. Schreiber no. 32 (new no. 98). *See Plate 59.*

A72 *Pug Dogs* (pair), 3in (7.6cm). Recumbent with heads rotated in opposite directions. Freeman pls 246–7. *See Plate 60.*

A73 *Pug Dogs* (pair), 4¾in (12.1cm). Recumbent on tasselled cushions. Schreiber pl. 9, no. 147 (new no. 4). *See Plate 61.*

A74 *Pug Dogs* (pair), 3¾in (9.5cm). Both stand on oval bases encrusted with flowers. Schreiber pl. 9, no. 149 (new no. 3). *See Plate 62.*

A75 *Pug Dogs* (pair), 3½in (8.9cm). Seated wearing studded collars, on rectangular bases. Sotheby's 25.2.86, lot 124.

A76 *Retriever barking with Game*, 3¼in (8.3cm). Stands with one paw upon a game-bird. Schreiber pl. 9, no. 701 (new no. 21); Sotheby's 6.12.77, lot 13. Version lacking game-bird, Christie's 25.11.91, lot 100. *See Plate 63.*

BIRDS

A77 *A Crane* (taperstick), 6in (15.2cm). Schreiber pl. 9, no. 151 (new no. 9); Hughes pl. 9.

A78 *Herons* (pair), 6½in (16.5cm). Standing with bulging eyes and bedraggled feathers. Museum of Fine Arts, Boston. *See Plate 64.*

A79 *A Pheasant*, 6¾in (17.1cm). Perched on a rocky mound. Schreiber pl. 9, no. 149 (new no. 7); Hughes pl. 9. *See Plate 65.*

A80 *Tawny Owl*, 8¾in (22.2cm). *Trans. E.C.C.*, 1966, Vol. 6, pt. 2, pl. 56. *See Plate 66.*

A81 Unidentified *Bird Group*, 6½in (16.5cm). Two birds, possibly finches, perch in a tree, watched by a dog. Sotheby's (as illustrated). *See Plate 67.*

MISCELLANEOUS

A82   *Caryatid Candlesticks* (pair), 17¾in (45.1cm). Each formed as a standing youth in
       classical dress, bearing a basket upon his head. Victoria & Albert Museum, Lane pl. 43.
       See Plate 68.

A83   *Sucrier supported by Putti*, 10in (25.4cm). A basket (taken from A61) supported by
       two putti (taken from A35). Freeman pl. 183.

---

13 BOW PORCELAIN MODELS C.1754–64

MODELLING

THE LESSONS AFFORDED FROM THE STUDY OF MEISSEN *Porzellanfiguren* were
soon learned and, by c.1754, many of the features hitherto represented in the round
were instead suggested by placements of enamel. Heads were more correctly
proportioned, faces became oval, noses *retroussé*, whilst mouths, nostrils, eyelids
and lashes were delineated with pencilling. Children are depicted with widely
spaced oval eyes, curvaceous cheeks, snub noses and mouths which have a broad
upper and a narrow lower lip. Folds of drapery became shallower with elimination
of most minor creases, whilst frogging of garments became superfluous and
sprigging was now reserved for ornamentation of bases. Many Bow figures of this
middle period have the semblance of toy-like animation distinguishing them from
their more stately Chelsea cousins and stiffly posed Derby relatives. This admirable
quality is in part due to an often impish inclination of the head, an unnatural
rotation of the torso just above the hips, and to the posture of both legs with slight
flexion of the knees. In addition, a few figures of men, including *Pedrolino* (B12,
Plate 75, Col. Plate II), a *Turk* (B59, Plates 117 and 118, Col. Plate XII) and a
Huntsman (B110, Plate 153, Col. Plate V) have rounded paunches and appear to
lean backwards. The Muses Modeller evidently played a leading role in these
developments for his style, although muted, remains discernible until c.1760.

BASES

UNTIL c.1755 some bases are adorned with clumsy moulded scrolls lined with a
dark purplish-grey but the vast majority are white pads or mounds, sparsely

sprigged with enamelled leaves and flowers; in a few examples floral sprays are painted instead upon the upper surface. Underneath, bases were ground flat free of glaze and, in this process, the outer circumference was frequently chamfered (Fig. 8).

The ventilation hole is cylindrical, small to intermediate in size, and there may be a second aperture that pierces the back of the figure or its support, and passes horizontally to enter the central cavity. This is usually square (Fig. 9), less often triangular, rarely round. Ceramic supports adjacent to figures were, until c.1755, sometimes combed vertically before firing to simulate the bark of a tree.

Mound bases after c.1756 became steeper, reduced in diameter, and decorated with shallow moulded scrolls arranged in asymmetrical designs picked out in turquoise and green enamels and accented with gilt. A few examples have scrolls and arabesques pencilled in gold as the only ornament. Upper surfaces were either left white or covered by a green wash, and sparsely sprigged with enamelled leaves, flowers and/or appropriate trophies. About 1756 a shallow glazed concavity may be present in the centre of the flat ground undersurface (Fig. 10) which, by c.1758, increased in both depth and diameter to leave only a circumferential rim (Fig. 11). Chelsea model bases show similar change at approximately the same time.

Fig. 8 (B66) Flat ground undersurface of a *Boy Toper*, showing a small ventilation hole and a chamfered circumference.

Fig. 9 (B103) A square aperture behind the base of a *Musician*.

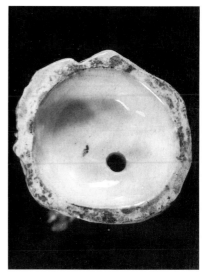

Fig. 10 (B12) Undersurface of *Pedrolino*, showing a small ventilation hole and a central shallow glazed concavity.

Fig. 11 (B103) Undersurface of a *Musician*, showing a deep glazed concavity with a circumferential flat ground foot-rim.

Also, bases elevated upon four short cabriole legs, like doll's house tables, made their debut. A pierced dependent U-scroll of asymmetrical form was placed between the front pair whilst the back two were occasionally replaced by a single vertical prop. The scrolls were lined with a brilliant vermilion and the upper surface decorated and sprigged in the usual manner. Underneath, bases are concave, glazed, pierced by a small cylindrical ventilation hole, and points of contact with the table-top ground to ensure stable and level stance. Initially these four-footed plinths were relatively simple in form, low in profile and decorated only with vermilion but, as the 1760s advanced, they became increasingly sculptural and were embellished with several colours accented with gilt.

LEAVES, FLOWERS AND BOCAGE

MOULDED BOW LEAVES are thicker than those made at Derby and larger than those of either Chelsea or Derby. Most often lanceolate, but occasionally heart-shaped, they are bluish-green with smooth edges. After c.1756 leaves became emerald green with spiky contours and branching dorsal veins pencilled in black or dark brown. During the 1760s moulded mid-ribs increasingly replaced painted veins, whilst a yellow-green was often laid beside the emerald producing a variegated effect. A few moulded flowers resemble small flat cog-wheels but most are large and saucer-

Fig. 12 (B46) Metal fitments attached to porcelain florets,
appended to two models from the *Seated Rustic Seasons*.

shaped with petals that are either long and pointed, or pear-shaped when they
radiate from a yellow or dark brown raised centre; a circumferential ring of brown
dots (Plate 144) is more commonly a Chelsea feature.

The sprigging of supporting tree-stumps with leaves and flowers steadily
increased and by c.1756 formed fan-like accretions which initially did not extend
above the model's waist but, during the 1760s, evolved to become arbours, or
bocages, that sometimes overhung and flanked the subject on both sides. Leaves
were twisted before being luted into position to create the appearance of natural
foliage. Frequently more than 100 castings were assembled by the repairer who
must have needed the patience of Job and the application of an obsessional to
complete his task.

The bocage is essentially an English innovation although a few Continental
factories mounted some figures before a flower-encrusted rococo trellis. During the
1750s and 1760s Vincennes and Sèvres embellished many figures and decorative
items, both from the factory and from abroad, with ormolu mounts, some bearing
candle-sconces, leaves and stems attached to flower-heads made of Chantilly
enamel. In England less sophisticated brass fitments with large porcelain florets
were preferred, which could be slotted into apertures behind the models (Fig. 12),
earlier described. These were soon replaced by less costly all-porcelain bocages that
did not require the services of skilled metal workers.

ENAMEL DECORATION 1754–6

AFTER 1754 THE number of models left white steadily declined. The factory palette included vermilion, a streaky pink (gold-purple) a dry powdery brownish-red (sealing-wax red), an opaque light blue (sealing-wax blue), both a lemon and a primrose yellow, a deep bluish-green and a lighter yellow-green and a sparkling dark blue with a violet tinge, together with dark brown, grey and black, all of which have a purplish cast.

Flesh tints, sometimes omitted altogether, are pale buff heightened with a faint orange blush; human hair was portrayed by coarse and evenly spaced dark brown pencilling laid upon washes of either grey or buff or light brown. The same brown was used to denote nostrils, eyebrows, eyelashes and eyelids. Pupils are black set in brown or grey irises but increasingly these were orange-pink after the Meissen style, and very rarely a violet-blue.[1] Mouths, no longer appearing to be smudged, were neatly painted in sealing-wax red or vermilion.

Garments were covered by plain washes of colour between large passages of white. Gilding was rarely employed and buttons, button-holes, pocket flaps and seams were pencilled in a dark colour or in black. Decorative small-scale floral sprays were usually executed in the Oriental fashion, devoid of perspective drawing or shading, known at Meissen as *indianische Blumen* (Col. Plates VI and X). Less often, and larger in size, stylised leaves and stems were painted in puce, incorporating blue florets with yellow centres (Col. Plate XIII). Floral sprays in the European style of *deutsche Blumen* are relatively uncommon at this time.

ENAMEL DECORATION c.1757–64

THE PALE GOLD-PURPLE was replaced by a rose colour that has a more even texture and a richer appearance, whilst the sealing-wax blue assumes a darker tone. Fresh colours include a transparent and vibrant emerald, a variety of purples and mauves and an opaque turquoise that often looks muddy due to overfiring. A peach colour was much employed for hats and head-dresses. A burnt orange introduced a discordant note but mercifully rarely appears on models. Other enamels from the earlier palette were mostly retained. Gilding was now routinely applied to buttons, shoe-buckles, the edges of garments, accessories such as musical instruments and to accent scrolls decorating bases.

Flesh tints became darker and the orange blush more pronounced. Pencilling of human hair is finer, more irregular and less conspicuous, but the manner in which other features were portrayed remained substantially unaltered. Painted floral sprays are now more commonly in the European manner. These may be small in scale and include a pink and a yellow rose, a yellow harebell and a blue blossom, possibly a campanula or dianthus (Col. Plate IV). Rarely, the same flowers may be depicted in a puce monochrome (Col. Plate X). Larger sprays including a cream and pink rose together with eight to twelve small leaves are especially attractive (Col. Plate XI).

During the 1760s washes of colour upon garments were broken by reserves, some oval and crenated, others trefoil or quatrefoil and framed by thin gilt scrolls, containing diaper patterns simulating brocades. Such sumptuous adornment of pastoral models is often at variance with the supposedly lowly social status of the subject.

THE MODELS

THE HISTORY OF the *Commedia dell'Arte* has been reviewed by Pierre Duchatre[2] and is summarised in Appendix A, while etchings of the *dramatis personae* by Giacomo Calotto (Fig. 13) have been presented by Howard Daniel.[3] Nearly all Bow Comedy models echo Meissen originals and *Arlecchino* (B1, Plate 69) in mask and motley, leaning against a tree-stump holding slap-sticks, reflects Kändler's 'Scowling Harlequin';[4] the low relief of detail suggests the copy was cast in a mould taken from the original. *Arlecchino* (B2, Plate 70) seated with bagpipes and *Columbina* playing a hurdy-gurdy also reflect Kändler's work,[5] who based the male model on a

Fig. 13 Etching by Giocomo Calotto of *Pantaloon*, sometimes called Cassandre c.1618

bronze 'Piping Shepherd Boy' by Giovanni da Bologna.[6] The same pair were issued at Chelsea[7] and Longton Hall,[8] whilst at Bow the *Boy Bagpiper* (B88) was issued both as a free-standing model and as the finial of a pot-pourri vase.[9] Most other Bow models of the *Commedia* were based on their counterparts in the Weissenfels series, earlier mentioned, created by Kändler and Reinicke in 1743/4.[10] *Columbina* (B3) wearing a brimmed hat, bodice and skirt, dancing with both her arms swinging to her right, is paired with *Arlecchino* clad in a cap, mask and motley, standing with his right hand close to his chin. The same model of *Columbina*, her right hand repositioned to touch the brim of her hat (B4, Plate 71, Col. Plate VII), was made as the partner of another model of *Arlecchino*, after an unpaired Meissen original,[11] standing with his left arm upraised.

Other Bow copies of the Weissenfels series include *Pantalone* (B11, Plate 74), in skull-cap, falling-ruffle, jacket, breeches and slippers, who stoops forward wrapped in a *zimara* (cloak) holding a money-bag before him. *Dottore Boloardo* (B7, Plate 72), in a wide-brimmed hat and zimara, strikes a pose with right hand on hip and left upraised; *Pedrolino* (B12, Plate 75, Col. Plate II) the ever faithful servant in Pierrot costume, holds up both hands in horror; *Mezzetino* (B9) the love-sick varlet, and his less amiable double *Scapino* (B13), are both attired in a soft cap, falling-ruffle, doublet, breeches and *tabarro* (cape); while *Narcissino* (B10, Plate 73), another menial, wears a brimmed hat, doublet, linen tabs at his throat, sash and baggy breeches as he stands with his zimara thrown over his shoulder. Often he has been misidentified as 'Il Capitano',[12] but his true nature is proclaimed both by the Weissenfels models and François Joullain's engravings upon which they were based (Figs 14 and 15).[13] *Capitano Rodomondo* was not represented at Bow but the Meissen model portrays him with upturned moustache wearing a tricorn hat, tight-fitting jacket, breeches, buckled shoes and gauntlets, standing with a huge sword at his side with arms akimbo. He was a braggart who, like the aging Menelaus in Rupert Brooke's poem[14] 'sacked a hundred Troys twixt noon and supper!' More sophisticated copies of Kändler and Reinicke's models were made at Chelsea,[15] but the Bow figure of *Isabella* (B8, Plate 72) standing bareheaded holding out her long gown with one hand, seems unique to the factory. *Children in Masquerade* (B6), in the costumes of Arlecchino and Columbina, may have been adapted directly from an engraving after Watteau, entitled 'Heureux Age d'Or'[16] since Meissen versions do not seem to have been issued until c.1765.[17]

Julia Poole[18] has traced the sources of the set of *Four Elements* (B41, Plates 94 and 95), common to Chelsea,[19] to marbles in the gardens at Versailles. *Juno*, her veil and hair blown out by the wind, standing beside an eagle, was based on sculpture emblematic of 'Air' by Étienne Le Hongre (1628–90),[20] located at the *Fontaine du Soire, ou Cabinet des Combats d'Animaux. Ceres*, standing with a cornucopia beside a lion, echoes the statue emblematic of 'Earth' by Benoit Massou (1627–84),[21] at the *Pourtour du Parterre du Nord. Neptune*, as a bearded man, pouring water from an

Fig. 14 Etching by François Joullain of *Narcissino* (Narcissus) c.1728

Fig. 15 Etching by François Joullain of *Il Capitano* (the Captain) c.1728

urn beneath his left arm and standing beside a dolphin, is a transposed adaptation of a marble nereid, representing 'Water', by Pierre Le Gros (1629–1714),[22] at the *Fontaine du Point du Jour*. *Vulcan* is depicted as an effeminate youth standing before a flaming urn, a phoenix at his feet, adapted from a marble nymph emblematic of 'Fire', shown in like fashion but with a salamander by Nicolas Dossier (d.1701),[23] at the *Rampe Soud du Parterre de Latone*. Poole points out that the porcelain modellers may have referred to intermediate sources, such as were provided by reduced bronzes, once in the Grünes Gewolbe in Dresden, or transposed engravings of the marbles made by Simon Thomassin.[24]

A fine pair of *Neptune riding a Dolphin* (B29) and *Jupiter astride an Eagle* (B24, Plate 83), once erroneously ascribed to Derby,[25] possess dynamic qualities suggesting they were derived from baroque bronzes. A refurbished *Mercury* (B27, Plate 85), after J. F. Eberlein,[26] now holds a money-bag as well as the caduceus; he stands before a casket placed upon two bales, an ink-well and a quill at his feet, symbolising 'Commerce'. *Apollo* (B14, Plate 76) wearing a laurel chaplet and robe,

Fig. 16 Archaic Greek marble, known as *Artemis Chasseuse*, with a stag, now in the Louvre, Paris.

stands playing his lyre looking up at the firmament for inspiration. A slightly different version (B15) portrays him leaning with his right hand upon his instrument, with trophies of the 'Arts' about him. Both were loosely adapted from a model by Eberlein.[27] *Diana* (B19, Plate 78), like her Derby sister,[28] holds a longbow in her left hand and selects an arrow with her right from a quiver behind her right shoulder, and has a hunting-dog at her side. This reflects Eberlein's group, based upon a seventeenth-century French bronze which, in turn, was inspired by an archaic Greek marble of 'Artemis Chasseuse' now in the Louvre (Fig. 16).[29] The tunic of the marble is lengthened to form a robe in the porcelain examples and the stag replaced by a hound. *Mars* (B25, Plate 84), clad in a helmet and Roman armour, stands holding a spear and oval shield and has affinities with Kändler's model of c.1747.[30] Another example (B26, Col. Plate VIII) shows the god bareheaded with one arm outstretched, standing upon a tall plinth. A large model of *Minerva* (B28) wears a crested helmet, cuirass, thonged skirt and sandals and she too carries a spear and shield upon which is a replica of Medusa's head. She, like her Longton Hall counterpart, may have been based on the finial of a decorative clock, made by Thomas Tompion for the bedchamber of King William III at Hampton

Court Palace.[31] Alternatively, the English models may reflect the porcelain figure surmounting Kändler's *Temple of Minerva* of c.1745.[32] A similar, but smaller, model called *Bellona* (B16) stands beside a little owl, symbolising *Wisdom*, and has GR III pencilled upon the front of her helmet; she may have been issued in 1760 to mark George III's accession to the throne.

The Bow *Flora Farnese* (B21, Plate 80) measures $17\frac{3}{4}$in (44.5cm) tall and is the largest model to have been made at the factory. Possible sources have been discussed by R. J. Charleston and Geoffrey Willis.[33] In 1762, Michael Rysbrack (1694–1770) sculpted the subject in marble for Sir Richard Hoare of Stourhead but, since the artist had never visited Florence, he must have referred to a three-dimensional replica. Peter Scheemakers sold a set of terracottas that included Flora from his studio in 1757,[34] whilst Rysbrack himself made another that is signed and dated 1759. Further, John Cheere made plaster models of gods and goddesses, some of which were painted to simulate bronze after the work of other sculptors.

An entirely different model, common to Bow (B22, Plate 81) and Chelsea,[35] is sometimes called 'Flora', portraying a woman wearing a long robe and veil who stands holding a posy to her nose, before a flower-encrusted plinth upon which rests a perfume vase. This may be mounted either on a rectangular base painted to simulate marble, or a four-footed plinth, and is a copy of Eberlein's figure, emblematic of 'Smelling', from a Meissen set of the 'Five Senses'.[36] Some Bow examples are inscribed 'Faustina', a name mentioned in an account sent to John Bowcock by Richard Dyer, dated 12 May 1760: '3 Fostinas at 3s 6d each @ 10s 6d'. Faustina Bordoni (1693–1786) was the leading soprano in the Dresden Court Opera Company who married the *Kapellmeister*, Johann Adolf Hasse, and paid her first visit to London in 1733. Margaret Newton[37] has reminded us of an amusing anecdote recorded in Jean Plaidy's *Caroline the Queen*. Handel had engaged Faustina and her great rival Cuzzoni to appear in his opera *Alesseandro* at the King's Theatre in the Haymarket, but the two prima donnas refused to share the same stage. The maestro felt constrained to employ unorthodox methods of persuasion and, lifting Cuzzoni up in his arms, he carried her to the open window and threatened to hurl her into the street below unless the two agreed to sing. Apparently, in this way, both emotional and musical harmony were restored!

A new group emblematic of *Charity* (B18, Plate 77), common to Chelsea,[38] was issued to replace the old one (A17, Plate 15), possibly based on a Meissen original, comprising a seated woman breast-feeding an infant, a seated and a standing child on either side of her. *Fame* (B20, Plate 79), in accord with tradition, is represented by a winged angel blowing a trumpet whilst *Venus* (B31, Plate 87) stands bareheaded and barefoot scantily draped with one breast exposed, with either doves (emblematic of 'Love') or sparrows (denoting 'Lust') at her feet.

Although a handful of talented modellers like J. J. Kändler of Meissen, Anton Bustelli of Nymphenburg and Nicolas Lecreux of Tournai made some exquisite devotional porcelain images, this aspect of their work had scant appeal in what was then a staunchly Protestant England. It was, accordingly, unexpected that Bow should have issued a model of a *Bishop* (B33, Plate 88), in full canonicals, his hand raised in blessing, possibly inspired by Kändler's *Prelate* giving Benediction with a monstrance.[39] An *Abbess* (B35, Plate 91), standing with one hand upon her breast, also has affinities with Kändler's *Nun of the Order of St John*,[40] and is paired with an *Abbot*. The *Priest* (B39) wearing a biretta, surplice, cassock and cape, who stands reading his Breviary, and *Abbess* pointing to the text of an open book, have been, perhaps hopefully, identified as Peter Abelard and Héloïse.

Between c.1740 and 1755, Kändler created several quasi-humorous models of *Monks and Nuns*, based upon engravings in diverse works published in the seventeenth and eighteenth centuries depicting the several habits worn by Religious Orders.[41] These prompted numerous English copies, especially at Bow. Nuns are clad in habit and veil, the monks have their tonsured pates exposed, and most are portrayed seated reading books (B34, 36 and 37; Plates 89 and 92, Col. Plate IX), although a few (B38) may hold a cross or a rosary. Open pages of the tomes often bear Latin inscriptions such as 'Omnia Gloria', 'Super Omnium', 'Momento Mori', or 'Omnia Vanitas', phrases more likely to feature in devotional literature, or the Divine Office, than in the Vulgate. Much of their charm relates to their tasteful decoration with nuances of purple and mauve between large passages left white, sometimes with the simulation of ermine upon capes and copes, and sparse gilding.

Seated models of an *Abbess* and a *Novice* (B34, Plate 89) show the older woman supporting a tome with her right hand and her left upon her knee, whilst the postulant holds what may be an Horae Diurnae in both hands. The *Abbess* also appears after seemingly undergoing a sex change, seated beside a pile of round-shot and a canon, as Roger Bacon (1214–94), the friar credited with the discovery of gunpowder.[42] Most of the Religious hold their books in both hands (B35 and 36, Plate 91), but a rare few (B37, Plate 92, Col. Plate IX) have one hand poised as if about to turn over to a fresh page. A Bow example, like its Meissen prototype,[43] wears a cream habit and veil spangled with gold stars, but coloured copies made at Richard Chaffers's Liverpool factory are charmingly but inappropriately decorated with floral sprays.[44]

Julia Poole[45] has shown that Bow versions of the *Four Quarters of the Globe*, known as paired groups (B42), chamber candlesticks (B43, Plates 96 and 97) and a set of semi-miniatures (C25, Plate 205), were based on marbles in the gardens at Versailles. *Africa*, as a scantily draped negress in an elephant head-dress, standing beside a lion, follows a marble by Jean Cornu (1650–1710);[46] *Asia*, daughter of Oceanus and Thetis, is a bareheaded maiden bearing a perfume vase, after sculpture by Leonard Roger (d.1693);[47] *America*, a Red Indian girl clad in a feathered skirt and head-dress, holding a longbow, standing beside an alligator, echoes a statue by

Giles Guérin (1609–78);[48] *Europe*, portrayed as a woman wearing a crested helmet, cuirass, thonged skirt and sandals, was based on a marble by Pierre Mazeline (1632–1708).[49] According to popular belief 'Europe' was fashioned in the likeness of Madame de Montespan and, for all eternity, looks across the *Parterre du Nord* at her lover, Louis XIV, representing 'Epic Poetry' in Jean Drouilly's statue.[50] The imagined resemblance between notables and allegorical sculpture recalls happenings in 1763 when a bronze of Louis XV on horseback was erected in the Place de Louis Quattorze in Paris, set upon a plinth with scantily clad nymphs by Jean-Baptiste Pigalle representing 'Force', 'Prudence', 'Peace' and 'Justice' at the four corners. When these were unveiled, the spectators cried out in delight: 'Vintmille, Mailly, Chateauroux et Pompadour. Ici comme a ce pays-ci c'est la même chose — fabriquées en pierre, sans cœur et sans entrailles!'[51]

The *Five Senses* (B44, Plates 98–102) incorporate seated peasants in seventeenth-century dress with rather small heads and long torsos, possibly adapted from French engravings. *Feeling* is a woman caressing a dog that has one paw upon her lap; *Seeing* is a girl holding a square mirror at arm's length, adjusting her coiffeur with her left hand; *Smelling* is a maiden seated beside a pannier of flowers, leaning to her right to smell a posy; *Hearing* is a troubador who sings and plays a guitar; *Tasting* is a youth astride a wine-keg, holding a goblet to his lips and grasping a flask — the model was later reissued in more sophisticated guise as a *Boy Toper* (B67, Plate 125).

Bow, like most other contemporary factories, issued a number of sets emblematic of the 'Four Seasons'. The *Antique Seasons* (B45, Plates 103–4) consist of the four deities *Flora* (Spring), *Ceres* (Summer), *Bacchus* (Autumn) and *Vulcan* (Winter), each standing before a rococo urn from which emerge, respectively, flowers, corn, grapes and flames, after F. E. Meyer.[52] The *Classical Seasons* (B48, Plates 108–10), after Eberlein,[53] include different models of the same divinities each separated from an attendant putto bearing appropriate accoutrements by a rococo candlestick. The *Seated Rustic Seasons* (B46, Plates 105–6) possess a simple grace, especially in early white examples mounted on plain uncluttered mound bases. *Spring* and *Summer* are both women wearing wide-brimmed hats holding, respectively, flowers and corn; *Autumn* is a *vendangeur* holding aloft a bunch of grapes, while *Winter* is a bearded man with the cowl of his coat pulled over his head, warming his hands over a brazier. Frank Hurlbutt considered they were based on Meissen originals but, although this is likely, examples are unknown to the author. A set of *Standing Rustic Seasons* (B49, Plate 111) wearing similar garments are far less pleasing, while the *Adolescent Seasons* (B47, Plate 107) are represented by smartly dressed girls and boys, better known in paired bocaged groups (C28, Plates 209–12). Minor variations are common and one delightful version of *Winter* is a youth holding an opulent fur muff with ear-flaps attached to his tricorn hat, doubtless intended as a lampoon of the extravagant dress favoured then, as now, by the young blood about town. Stiffly posed standing *Four Putti as Seasons* (B50, Plate 112), known both with and without bocages, wear chaplets and diagonally slung belts composed of, respectively, flowers, corn, grapes and holly, and carry bundles of the same. The *Child Seasons* (B51, Plate 113), after F. E. Meyer, comprise scantily clad seated children, three of them wearing chaplets and proffering flowers, corn and fruit, the fourth wrapped in a mantle warming his hands over a charcoal burner balanced precariously upon one knee. All examples known to the author are either patch-marked Derby c.1760–5, or Chelsea-Derby incised no. 6. It may be that Hurlbutt ascribed them to Bow erroneously by reason of the square apertures behind some examples, but genuine Bow versions may exist. *Bustos as the Four Seasons* (B52, Plate 114), on waisted plinths, include Flora, Ceres, Bacchus and Saturn, and recall the much finer Chelsea busts of *Pagan Gods*.[54]

The dawning of the eighteenth century saw the birth of those Occidental fantasies of the Orient known as chinoiseries and japonaiseries that were soon incorporated into the rococo style to find expression in painting, sculpture, furniture, engraving, architecture and porcelain. However, by c.1755, the popularity of this art form had waned and few Bow examples are known of this period. The *Chinese Magician's Family* (B53, Plate 115), after Reinicke,[55] includes a Chinaman wearing a conical hat and robe standing regarding a child seated upon a stool, watched by his wife who has a top-knot; a second child stoops to feed a monkey with nuts. A simplified version omits the lady and stooped child and replaces the monkey with a bear (B54), while the *Putto and Monkey* (B195, Plate 193) were issued as a separate group.

Bow models of Middle Eastern persons mostly echo Meissen, possibly adapted from engravings in a folio *Recueil de cent estampes représentant différentes Nations du Levant, tirées sur les tableaux peints d'après Nature en 1707–1708, par ordre de M. Ferriol*.[56] The patron was French Ambassador to the Sublime Porte (1700–10) who, when presenting his credentials to the Sultan, had refused to divest himself of his sword in the belief that to do so would tarnish the honour of his sovereign, and narrowly escaped mutilation and death for this infringement of Islamic law. Meissen modellers may have referred to an abridged folio containing only 65 of the original 120 plates, published by Christoph Weigel c.1719 at Nuremberg. Plate 5, 'Le Capi Aga ou Chef des Eunugues blanc' prompted Eberlein's *Turk* standing in a cylindrical hat, paired with a *Levantine Lady* adjusting her tall head-dress.[57] Both were copied at Chelsea,[58] but at Bow the male figure was replaced by a turbanned *Turk* wearing a fur-trimmed cloak (B59, Plate 118, Col. Plate XII) adapted from the engraving 'Le Bostangi Bachi'. Rather similar models, after Eberlein,[59] of a seated *Turk* and *Levantine Lady* (B60, Plates 119 and 120), each holding shell containers, were also copied at Chelsea. Two pairs, one of *Turkish Dancers* (B62, Plate 121), the other of a *Turkish Boy and Girl* (B61) and later reissued as a group (B63), all have small heads and stylistically recall work by F. E. Meyer. *Turkish*

Children (B55) made their debut at Meissen as Blackamoors which were copied at Derby,[60] before their metamorphosis into pale-skinned Turks.[61] Models representing *Africa* and *America*, from the *Four Quarters of the Globe* (B42 and 43, Plates 96 and 97) were also refurbished as a *Negro* and *Negress* (B56) by repainting the Red Indian girl's skin black after some minor postural adjustments. A *Negro Page* (B58), wearing turban and livery, carrying a tray of refreshments, paired by a *Negress* bearing a basket of fruit and adjusting a tall head-dress, follow originals by Reinicke.[62] Kändler incorporated the Page into a group known as *The Hand Kiss* portraying a lady wearing a hooped skirt accepting a cup of chocolate from the servant while ignoring her ardent suitor who kneels to kiss her proffered hand.[63] The Blackamoor also reappears in a later Bow *Tea Party Group* (B127, Plate 167).

Bow versions of 'Paris Cries' after Bouchardon include a pair of *Cooks* (B69, Plate 127, Col. Plate III), the man wearing a turban, the woman a linen cap, both with aprons, carrying platters of two trussed ducks and a leg of lamb respectively. Possibly they were adapted from the engravings since no Meissen prototypes have yet been identified.[64] The *Savoyard Drummer* (B100), after Kändler,[65] clad in a tricorn hat, stands playing a flageolet as he beats a tall drum. A pair of *Woodcutters* (B87, Plates 140–1), also after Kändler,[66] shows one in a brimmed hat splitting logs with an axe, the other sitting in a fur cap cutting a baulk of timber upon a trestle with a small saw held in his right hand. Bouchardon depicted both men bareheaded, the second standing holding a large saw with both hands, one foot upon the timber.[66a] The figure of the *Alchemist* (B64) standing with his tray of bottles is likely to echo a Meissen original. There is, also, a very ugly pair of *Pedlars* (B77, Plate 133) that comprise a ragged beggarman with his bowl, and an old woman wearing a turban-like head-dress, a scarf, and coat left unbuttoned, carrying a rucksack upon her back on which a squirrel is perched; she supports a tray of medicine bottles and a scroll inscribed 'Powder [to] kill'. Some believe she may be the companion of the *Rat Catcher* (B81), but her sinister mien raises the suspicion that she is a sorceress as ready to poison humans as rodents! She first appeared in Antoine Watteau's painting of 'La Diseuse d'Aventure', engraved by Laurent Cars,[67] and later returns in Robert Hancock's etchings after Boitard of the same subject and in some versions of the 'Tea Party', finally prompting the Bow model of a younger female *Pedlar* (B78, Plate 134).

Bow models of the 'Cries of Paris', after Christophe Huet's water-colour sketches, were mostly copied from the intermediate sources of Meissen versions. A *Street Cook* (B68, Plate 126), after Reinicke,[68] clad in toque and apron, stands holding a saucepan of vegetables over a brick stove, tasting his forefinger. The *Itinerant Peep-showman* (B75, Plate 132), also after Reinicke,[69] carries his magic lantern upon his back and turns the handle of what appears to be a musical box. The *Knife Grinder* (B76) does not seem to have been illustrated, whilst a *Tinker* (B85), clad in a tricorn hat standing amid pots and pans, differs from Kändler's model which shows him seated beside a metal stove, tinning a saucepan.[70] The *Rat Catcher* (B81), wearing a plumed cap, sits beside a wooden box, holding either a ferret or a rat by its tail, subsequently adapted by replacing the animal with a stick to provide a *Salt Box Player* (B101, Plate 146) and both versions were also issued by Chelsea.[71] An entry in the Bow Memorandum Book for May 1756 reads: 'What is meant by 36 white men with salt boxes?' Also apposite is a passage from Croker's edition of Boswell's *Life of Dr. Samuel Johnson* (p. 143): 'At Ranelagh Gardens, about this time, a song was given by Beard, accompanied on the salt box by Brent, the fencing master, whilst Skeggs played broomstick as bassoon'. Afterwards the company sang recitative choruses in masquerade costumes.

Models of adolescents include a *Vendangeur and Flower Girl* (B72, Plates 129 and 130) after Kändler and Reinicke, who based the female figure on a drawing of 'Two Flower Girls' by Boucher.[72] She stands bareheaded, proffering a posy, with flowers gathered in her apron while her companion carries a tall pannier of grapes upon his back. Stylistically similar are a seated pair of *Grape Sellers* (B74, Plate 131) and also two *Boy and Girl Fish Sellers* (B65, Plate 122) after Eberlein.[73] The boy may wear a soft cap,[74] but usually both stand bareheaded and barefoot, he beside an up-ended oval creel, she with a basket of fish over her arm. A *Boy Toper* (B67, Plate 125), wearing a plumed conical cap, straddles a tree-stump, holding a tankard in either hand, with an expression of bewilderment at having become intoxicated for the first time. A later version (Plate 124) shows his jacket decorated with playing cards in a manner more often used on the clothing of characters from the *Commedia dell'Arte*. Another *Boy Toper* (B66, Plate 123, Col. Plate VI) in a brimmed hat, sits astride a wine-keg, and was based on an earlier model emblematic of *Tasting* (B44, Plate 101).

The *Piedmontese Bagpiper* (B79, Plate 135), readily identified by his broad-brimmed hat, long cloak, and the huge chanter and drones of his instrument, echoes Kändler's model based upon Jean Daullé's engraving after J. Dumont le Romain.[75] A group of *Tyrolean Dancers* (B86, Plate 139), after Eberlein,[76] portray a rustic swain in a brimmed hat, falling-ruffle, jacket and breeches, dancing a wild gavotte with a peasant maid whose plaits and dress swirl outwards as the couple gyrate. A Derby group is similar,[77] but at Chelsea the youth wears a grotesque mask,[78] whilst a droll Chinese version is known.[79]

A *Gardener and Companion* (B73) show the lady with flowers in her apron proffering a nosegay to her escort, who leans awkwardly on his spade and declines the favour by a gesture; they appear to be members of the aristocracy in masquerade. A *Flower Girl* (B71, Plate 128, Col. Plate XIII), wears a brimmed hat, jacket and skirt which she elevates to reveal her petticoat, and has a pannier of flowers over her arm and holds a posy. The Saltram House collection contains two examples, both paired with models of Pedrolino (nos T.260 and T.263), so that she may represent *Columbina*, although based upon a red-anchor Chelsea figure emblematic of 'Spring'.[80] A rare *Pilgrim* (B80, Plate 136) stoops, staff in hand, beneath his rucksack and is mounted upon a square base. He was probably copied from either a bronze or a lime-wood carving[81] of Flemish origin.[82] Seafarers are represented by a *Fisherman* (B70) clad in a tricorn hat, standing with a casting-net in both hands. A *Sailor* (B83, Plate 137) in similar headgear, cravat, jacket and knickerbockers, dances with arms outstretched and another *Sailor* paired with a *Lass* (B82) in like attire, stands hand on heart, while his lady, clad in a small round hat and gown, holds before her in both hands an object that is either a handkerchief with which to dry the tears of separation, or a purse containing the wages of sin! The pair were later reissued as a group (C59). Another dapper little fellow, either a *Midshipman* or *Dandy* (B84, Plate 138) holds a gold-headed cane and strikes a pose.

The Bow orchestra embraces a wide spectrum of instrumentalists of which a few faithfully follow Meissen originals. A peasant woman clad in a head-scarf playing a guitar (B95), and male *Fiddler* (B95), after Reinicke,[83] have Chelsea[84] and Bloor Derby[85] counterparts. Two *Boys with Drum and Fife* (B89), after Kändler, wear broad-brimmed plumed hats, military style jackets and breeches and buckled shoes; examples of c.1760 stand upon rectangular plinths with chamfered corners, painted with panels of floral sprays alternating with musical trophies, but later reappear on four-footed bases. Other Bow musicians were but loosely based on Meissen *Porzellanfiguren* and the majority were issued as standing or seated pairs (B88–104, Plates 142–8, Col. Plate XI). Notable amongst them are the *Idyllic Musicians* (B103, Plate 147), so named by Egan Mew, comprising the man with flageolet and tabor and the girl holding a triangle, with triple plumes adorning the gentleman's hat and lady's coiffeur. The female model was refurbished as a partner for a *Trumpeter* (B102). Earlier mention has been made of the *Salt Box Player* (B101, Plate 146), adapted from the *Rat Catcher* (B81) sometimes paired with a seated lady *Flautist* (B99, Plate 145). The seated male *Drum Player* with a flageolet, and his lady playing a zither (B104, Plate 148, Col. Plate XI) are enamelled with washes of delicious pale colours, embellished with sprays of roses in the manner of *deutsche Blumen*, and are extremely attractive. The vertical row of small bows on the lady's stomacher, known as '*parfait contentements*', may be seen upon the gown worn by the Marquise de Pompadour in a portrait of c.1757 by François Boucher.[86] Another seated pair of male *Hurdy-gurdy Player and Cellist* (B96), known also in Chelsea versions,[87] are finely sculptured and mounted upon four-footed bases although they are a trifle large to have universal appeal.

Two *Dancers* (B105, Plate 149), both wearing brimmed hats, show the man with his right arm upraised and the girl holding out her skirts in a fan, adopted from Kändler's *Dancing Columbina*[88] in a bandeau, reflected also at Chelsea.[89] The *Dutch Dancers* (B107, Plate 151), clad in bicorn hat and linen cap, dance with arms akimbo; their dynamic quality suggests Meissen prototypes and they contrast with stiffly posed *Dancers* (B106, Plate 150) standing in shadow positions. The *New*

Dancers (B106, Plate 150) consist of adolescents in wide-brimmed plumed hats, standing with both hands raised before them. They number amongst the commonest Bow models and later reappeared (C49–51) in several variations. Their prototypes appear to be smaller and simpler models that were issued both by Longton Hall[90] and Derby[91] in about 1754.

Bow porcelain modellers ignored the local fox-hunting scene and were content simply to copy Meissen versions of the chase which in reality amounted to little more than ritual slaughter, when wild animals were driven into a forest glade, or even a town square, to be shot to death at point-blank range by courtiers and their ladies. Sometimes Bow craftsmen failed to retain the proper pairing of the Meissen originals so that, for example, a *Huntsman* (B110, Plate 153, Col. Plate V) with gun and dog, acquires a *Lady Falconer* as his improbable companion. Each model was taken from a different pair by Eberlein comprising a *Huntsman and Lady*, each holding a gun, and a couple of *Falconers*.[92] Other Bow sporting pairs show a better appreciation of the subject and include a *Huntsman and Lady* (B111) wearing brimmed hats carrying flintlock guns, and a second pair in tricorn hats (B112, Plates 154 and 155) with gun and pistol. There remain two bocaged groups (B123) illustrating the equestrian feats of a certain Mr Price, performed during the 1760s in Dobney's Tea Gardens; in one he stands and in the other kneels upon the backs of two horses.

Pastoral subjects copied from Meissen models may often be traced back to engravings after French artists such as Boucher and Lancret who first created and then sustained the 'Idyllic Pastoral Myth'. In this, bewigged courtiers wore shepherds' costumes made of rich materials, gold-buckled shoes and buttons to match, whilst their ladies with powdered coiffure were attired as shepherdesses in silken gowns and satin slippers. They posed amongst faithful dogs and sheep in an Arcadian setting, creating a charade in miniature that reflected the masked balls and the masquerades enacted by courtiers at Versailles or the Opéra Comique. Ladies at the Court of Württemberg wore blue satin slippers only if they had granted their favours to their Duke, Karl Eugene! A *Boy Shepherd Piper* and his *Dancing Shepherdess* (B115, Plate 158, Col. Plate X) wear fine clothes and even the attendant lamb has a scarlet ribbon about its neck! Either they were copied from larger dry-edge Derby models,[93] or share with them a common source, and at both factories reappear in Scottish dress.[94] The *Shepherd playing a recorder* (B116, Plate 159) and *Shepherdess* with flowers, follow Meissen originals,[95] while a larger *Shepherd Bagpiper and Shepherdess* (B117), each with two sheep and a dog, do likewise.[96] In some examples the mouthpiece of the bagpipes is inscribed with the initials IB over 1757 within an oval.[97] The *French Shepherds* (B109) comprise a pair of bareheaded children, the boy holding aloft a ball and supporting with his right hand a dog that has leapt up on to his chest, the girl clasping a lamb. They are better known in Chelsea-Derby versions inscribed no. 57, depicting them barefoot. Emasculated models of *Liberty and Matrimony* (B113, Plate 156), common to Derby,[98] portray a youth bearing a nest of fledglings and girl holding a lantern-like bird-cage, and a primitively modelled group illustrates the same theme (B114, Plate 157).

Frederick the Great (1712–86), whose mother Sophia Dorothea was a daughter of George I, was hailed in England as 'The Prussian Hero' for his espousal of the Protestant cause in the Seven Years War against Maria Theresa. His Bow model (B119, Plate 162), probably after a Meissen original of c.1757, shows him bareheaded, standing in uniform amidst the trophies of battle. John Manners (1721–70), Marquis of Granby and the third son of the Duke of Rutland, became Colonel of the Leicestershire Blues raised in 1745 to defeat Bonny Prince Charlie. The regiment was disbanded after the victory of Culloden and for a while King George II was reluctant to agree to appoint the marquis Colonel-in-Chief of the Horse Guards, on account of his heavy drinking. However, in 1758 King George relented and within months Granby was engaged on active service in the Seven Years War, under the supreme command of Frederick Duke of Brunswick. Despite the court-martial of Lord George Sackville, who was his immediate superior, for incompetence, Granby was highly commended for his conduct at Minden in 1759. The following year at Warburg he led a charge of the Blues to victory during which, bereft of hat and wig, his bald pate became a rallying point in the ensuing *mêlée*. Richard Houston's engraving of Sir Joshua Reynolds' commemorative painting[99] provided the basis of the Bow portrait model (B124, Plate 165). Major-General James Wolfe (1727–59) had fought at Dettingen and Culloden before taking command of the British force in Canada against the French, under Louis-Joseph Marquis de Montcalm, who had taken up seemingly impregnable defensive positions before the city of Quebec. Wolfe crossed the St Lawrence River under cover of darkness on 13 September 1759, led his troops up the unguarded Heights of Abraham, to surprise the enemy and capture the city, but was slain in the hour of triumph. The portrait model (B128, Plate 168), based on Houston's engraving of a sketch made by a certain Captain Harvey Smith, shows the general wearing a cocked hat and uniform, standing with a musket slung across his back, holding a rolled map of Quebec, amid the trophies of war.

Captain Marcellus Laroon, the son of a Flemish painter, was part time opera singer, actor and soldier. He was a friend of William Hogarth and, when resident in London, was an *habitué* of taverns and more disreputable establishments of Drury Lane and frequently in trouble for drunkenness and unruly behaviour. Surprisingly he found time to sketch many of the strange characters whom he met and 70 of his drawings were engraved by Pierce Tempest and published in his *Cryes of the City of London* in 1711. They include plates of a notorious London pimp, named either the 'Marquis' or 'Squire of Alsatia', together with one of his courtesans, which were the basis of models by Peter Reinicke of c.1750. Christophe Huet during the 1740s made several water-colour sketches loosely following Tempest's engravings, including one in which the 'Marquis' and his coquette were altered to portray a *Gallant and Lady*, which prompted further models by Reinicke c.1758 that were copied at Bow (B121, Plate 163).[100] They portray a dandy holding his hat beneath his arm and companion lady carrying an open fan. A pair of *Gallant and Lady Topers* (B120) recline in mirror poses, the man with a flagon, the woman with a goblet, in their upraised hands, while standing figures of a *Gallant and Lady* (B122, Plate 164) may, by reason of the histrionic gestures they make, be unrecognised stage personalities. A group depicting a *Tea Party* (B127, Plate 167), brings together models of a standing *Gallant* (B121, Plate 163) and *Negro Page* (B57, Plate 116), previously issued as members of two unrelated pairs, with a seated Lady drinking tea in a garden setting.

Paired engravings by Pierre Filloeul, after J. B. Pater, 'Le Baiser Rendu' and 'Le Baiser Donné', prompted two Höchst groups by J. F. Lück. The first shows a peasant kissing the spouse of a nobleman who regards the scene with amusement;[101] in the second, the count embraces the wife of the yokel, who exclaims:

> Ah, que ma joye auroit été complète,
> Si Monsieur eut voulu coucher avec Lizette!

Kändler preferred to create a pair of models based on 'Le Baiser Rendu', replacing the peasant with a gallant attired in a tie-wig and dressing-gown, who stoops forward to blow a kiss. The object of his attention is the nobleman's wife portrayed bareheaded, wearing a blouse and hooped skirt and holding an open fan; the pair is often called *The Blown Kiss*.[102] Early Bow copies (B118, Plate 161), like their prototypes, have no bases and are supported only by the arrangement of their garments. Later, the old paramour was replaced by a new one wearing a small hat, mantua and hooped skirt adorned with flounces, without any fan (C64, Plate 229), and the two mounted upon tall pedestals. A pair of *Hussars* (B125, Plate 166) stand in arrogant poses, whilst a *Hussar on Horseback* (B126) with left arm upraised astride a dapple-grey charger follows a miniature Meissen original by Kändler.[103]

Cupids (B129, Plate 169) or more properly *Putti*, for there was only one Cupid, stand stiffly decked in chaplets and diagonal belts of flowers holding a basket of flowers or a pot-plant or puppy. Girls have narrower faces, a queue of hair and drapery which hangs from the hip downwards and to the left, a direction reversed for boys. Seated *Putti Musicians* (B130) hold a mandoline and fiddle and others, representing *Astrology* and *Music* (B131, Plate 170) sit on shaped plinths with a celestial globe and a lyre. Most are loosely based on F. E. Meyer's originals. However, the *Infant Bacchus* (B132, Plate 171) feeding grapes to a recumbent leopard, and scantily draped *Girl* seated upon a lion, echo Kändler's work[104] together with a pair of naked *Putti* (B134, Plate 172) seated in mirror poses each with a vase.[105] There are two charming groups of *Putti garlanding a Goat* (B133) portraying three putti festooning the animal with flowers and two putti garlanding a nanny-goat that suckles a kid.[106] *Putti Candlesticks* (B135, Plate 173) were also made, while *Putti as Pugilists* (B136, Plate 174) show them stripped to the waist, each leading with his bare left fist, their discarded garments beside them.

The concept of monkeys wearing human clothing, smoking pipes, playing music, drinking tea or hunting, probably arose in the Orient and was introduced to Europe in works by Audran, Watteau and Huet. Indeed, Christophe Huet's murals of *singeries* executed at Chantilly were subsequently engraved[107] and may have prompted Kändler's *Affenkapelle* of c.1752.[108] Not less than ten of these monkey musicians were copied at Chelsea,[109] but none were made at Bow. Instead a pair of *Singerie sweetmeat containers* (B139, Plate 175) decorated with monkeys attired as Gallant and Lady were issued.

Decorative Rococo Clock Cases (B137), after Meissen originals, were refurbished to commemorate the death of George Frideric Handel (1685–1759). The most elaborate example is surmounted by the figure of *Father Time*, flanked by seated *Putti Musicians*, with enamel decoration that includes fanciful musical scores. Three simpler ones are known together with one other unrelated to the maestro. There are also *Handel Vases* (B138) of double ogee form with twin handles, and three putti, representing Dance, Drama and Music, mounted upon the foot.

Birds were among the first small-scale models to be created by Kändler during what he described as *Feierabendarbeit* (leisure time). He was able to recapture the *Gestalt* of each creature in a few square inches of paste that could only have been possible after hours of personal observation. Most of the large Bow aviary was loosely based upon his work and, despite limitations imposed by the materials, manage to reflect something of his *élan*. They are larger and engender a greater sense of animation than Chelsea or Derby counterparts and are often brilliantly coloured with a purely fanciful plumage. Many are mounted upon white truncated cones, or tree-stumps, sparsely encrusted with different permutations of enamelled leaves, flowers, insects, fungi, moss or fruit.

A pair of *Bullfinches* (B143), after Kändler,[110] have purplish-brown feathers, russet breasts and throats, and perch with heads rotated in opposite directions. *Buntings*, both yellow (B144, Plate 176) and purple and green (B145, Plate 177), are presented in a similar manner, as well as a group of two *Buntings in a cherry branch* (B147) with a nest of fledglings. There is a veritable charm of *Goldfinches* (B153–8) after Kändler,[111] and the pair of green *Parrots Eating Nuts* (B163, Plate 182) also echo his work,[112] although a group of two small *Parrots in a Bocage* (B164) may have been created at Bow. The preference for brilliantly coloured and often unnatural plumage is perhaps exemplified by a *Peacock and Peahen* (B165, Plate 183) in which the cock bird has a slate-blue neck, a brown body with wings pencilled in purplish-black, and emerald-green tail feathers, likewise by a *Cock and Hen Pheasant* (B167) which have lavender-blue beaks and legs while their plumage is suggested by broad streaks of brown, purple, yellow and red enamel. *Cockerels and Hens* (B148–50, Plate 179), after Meissen originals,[113] were made both as pairs and groups, sometimes in the latter incorporating other farmyard stock. Two *Cormorants* (B151, Plate 180) with their wings outstretched, and pairs of *Tawny Owls* (B161–2), however, cannot be traced to Meissen prototypes. The Bow Memorandum Book mentions 'Birds on Pedestals', which probably referred to buntings, but the 'Swans' and 'Swans, wings open', are unknown to the author.

The hegemony of Meissen over the Bow figure department extended to include models both of domestic and wild animals. Indeed, Kändler's original models of seated *Cats*[114] copied both with and without prey at Bow (B174–5, Plates 184–5), first appeared at Meissen c.1736. His flocks of *Sheep* and herds of *Cattle*[115] were somewhat loosely adapted at Bow to provide pairs, both recumbent and standing, of *Ewe and Ram* (B179–80), and *Cow and Bull* (B176–7, Plate 186), which have their counterparts in Chelsea[116] and Derby[117] versions. A seated *Fox* (B181), after Kändler,[118] and a pair of *Goats* (B182), the female suckling a kid, also reflect his work.[119] A delightful pair of seated *Hares* (B184, Plate 234) and another evidently enjoying a good scratch (B183, Plate 187), reflect originals by Peter Reinicke.[120] A *Hound Dog and Bitch* (B185, Plate 188), may have been adapted from smaller versions mounted beside models of shepherds and huntsmen, but are even more noble by themselves as they sit with ears pricked up and heads half turned awaiting their master's summons. They recall an earlier pair which have bulging eyes made c.1751 at the enigmatic Girl-in-a-Swing factory.[121] The kennel of *Pug Dogs* (B190–3, Plates 190–2) includes both old friends and new arrivals, and there is also a *Puppy* (B194) of uncertain pedigree.

The '6 White Boars', mentioned in the Bow Memorandum Book as having been sold to the dealer Mr Fogg, have vanished without trace, although dry-edge Derby examples are well known.[122] A pair of seated *Lion and Lioness* (B186, Plate 189) each with one paw resting upon a globe, may be reduced adaptations of Kändler's originals,[123] and there is a large pair of recumbent *Lion and Lioness* (B187) on platform bases. Other members of the Bow pride have earlier been presented. *Monkeys* (B188), like their Meissen precursors[124] are depicted eating nuts, the female carrying a baby upon her back. The *Stag and Doe* (B196) at lodge also echo the *Modellmeister*'s work.[125] Perhaps the most endearing of the Bow animals is a pair of red *Squirrels* (B197) eating acorns. They look far happier than their Meissen cousins[126] which have metal collars with attached chains, and they are spared the indignity of wearing blue ribbons about their necks evident on the Chelsea[127] and Derby[128] animals. They usually appear upon four-footed bases and may be identified instantly by their long ear-tufts.

69 (B1) White model of *Arlecchino* scowling 5½in (14cm) c.1760

70 (B2) *Arlecchino and Columbina* seated with bagpipes and a hurdy gurdy 6¼in (15.9cm) c.1758

69

70

71

72

71 (B4) *Arlecchino and Columbina* dancing in mirror positions 6¼in (15.9cm) c.1760

72 *Left*, (B7) *Dottore Boloardo* striking a histrionic pose; *Right*, (B8) *Isabella*. Both 7½in (19.1cm) c.1764

73 (B10) *Narcissino* (Narcissus), often mistaken for 'The Captain' 7½in (19.1cm) c.1764

74 (B11) *Pantalone* (Pantaloon), holding a money-bag (missing) 4½in (11.4cm) c.1755

75 (B12) *Pedrolino* (Pierrot) 5½in (14cm) c.1760

73

74

75

76

77

78

79

76 *Right*, (B14) *Apollo* crowned with laurels, playing a lyre; *Left*, (B27) *Mercury* holding the caduceus (missing) and a money bag, emblematic of Commerce. Both 7in (17.8cm) c.1764

77 (B18) A group representing *Charity* 5½in (14cm) c.1760

78 (B19) *Diana* with a hunting-dog 7¼in (19.7cm) c.1764

79 (B20) Winged *Angel* blowing a trumpet, emblematic of Fame 7½in (19.1cm) c.1760

80 (B21) Model of the *Flora Farnese* 10in (25.4cm) c.1760

81 (B22) A model adapted from J. F. Eberlein's 'Smelling', sometimes called *Flora* or inscribed *Faustina* 10in (25.4cm) c.1760

82 (B23) *Juno with a Peacock* 6¾in (17.1cm) c.1760

80

81

82

83

83 (B24) *Jupiter astride an Eagle* 6in
(15.2cm) c.1754

84 (B25) *Mars* 10in (25.4cm) c.1761

84

86

85

85 (B28) *Minerva* 13¾in (35.1cm) c.1764

86 (B30) *Neptune* riding a Dolphin 6¾in
(17.1cm) c.1754–6

87 (B31) *Venus* with Doves 10in (25.4cm)
c.1764

87

88 (B33) *Bishop* giving Benediction 11¾in (29.8cm) c.1760

89 (B34) *Abbess and Novice*, seated reading the Divine Office 5¾in (14.6cm) c.1758

88

89

90

91

90 (B35) *Abbot* holding a crucifix in his
right hand (missing) 7in (17.8cm) c.1755

91 (B35) Companion *Abbess*, holding an
open book in her left hand (missing), and
her right upon her breast, idem.

92 (B37) Seated *Nun* in a star-spangled veil
5¾in (14.6cm) c.1756

92

93

93 (B40) Standing *Prior and Prioress* 5¾in (14.6cm) c.1760

94 (B41) *Ceres*, emblematic of *Earth*, from a
set of the *Four Elements* 7½in (19.1cm)
c.1758

95 (B41) *Juno* and *Neptune*, emblematic of
Air and *Water*, idem.

94

95

96

97

98

99

100

101

96 (B43) Candlestick Group representing *Asia and Africa*, from the *Four Quarters of the Globe* 7¾in (19.7cm) c.1762

97 (B43) Companion Candlestick *Group of America and Europe*, ibid.

98 (B44) *Troubadour*, emblematic of *Hearing*, from a set of the *Five Senses* 6in (15.2cm) c.1754

99 (B44) *Lady* holding a mirror, adjusting her coiffure, emblematic of *Seeing*, ibid.

100 (B44) *Girl* with flowers and a posy, emblematic of *Smelling*, ibid.

101 (B44) *Toper* astride a wine-keg, emblematic of *Tasting* 6½in (16.5cm), ibid.

102 (B44) *Lady* caressing a dog, emblematic of *Feeling* 5¼in (13.3cm), ibid.

102

103

104

105

I

(*Above*) The muses *Polyhymnia* (A30) and *Urania* (A33), showing the characteristic modelling traits and decoration with plain washes of pale enamel colour.

(*Left*) *Pedrolino* (B12), wearing a peach-coloured hat and yellow costume with gilt facings and buttons, standing before a white tree-stump sprigged with emerald green leaves.

II

III

IV

V

(*Above*) *A Huntsman and Lady
Falconer* (B110), decorated
predominantly in gold-purple. Both
mound bases are sprigged with
enamelled leaves and flowers, but
painted floral sprays also occur on the
upper surface of the male figure.

(*Left, bottom*) *Neptune* (B41),
representing *Water*, decorated
in polychrome and *Ceres*, emblematic
of *Earth* decorated in puce
monochrome with floral sprays in the
manner of *deutsche Blumen*.

(*Left, top*) A pair of *Cooks* (B69),
finely modelled and enamelled with
small scale floral sprays resembling the
Chinese *famille rose* decoration.

(*Right*) *A Boy Toper* (B66), enamelled
with sealing-wax blue and gold-purple,
with small floral sprays in the style of
indianische Blumen.

VI

(*Above*) *Arlecchino and Columbina* (B4), attired in motley, dancing in shadow positions that recapture something of the *elan* of their Meissen prototypes.

(*Right*) A seated *Nun* reading the Divine Office (B37), wearing a cream coloured habit and veil adorned with gold stars.

(*Left*) *Mars* (B26), a rare model showing the god standing upon a rectangular plinth, bareheaded, in Roman armour.

X

XI

XII

(*Left, top*) *Boy Shepherd Piper and Dancing Shepherdess*
(B115). The boy's white jacket is adorned with small scale
floral sprays in polychrome after the manner of *indianische
Blumen*, and the girl's apron has *deutsche Blumen* in puce
monochrome.

(*Left, bottom*) A pair of seated *Musicians* (B104), the man
with flageolet and drum, the lady with a zither. Decoration
includes sprays, each of two roses with emerald green leaves
that are rather large in scale.

(*Above*) *A Turk and Levantine Lady* (B59), decorated in
sealing-wax red and blue, gold-purple and pale yellow.

(*Right*) A *Flower Girl* (B71), after a red anchor Chelsea figure,
emblematic of 'Spring'. Her rose-pink jacket is edged with
gold and her skirt is decorated with stems and leaves of puce,
and large blue daisy heads with yellow centres.

(*Above*) A pair of *New Dancers* (B108), decorated in colours
of the late Bow palette and rather brassy gilding.

XIII

XIV

106

103 (B45) *Flora* standing beside an urn filled with flowers, emblematic of *Spring*, from the *Antique Seasons* 9½in (24.1cm) c.1758

104 (B45) *Bacchus* likewise before an urn filled with grapes, emblematic of *Autumn*. Companion model but on a different base 10in (25.4cm)

105 (B46) *Two Ladies* with flowers and corn, representing *Spring* and *Summer*, from the *Seated Rustic Seasons* 5in (12.6cm) c.1755

106 (B46) Companion models of a *Vendangeur* and *Old Man* warming his hands, emblematic of *Autumn* and *Winter*.

107 (B47) *Youth* wearing a tricorn-hat with ear-flaps, holding a fur muff, emblematic of *Winter*, from a set of the *Adolescent Seasons* 6½in (16.5cm) c.1764

107

108   109

108 (B48) *Flora and a Putto*, emblematic of *Spring*, from a set
of the *Classical Seasons* 11in (27.9cm) c.1762

109 (B48) *Bacchus* with grapes and an attendant *Putto*,
emblematic of *Autumn*.

110

110 (B48) Companion groups to **108** and **109** of *Ceres with a Putto* and *Vulcan* likewise, emblematic of *Summer* and *Winter*.

III

112

113

114

111 (B49) The *Standing Rustic Seasons* 9in (22.9cm) c.1760

112 (B50) Standing *Putti*, representing the *Four Seasons* 6in (15.2cm) c.1764

113 (B51) The four *Child Seasons*. These are Chelsea-Derby, incised *No. 6*, and patchmarked, but closely resemble those ascribed to Bow by Hurlbutt 5¼in (13.3cm) c.1773

114 (B52) *Bustos of Flora, Ceres,* and *Bacchus*, omitting *Saturn,* representing the *Four Seasons* 6in (15.2cm) c.1746

115 (B53) Group portraying the *Chinese Magician's Family* 6½in (16.5cm) c.1762

115

116

117

116 (B57) *Negro Page and Maid* 7¼in (18.4cm) c.1760

117 (B59) Model of a standing *Turk*, shown by X-Ray tomography to be solid cast 7¼in (18.4cm) c.1755

118

118 (B59) Standing *Turk and Levantine Lady* 8in (20.3cm) c.1760

119 (B60) Seated *Turk* holding a shell container 5¾in (14.6cm) c.1756

120 (B60) Companion *Levantine Lady* 5½in (14cm)

119

120

121

122

123

124

121 (B62) Pair of *Turkish Dancers* 7¾in
(19.7cm) c.1762

122 (B65) *Boy and Girl Fish Sellers* 6in
(15.2cm) c.1758

123 (B66) *Boy Toper* 5¼in (13.3cm) c.1756

124 (B66) Late version of *Boy Toper*,
decorated with playing-cards.

125 (B67) *Boy Toper* astride a wine-keg,
adapted from B44, *Tasting* 5¾in (14.6cm)
c.1760

125

126

126 (B68) *Street Cook* 6in (15.2cm) c.1760

127 (B69) Pair of *Cooks* bearing platters of food, including two trussed ducks with orange slices, and a leg of lamb 6½in/6¾in (16.5cm/17.1cm) c.1756

127

128

129

130

128 (B71) *Flower Girl*, after a Chelsea
model, emblematic of *Spring* $5\frac{3}{4}$in (14.6cm)
c.1756

129 (B72) *Vendangeur* carrying a hod of
grapes 7in (17.8cm) 1762

130 (B72) *Companion Flower Girl*, after
Boucher, ibid.

131

132

134

133

135

131 (B74) Pair of seated *Grape Sellers* 5¾in
(14.6cm) c.1762

132 (B75) *Itinerant Peep-Showman* 5½in
(14cm) c.1758

133 (B77) Traditionally known as *Pedlars*,
but probably *Beggar and a Sorceress* 6¾in
(17.1cm) c.1758

134 (B78) *Female Pedlar* 7in (17.1cm)
c.1760

135 (B79) *Piedmontese Bagpiper* 9½in
(24.1cm) c.1754

136

137

138

136 (B82) *Sailor's Lass* 7¼in (18.4cm) c.1755

137 (B83) Dancing *Sailor* 8in (20.3cm)
c.1764

138 (B84) *Midshipman*, or possibly *Dandy*,
striking a pose 7¾in (18.4cm) c.1758

139 (B86) *Tyrolean Dancers* 6in (15.2cm)
c.1756

139

140   141

140 (B87) *Woodcutter* sawing timber on a trestle 5¾in (14.6cm) c.1760

141 (B87) Companion *Woodcutter* splitting logs with an axe (missing), ibid.

142 (B89) *Drummer Boy*, mounted upon a tall plinth 10in (25.4cm) c.1760

143 (B96) Seated male *Cellist* and *Hurdy-Gurdy girl* 6¾in (17.1cm) c.1762

144 (B97) *Lady* playing a lyre 8in (20.3cm) c.1760

142

144

143

144

145

145

146

145 (B99) Seated male *Flautist* and *Lady with a mandoline* (mandoline missing) 7in (17.8cm) c.1756

146 (B101) *Salt Box Player* 5in (12.7cm) c.1758

147 (B103) *Musician with flageolet and tabor*, and *Lady playing a Triangle* 7in (17.8cm) c.1760. Known as the 'Idyllic Musicians'.

148 (B104) Seated male *Drum Player* with a flageolet, and lady *Zither player* 6½in (16.5cm) c.1758

147

148

149

149 (B105) Group of two *Dancers* 9½in (24.1cm) c.1760

150 (B106) Pair of two *Dancers* in shadow positions 6in (15.2cm) c.1762

151 (B107) Pair of *Dutch Dancers* 7½in/7¾in (19.1cm/20.3cm) c.1762

150

151

152

153

154

155

152 (B108) *New Dancers* 7¾in/7½in (19.7cm/ 19.1cm) c.1762

153 (B110) *Huntsman and Lady Falconer* 7½in (19.1cm) c.1755

154 (B112) *Huntsman* holding a gun 5½in (14cm) c.1760

155 (B112) Companion *Lady* with a gun, idem.

156 (B113) *Lady* with a Bird-cage, emblematic of *Matrimony* 7½in (19cm) c.1764

156

157

158

159

157 (B114) Primitively modelled group representing *Liberty and Matrimony* 6¼in (15.9cm) c.1758

158 (B115) *Shepherd Boy Piper* and *Dancing Shepherdess* 5¾in (14.6cm) c.1755

159 (B116) *Shepherd playing a Recorder* and *Shepherdess with Flowers* 6in (15.2cm) c.1755

160 (B117) *Shepherd bagpiper and Shepherdess* 10½in (26.5cm) c.1757

160

161

162

163

164

161 (B118) *Gallant blowing a kiss* 7in
(17.8cm) c.1755. Usually paired with *Lady
holding a fan*.

162 (B119) *Frederick the Great* 9¾in (24.8cm)
c.1760

163 (B121) *Squire of Alsatia and a Courtesan*
7½in (19.1cm) c.1762

164 (B122) *Gallant and Lady*, possibly an
Actor and Actress 7½in (19.1cm) c.1760

165 (B124) *Marquis of Granby* 14in (36cm)
c.1760

165

166

168

167

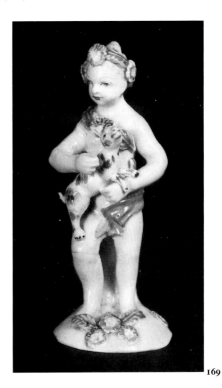

166 (B125) *Hussar* standing in an arrogant pose, one of a pair 4in (11.4cm) c.1758

167 (B127) *Tea Party* (group) w.10in (25.4cm) c.1764

168 (B128) *Major-General James Wolfe* 13in (33cm)

169 (B129) Female *Putto holding a puppy* 4¾in (12.1cm) c.1760

170 (B131) Two *Putti* representing *Music* and *Astrology* 7½in (19.1cm) c.1760

169

170

171

172

171 (B132) *Infant Bacchus* feeding grapes to a leopard, and
Girl with a lion 4in (10.2cm) c.1758

172 (B133) Two groups, each portraying *Putti garlanding a
Goat* with flowers 7in (17.8cm) c.1760

173 (B134) Pair of naked *Putti with vases*, seated 3½in (8.9cm)
c.1760

174 (B135) Pair of *Candlesticks*, each incorporating a seated
Putto 7½in (19.1cm) c.1760

173

174

175

175 (B139) Pair of Rococo *Sweetmeat Containers* decorated with *singeries* 6¼in (15.9cm) c.1762

176 Clockwise from left, (B144)Pair of *Buntings* 3¾in (9.5cm) c.1760; (B170) *Pigeon* 1¼in (3.2cm) c.1762; (C79) *Goldfinch* on a four-footed base 3¾in (9.5cm) c.1762

177 (B145) Pair of purple and green *Buntings* 2½in (6.4cm) c.1760

178 (B146) *Bocaged Candlesticks*, each with a pair of nesting *Buntings* 7in (17.8cm) c.1764

176

177

178

179

179 *Left*, (B149) *Cockerel and Hen Group* 4½in (10.8cm); *Right*, (B184) Seated *Hare* 5¾in (14.6cm). Both c.1765

180 (B151) *Cormorant* with wings outstretched 3½in (8.9cm) c.1760

181 (B153) Pair of *Goldfinches* 3¾in (9.5cm) c.1760

182 (B163) Pair of *Parrots eating Nuts* 7in (17.8cm) c.1762

180

181

182

183

184

185

C.1754-64

186

183 (B165) *Peacock and Peahen* 6½in
(16.5cm) c.1760

184 (B174) Seated *Cat* 2½in (6.5cm) c.1760

185 (B175) Seated *Cat with a Mouse* 3in
(7.6cm) c.1762

186 (B176) *Cow and Bull*, each standing
before a flowering tree 8¼in (21cm) c.1760

187 (B183) Seated *Hare* scratching 5½in
(14cm) c.1760

187

188

189

188 (B185) Pair of seated *Hounds* 2¼in (5.7cm) c.1760

189 (B186) Recumbent *Lion and Lioness*, each with one front paw upon a globe 4½in (11.4cm) c.1754

190 (B191) *Pug Dogs* standing 3¾in (7cm) c.1764; (B193) Recumbent *Pug Dog*, one of a pair w.3¼in (8.3cm) c.1762

191 (B192) *Pug Dog* seated, wearing a studded collar, one of a pair 2¼in (7cm) c.1755

190

191

192

192 (B194) Recumbent *Puppy* 1¾in (4.3cm) c.1760

193 (B196) *Stag* (lacking antlers) and *Doe* at lodge 3½in (8.9cm) c.1760; (B175b) Seated *Cat with a Mouse* 3in (7.6cm) c.1758

193

BOW PORCELAIN MODELS C.1754–64

ITALIAN COMEDY

B1　*Arlecchino*, 5½in (14cm). He stands leaning against a tree-stump with slap-sticks under his arm, touching his hat brim with his right hand. Hurlbutt pl. 43a; *E.C.C.* 1948 Ex. Cat. pl. 40, no. 147; author's collection. *See Plate 69*.

B2　*Arlecchino and Columbina* (pair), 6¼in (15.9cm). Both seated, he in a brimmed conical hat and motley with bagpipes; she in hat, bodice and skirt playing a hurdy-gurdy. Sotheby's 23.2.87, lot 102; ibid. 29.9.87, lot 105; Christie's 2.6.86, lot 307. *See Plate 70*.

B3　*Arlecchino and Columbina* (pair), 6in (15.2cm). Both stand, he in hat, mask and motley, with right hand upon his breast; she in a brimmed hat, bodice and skirt, dancing with both arms swinging towards her right. Stoner pl. 71.

B4　*Arlecchino and Columbina* (pair), 6¼in (15.9cm). Both stand attired as in B3, he with left hand raised to his chin; she touching the brim of her hat with her right hand. Schreiber pl. 2, no. 198 (new no. 48); B. and T. Hughes pl. 10b and d (middle row). *See Plate 71, Col. Plate VII*.

B5　*Boy Singer*, 6in (15.2cm). He stands clad in a hat, jacket and breeches, holding a song-sheet in his left hand while conducting with his right. Hurlbutt pl. 46a.

B6　*Children in Masquerade* (pair), 5in (12.7cm). They stand in costumes of Arlecchino and Columbina. *Antique Dealer & Collector's Guide*, February 1973, 102.

B7　*Dottore Boloardo*, 6½in (16.5cm). He wears a brimmed hat, jacket, falling-ruffle, waistcoat, breeches and zimara and stands with right hand on hip and left upraised. Christie's 1.10.90, lots 75 and 140 (on mound bases); Hughes pl. 4 (four-footed base); Sotheby's 5.10.76, lot 120. *See Plate 72*.

B8　*Isabella*, 7½in (19.1cm). She stands bareheaded holding out the skirt of a long dress with her right hand whilst gesturing with her left. Victoria & Albert Museum, Hughes pl. 4. *See Plate 72*.

B9　*Mezzetino*, 5½in (14cm). He wears a soft cap, doublet, breeches and tabarro, and walks with arms outstretched. *E.C.C.* 1948 Ex. Cat. pl. 41, no. 146.

B10　*Narcissino*, 6in (15.2cm). He stands, a cloak thrown over his left shoulder, wearing brimmed hat, sash and baggy breeches. Private collection. *See Plate 73*.

B11　*Pantalone*, 4¼in (10.8cm). Clad in skull-cap, jacket, breeches and zimara, he stoops forward holding a money-bag. Sotheby's 6.12.77, lot 27; Bradshaw pl. 61 (white). *See Plate 74*.

B12　*Pedrolino*, 5½in (14cm). He stands in Pierrot costume with both hands raised in horror before him. Christie's 23.2.87, lot 239; Freeman pl. 223. *See Plate 75, Col. Plate II*.

B13　*Scapino*, 5½in (14cm). Reissue of A12, mounted on a mound base. Private collection.

MYTHOLOGY

B14　*Apollo*, 7in (17.8cm). Wearing a laurel chaplet and scantily draped, he stands playing a lyre held in his left hand. Sotheby's 26.11.74, lot 137. *See Plate 76*.

B15　*Apollo*, 7¼in (19.7cm). Attired as in B14, he stands leaning with his right hand upon a lyre, with trophies of the 'Arts' at his feet. Hurlbutt pl. 63.

B16   *Bellona*, 7½in (19.1cm). She stands, in crested helmet, cuirass, thonged skirt and sandals holding an oval shield and spear, an owl at her feet and GR III inscribed upon her helmet. Hurlbutt pl. 56b.

B17   *Ceres*, 3¼in (8.3cm). Bareheaded and scantily draped she stoops over a corn-sheaf. Freeman pl. 227. See B41.

B18   *Charity* (group), 5½in (14cm). A seated woman in a veil and robe suckles a babe and has a seated and a standing child on either side of her. Sotheby's 1.7.75, lot 88; ibid. 1.7.86, lot 177. *See Plate 77.*

B19   *Diana*, 7¾in (19.7cm). She wears a crescent in her hair and long robe gathered by a sash, and stands selecting an arrow for her longbow. Hurlbutt pl. 63. *See Plate 78.*

B20   *Fame*, 7½in (19.1cm). A winged angel standing blowing a trumpet. Bradshaw pl. 73, private collection. *See Plate 79.*

B21   *Flora Farnese*, 17½in (44.5cm). She stands bareheaded and barefoot in a long robe, holding a cloak draped across her back with both hands. King fig. 10; Lane pl. 52; Freeman pl. 226. *See Plate 80.*

B22   *Flora*, 10in (25.4cm). She stands in a veil and robe holding a posy to her nose, before a perfume vase on a flower-encrusted plinth. Hurlbutt pl. 36; Hughes pl. 4b. *See Plate 81.*

B23   *Juno and Jupiter* (pair), 6¾in (17.1cm). Both stand crowned wearing regal robes, Juno beside a peacock, Jupiter holding thunderbolts in his upraised right hand, beside an eagle. Phillips 6.6.91, lots 384–5; Sotheby's 8.7.80, lot 90 (Juno only). See also B41. *See Plate 82.*

B24   *Jupiter astride an Eagle*, 6in (15.2cm). Crowned and in royal robes he sits astride an eagle, holding thunderbolts. Sotheby's 24.2.87, lot 104; *Connoisseur*, Vol. LXXVIII, 3, no. vi. *See Plates 83 and 91.*

B25   *Mars*, 10in (25.4cm). Clad in Roman helmet and armour and a cloak, he stands holding a spear and an oval shield. Sotheby's 13.11.73, lot 137. *See Plate 84.*

B26   *Mars*, 9½in (24.1cm). He stands bareheaded with his right arm outstretched, on a plinth. Savage, private collection.

B27   *Mercury*, 8¼in (21cm). Clad in a round helmet, cloak and winged sandals, he holds a money-bag and stands before a casket placed on top of two bales, with an ink-pot and a quill at his feet. Sotheby's 20.10.81, lot 118; ibid. 16.11.74, lot 103 (7½in/19.1cm version). *See Plate 85.*

B28   *Minerva*, 13¾in (35cm). A larger and more elaborate version of Bellona B6, mounted on a four-footed base. Victoria & Albert Museum, Lane col. pl. C; Hurlbutt pl. 56a. *See Plate 76.*

B29   *Neptune riding a dolphin*, 6½in (16.5cm). Crowned with seaweed and draped, he sits astride a dolphin, trident in hand. *Connoisseur*, Vol. LXXVIII, 3, no. vi. See B41 for different model.

B30   *Neptune*, 6¾in (17.1cm). He stands bareheaded and draped, astride a dolphin, gesturing with his left hand. Sotheby's 18.3.85, lot 208. *See Plate 86.*

B31   *Venus*, 10in (25.4cm). She stands bareheaded wearing a robe secured by a sash, her left breast exposed, with doves or sparrows at her feet. Schreiber pl. 2, no. 9 (new no. 88); B. and T. Hughes pl. 10d (bottom row). *See Plate 87.*

B32   *Winter*, 10in (25.4cm). A bearded man wearing a toque and fur-trimmed garments, stands before a flaming urn upon an architectural plinth. Hurlbutt pl. 53.

RELIGIOUS

B33   *A Bishop*, 11¾in (29.8cm). Attired in full canonicals he stands, his right arm raised in benediction. Schreiber pl. 2, no. 24 (new no. 91). *See Plate 88.*

B34   *Abbess and Novice* (pair), 5¾in (14.6cm). Both wear a veil and habit and sit reading books; the older woman supports the tome with her right hand, the postulant with both. Christie's 13.2.84, lot 170; Sotheby's 10.2.81, lot 60 showing enamel decoration simulating ermine; Freeman pl. 210 (Abbess only). *See Plate 89.*

B35   *Abbot and Abbess* (pair), 7in (17.8cm). The bearded Abbot, clad in a fur-trimmed cope, stands with arm outstretched and the Abbess with one hand upon her heart. Bradshaw pls 79a–b. Christie's 25.11.91, lot 97. Clean shaven Abbot and Abbess with right hand on her breast, holding a book in her left. *See Plate 91.*

B36   *Monk and Nun* (pair), 5½in (14cm). Both seated, the nun in habit and veil, the monk with pate exposed, holding books in both hands. Morley-Fletcher p. 100; same pair with nun supporting a cross, Christie's 23.2.87, lot 24.

B37   *Monk and Nun* (pair), 5¾in (14.6cm). Similar to B36 but with one hand poised in the air. Bradshaw pl. 78; Herbert Allen pl. 3, no. 6. *See Plate 92, Col. Plate IX.*

B38   *Monk and Nun* (pair), 4 and 4½in (10.1 and 11.4cm). Similar to B36, but the monk points to the text of an open book and the nun holds a cross and rosary. Lane pl. 51b.

B39   *Priest and Abbess* (pair), 5½in (14cm). Both stand, the priest in biretta, cape, and surplice reads his breviary, the Abbess holds an open tome and gestures with her right hand. Lane pl. 51a.

B40   *Prior and Prioress* (pair), 6in (15.2cm). Both stand, the Prior with hands clasped in prayer, the Prioress holding an open tome. Sotheby's (as illustrated). *See Plate 93.*

ALLEGORICAL

B41   *Four Elements* (4 figures), 7½in (19.1cm). *Air*, Juno standing beside an eagle, her hair and veil blown out by the wind. *Earth*, Ceres holding a cornucopia beside a lion, proffering fruits. *Water*, Neptune crowned with seaweed standing beside a dolphin, pouring water from an urn under his left arm. *Fire*, Vulcan shown as an effeminate youth, standing before a flaming urn upon a plinth, a phoenix at his feet. Bradshaw col. pl. E, Water and Earth (mound bases); Freeman pl. 245, complete set on tall bases, 11in (28cm). *See Plates 94 and 95, Col. Plate IV.*

B42   *Four Quarters of the Globe* (2 groups), 5¼in (13.3cm). *Africa and Asia*, a negress wearing an elephant head-dress, bodice and skirt stands beside a lion; a Levantine girl stands bareheaded with a perfume vase. *America and Europe*, a Red Indian girl in a feathered head-dress holding a longbow, beside an alligator; a white woman clad in a helmet, cuirass and thonged skirt, leans on an oval shield. Pallant House, Freeman pl. 231 (first group only).

B43   *Four Quarters of the Globe* (paired chamber candlesticks), 7¾in (19.7cm). Same groups as B42, with attached loop handles and sconces. Upton House, cat. no. 4. *See Plates 96 and 97.*

B44   *Five Senses* (5 models), 6–6½in (15.2–16.5cm), each depicted as a seated adult in contemporary dress. *Hearing*, a troubadour clad in a stocking-cap, cravat, shirt, jacket, breeches and hose rolled down, singing as he strums on a lute. *Seeing*, a lady holding a mirror at arm's length, adjusting her coiffure with her left hand. *Smelling*, a bareheaded maid beside a pannier of flowers leaning to her right to savour the aroma of a posy in her dependent right hand. *Tasting*, a youth in a brimmed hat, jacket and breeches, astride a wine-keg, holding a wine-flask and drinking. *Touching*, a lady wearing a mob-cap and dress caressing a dog seated beside her with one paw upon her lap. Stoner pl. 77, Hearing and Taste only; Plymouth Museum, set lacking Smelling; author's collection, lacking Feeling. See Plates *98–102*.

B45   *Antique Seasons* (4 figures), 9½in (24.1cm), four classical divinities standing beside rococo urns or vases. *Spring*, Flora, scantily draped, beside a vase of flowers. *Summer*, Ceres, clad in a *décolleté* dress, beside an urn from which emerges corn. *Autumn*, Bacchus bedecked in grapes and vine leaves, holds a goblet and bunch of grapes and stands before an urn from which grapes sprout. *Winter*, Vulcan, as an effeminate youth, standing before a flaming urn, a phoenix at his feet. Hurlbutt pl. 51a; Lane pl. 54, Spring only; David Love late stock, Summer only; Temple Newsam House, Autumn only. No example of Winter known to author but full set of Meissen originals illustrated by Hurlbutt pl. 51b. See Plates *103 and 104*.

B46   *Seated Rustic Seasons*, 5in (12.7cm), represented by four seated adults. *Spring*, a lady clad in brimmed hat and dress, a basket of flowers over her arm, proffering a posy. *Summer*, a lady, in similar attire, beside a corn-sheaf, proffering a handful of corn. *Autumn*, a *vendangeur* clad in brimmed hat and apron, holding aloft a bunch of grapes with a receptacle in his left hand. *Winter*, a bearded man in a heavy overcoat, a cowl pulled over his head, warming his hands over a brazier. Author's collection (white set); Freeman pls 204–5 (enamelled) lacking Summer; Savage pl. 64; Stoner pl. 88 (enamelled on scrolled bases). See Plates *105 and 106*.

B47   *Adolescent Seasons*, 7in (17.8cm), represented by four standing smartly dressed boys and girls. *Spring*, a girl clad in a brimmed hat, bodice and skirt with basket of flowers over her arm, proffering a bunch. *Summer*, a girl clad in brimmed hat, bodice, dress and apron, holding a sheaf of corn under her left arm. *Autumn*, a youth in a tricorn hat, jacket and breeches, holding a bunch of grapes. *Winter*, a youth in a tricorn hat, jacket and breeches, with both hands thrust into a fur muff. Hurlbutt pl. 49, Winter with ear-flaps attached to his tricorn hat. Other individual examples appear to be very rare, but paired groups are fairly common. See C28. See Plate *107*.

B48   *Classical Seasons*, 11in (27.9cm), represented by four classical divinities each with a putto, from which they may be separated by rococo candlesticks. *Spring*, Flora, scantily draped, standing beside a putto holding a basket of flowers. *Summer*, Ceres stooped over a putto bearing a sheaf of corn. *Autumn*, Bacchus decked in grapes and vine leaves, holding a bunch of grapes and a goblet, attended by a putto bearing a pannier of grapes. *Winter*, Vulcan wrapped in a mantle attended by a putto who warms his hands over a brazier. Morley-Fletcher p. 101; Hurlbutt pl. 50a, Autumn only; Freeman pl. 234, Spring only. All four Meissen prototypes are illustrated by Hurlbutt pl. 50b. See Plates *108–10*.

B49   *Standing Rustic Seasons* (4 figures), 9in (22.9cm). *Spring*, a woman wearing a round hat, dress and apron, her right hand resting upon her left shoulder, holding in her left a basket of flowers. *Summer*, a woman wearing a brimmed hat, bodice, skirt and apron, holding before her with both hands a corn-sheaf. *Autumn*, a man wearing a brimmed hat, holding aloft a bunch of grapes, a goblet in his right hand and a fruiting vine at his feet. *Winter*, a man clad in a brimmed hat and overcoat, warming his hands over a charcoal-burner attached to his belt. Stoner pl. 87; Hurlbutt pl. 54 (the same set). *See Plate 111.*

B50   *Four Putti as Seasons* (4 models), 6in (15.2cm). Each is decked in a chaplet and diagonal garland, composed of, respectively, flowers, corn, grapes and holly, and also carry bundles of the same. Bradshaw pl. 75; Lady Ludlow pl. 51, no. 116. Bocaged versions in a private collection. *See Plate 112.*

B51   *Child Seasons* (4 models), 7in (17.8cm). Each sits upon a tree-stump, scantily draped, a chaplet upon its head. *Spring*, with a basket of flowers, proffering a posy. *Summer*, with a corn sheaf, proffering corn. *Autumn*, with a pannier of grapes holding aloft a bunch. *Winter*, wrapped in a mantle, warming its hands over a charcoal-burner balanced precariously upon one knee. Hurlbutt pl. 48, Winter and Autumn only. All examples examined by the author have been Derby or Chelsea-Derby. *See Plate 113.*

B52   *Bustos as the Four Seasons* (4 models), 6in (15.2cm). Bustos of Flora, Ceres, Bacchus and Saturn, mounted upon square, waisted plinths. Bradshaw pl. 75 (3 only); Freeman pl. 208; *Connoisseur*, Vol. LXXVIII, 74, no. 1. *See Plate 114.*

FOREIGN PERSONAGES

B53   *Chinese Magician's Family* (group), 6½in (16.5cm). A Chinaman in conical hat and robes stands with left hand raised, facing a bareheaded lady with a top-knot; between them a child sits upon a stool, while in front a second child feeds a monkey with nuts. Freeman pl. 230. *See Plate 115.*

B54   *Chinese Magician Group*, 7¾in (19.7cm). The same as B53, less the Chinese lady and child feeding the monkey and with the monkey replaced by a bear. Hurlbutt pl. 42b.

B55   *Children, Turkish* (pair), 6½in (16.5cm). The boy is clad in a turban, long coat and trousers and stands left hand on hip; the girl wears a toque and long robe. Private collection.

B56   *Negro and Negress* (pair), 4in (10.2cm). Adapted from Africa and America with the Red Indian girl's skin repainted black, from B43. Freeman pl. 202.

B57   *Negro Page and Maid* (pair), 7¼in (18.4cm). A turbanned page carries a circular tray of refreshments; the maid has a basket of fruit over her left arm and adjusts her tall head-dress with her right hand. Hurlbutt pl. 34. *See Plate 116.*

B58   *Negro Page and Turkish Lady* (group), 10in (25.4cm). A page B57 proffers refreshments to a seated Turkish lady. Grosvenor House Antiques Fair, June 1976, cat. fig. 3.

B59   *Turk and Levantine Lady* (pair), 7¼in (18.4cm). Both stand, the Turk turbanned and clad in a fur-trimmed cloak and baggy trousers, right hand on hip and left outstretched; the lady in a long coat and trousers adjusts her tall head-dress with her right hand. Morley-Fletcher p. 100; Bradshaw pl. 62. *See Col. Plate VII. for solid cast model of Turk, and Plates 117 and 118, Col. Plate XII.*

B60   *Turk and Levantine Lady* (pair), 7in (17.8cm). Both seated holding shell containers, the Turk wearing a cylindrical head-dress, the lady similar to B59. Untermyer, pl. 80, fig. 245. *See Plates 119 and 120.*

B61   *Turkish Boy and Girl* (pair), 8¼in (21cm). Both stand, the boy clad in turban, waistcoat, baggy trousers and slippers; the girl in a tall head-dress, robe secured by a sash and a long coat. Sotheby's 10.12.73, lot 161.

B62   *Turkish Dancers* (pair), 7¼in (18.4cm). Attired like B61, saving the girl is bareheaded, they assume mirror poses with one hand on heart, the other upraised. Lady Ludlow pl. 99, no. 111; Honey p. 136, female only. *See Plate 121.*

B63   *Turkish Dancers* (group), 7¾in (19.7cm). Similar to B62, married on a single wide base with four short legs. Christie's 9.10.89, lot 211.

ARTISANS, PEASANTS AND MARITIME FOLK

B64   *Alchemist*, 8in (20.3cm). He stands, clad in tricorn hat, a tray of bottles beneath his right arm, a bottle in his left hand, a monkey perched on his back. Sotheby's 18.4.67, lot 178.

B65   *Boy and Girl Fish Sellers* (pair), 6in (15.2cm). Both stand bareheaded, the boy beside an up-ended oval creel, the girl holding a basket of fish. Christie's 1.6.87, lot 245; Schreiber pl. 1, no. 1 (new no. 51); *E.C.C.* 1948 Ex. Cat. pl. 40, no. 186. *See Plate 122.*

B66   *Boy Toper*, 5¼in (13.3cm). He wears a conical plumed cap, and straddles a tree-stump holding a tankard in each hand. Freeman pl. 203; Bradshaw pl. 65. *See Plates 123 and 124, Col. Plate VI.*

B67   *Boy Toper*, 5¾in (14.6cm). A more sophisticated example of B42. Sotheby's 5.10.76, lot 121; Herbert Allen pl. 2; Hoff Antiques late stock, *Antique Dealer & Collector's Guide*, June 1980, 58 (advertisement). *See Plate 125.*

B68   *Street Cook*, 6in (15.2cm). He stands clad in cap and apron, tasting his forefinger, holding a saucepan of vegetables over a brick stove. Christie's 10.10.88, lot 272; Sotheby's 5.10.76, lot 123. *See Plate 126.*

B69   *Cooks* (pair), 7in (17.8cm). Both stand in aprons, the man clad in a turban carries a platter of two trussed ducks; the woman in a linen cap likewise with a leg of lamb. Untermyer pl. 81, fig. 224; Lane pl. 50 (both mound bases); Stoner pl. 84 (four-footed bases). *See Plate 127, Col. Plate III.*

B70   *Fisherman*, 7in (17.8cm). He wears a tricorn hat, jacket and breeches, holding a net in both hands. Savage pl. 60.

B71   *Flower Girl*, 5¾in (14.6cm). She stands, clad in brimmed hat, jacket and skirt which she lifts to reveal her petticoat, whilst bearing a basket of flowers over her right arm and holding a posy in her right hand. Christie's 23.2.87, lot 238; author's collection. *See Plate 128, Col. Plate XIII.*

B72   *Vendangeur and Flower Girl* (pair), 7in (17.8cm). A young vendangeur stoops beneath a tall pannier of grapes upon his back; his companion wears a small hat, secures blossoms in her apron and has a basket of flowers over her left arm. Christie's 10.2.86, lot 290 (male only); ibid. 13.2.84, lot 132 (female only). *See Plates 129 and 130.*

B73   *Gardener and Companion* (pair), 7¼in (18.4cm). Both stand, the man in a tricorn hat leans upon a spade and gestures with his right hand; the lady wears a small hat, dress and apron, holds flowers in her apron and proffers a posy. Christie's 20.10.86, lot 202; ibid. 13.2.84, lot 136.

B74   *Grape Sellers* (pair), 5¾in (14.6cm). Both are seated; the boy, bareheaded, holds up a bunch of grapes and has a basket of fruit beside him; the girl in a brimmed hat holds a pannier of grapes upon her lap. Christie's 3.6.85, lot 155. *See Plate 131.*

B75   *Itinerant Peep-showman*, 5½in (14cm). Clad in a brimmed hat, coat and breeches, he stands bearing a magic lantern on his back and a wooden box suspended before him which has a handle that he turns. Sotheby's 7.5.68, lot 22; private collection (as illustrated). *See Plate 132.*

B76   *Knife Grinder*. Details unknown to author. Model cited in *E.C.C.*, 1968, Vol. 7, pt. 1, 'A Miscellany of Pieces'.

B77   *Pedlars* (pair), 6¾in (17.1cm). Both stand: the man, clad in a soft cap, jacket, knickerbockers and cloak, holds a bowl; the woman, in a turban-like head-dress and long coat, carries a pack upon her back on which a squirrel sits, and has a tray of medicine bottles and a scroll, the latter inscribed 'Powder [to] Kill'. Stoner pl. 79; Victoria & Albert Museum, C.145-1928; Sotheby's 18.4.67, lot 178. *See Plate 133.*

B78   *Pedlar*, 7in (17.8cm). Similar to B77, but portraying a younger woman wearing a cap instead of a turban, lacking the scroll. Private collection (as illustrated). *See Plate 134.*

B79   *Piedmontese Bagpiper*, 9½in (24.1cm). He stands wearing a brimmed hat and cloak, playing bagpipes which have a large chanter and drones. Freeman pl. 191; Savage pl. 57. *See Plate 135.*

B80   *Pilgrim*, 6⅜in (16.2cm). He wears a brimmed hat, coat and breeches, and stands stooped, stick in hand, bearing a rucksack upon his back. Lane pl. 49. *See Plates 29 and 136.*

B81   *Rat Catcher*, 5in (12.7cm). He sits, clad in a brimmed hat, jacket and trousers, beside a wooden box, holding either a ferret, or at arm's length a rat by its tail. Private collection (as illustrated). See B94.

B82   *Sailor and Lass* (pair), 7¼in (18.4cm). The sailor wears a hat, scarf, jacket and knickerbockers and stands left hand on heart; the lass, in a round hat and gown, holds a handkerchief or purse before her in both hands. Stoner pl. 76; Bradshaw pl. 67 (female only).

B83   *Sailor*, 8in (20.3cm). Attired as B82, dancing with both arms outstretched. King fig. 11; Lane pl. 55; Christie's 3.6.85, lot 154. *See Plate 137.*

B84   *Midshipman*, 6¾in (17.1cm). He stands clad in a bicorn hat, shirt, coat and breeches, holding a cane and with his left hand on hip. Private collection (as illustrated). *See Plate 138.*

B85   *Tinker*, 7½in (19.1cm). He stands clad in tricorn hat, jacket, breeches and apron, tinning a saucepan with other utensils at his feet. *Trans. E.C.C.*, 1968, Vol. 7, pt. 2, pl. 2a.

B86   *Tyrolean Dancers* (group), 6in (15.2cm). A rustic swain, clad in brimmed hat, ruffle, jacket and breeches, dances a gavotte with a peasant maid in a laced bodice and skirt. Stoner pl. 85; King fig. 8; Fitzwilliam Museum. *See Plate 139.*

B87   *Woodcutters* (pair), 5¾in (14.6cm). One, in a brimmed hat, splits logs with an axe, the other sits sawing timber on a trestle with a saw held in his right hand, and wears a fur cap. Sotheby's 5.10.76, lot 22; Bradshaw pl. 64 (axe man only). *See Plates 140 and 141.*

MUSICIANS

B88   *Boy Bagpiper*, 4¾in (12.1cm). He sits cross-legged wearing a brimmed hat, playing bagpipes. British Museum 1938 3–14–28, *Connoisseur*, 1927, Vol. LXXXIX, col. pl. on p. 10.

B89   *Boys with Drum and Fife* (pair), 10in (25.4cm). Both wear wide-brimmed plumed hats, tight-fitting jackets and trousers, and stand playing their instruments upon tall plinths. Untermyer pl. 82, fig. 247; King fig. 14 (Drummer only, 14in/35.6cm).

B90   *Dulcimer Player*, 7¾in (19.7cm). A seated female musician wearing a hat, bodice and skirt. Sotheby's 28.10.69, lot 104. *See Plate 142.*

B91   *Flautist*, 3¾in (9.5cm). A seated male musician wearing a soft cap, jacket and breeches. Freeman pl. 222; Christie's 10.2.86, lot 291; Sotheby's 21.5.85, lot 347.

B92   *Flautist*, 8¾in (22.2cm). A standing female musician. Sotheby's 27.4.76, lot 65.

B93   *Flautist*, 5in (12.7cm). Seated lady musician, often paired with the Salt Box Player, B102. Savage pl. 50.

B94   *Guitarist and Violinist* (pair), 9in (22.9cm). The lady guitarist wears a round hat, bodice and skirt and stands playing a guitar; the male, clad in a soft cap, stands likewise with a violin. Stoner pl. 90.

B95   *Guitarist and Violinist* (pair), 6½in (16.5cm). Both stand; the woman in headscarf, bodice, apron and skirt, plays a guitar, the male violinist is clad in a tricorn hat, breeches and jacket. Victoria & Albert Museum, Schmidt, p. 99; Christie's 18.6.84, lot 292; Poole cat. no. H12.

B96   *Hurdy-gurdy Player and Cellist* (pair), 6¾in (17.1cm). Both seated, the lady wears a round hat, bodice and skirt and plays a hurdy-gurdy, the man in a tricorn hat plays a cello. Stoner pl. 86.

B97   *Lyre Player*, 8in (20.3cm). A seated female musician in a hat, bodice and skirt, plays a lyre. Freeman pl. 221. *See Plate 143.*

B98   *Mandoline and Flageolet Players* (pair), 7in (17.8cm). Both seated, the lady in round hat, bodice and skirt plays a mandoline, the man in a soft cap plays a flageolet and small drum. Stoner pl. 82. *See Plate 144.*

B99   *Mandoline Player and Flautist* (pair), 7in (17.8cm). Both seated, the lady clad in brimmed hat and dress plays a mandoline, the man in a soft cap plays a flute. *Antique Dealer & Collector's Guide*, March 1973, 74. *See Plate 145.*

B100   *Savoyard Drummer*, 6¾in (17.1cm). He stands clad in brimmed hat, jacket and breeches, beating on a tall drum while holding a flageolet to his lips in his left hand. Late stock Newman & Newman.

B101   *Salt Box Player*, 5in (12.7cm). Adapted from B81 by the replacement of the ferret with a stick. Private collection. *See Plate 146.*

B102   *Triangle Player and Trumpeter* (pair), 7in (17.8cm). Both stand; the lady bareheaded, clad in bodice, blouse, apron and skirt plays a triangle, the man in a brimmed hat blows a trumpet. Hughes pl. 7; Sotheby's 22.10.25, lot 115.

B103   *Triangle and Flageolet Players* (pair), 7in (17.8cm). Both stand; the lady with plumes in her hair plays a triangle, the man in a brimmed hat with triple plumes plays a flageolet and tabor. Known as the 'Idyllic Musicians'. Hurlbutt pl. 62; Bradshaw pl. 69 (male only). See C45 for group. *See Plate 147.*

B104   *Zither and Drum Players* (pair), 6½in (16.5cm). Both seated, the lady with elaborate coiffure, jacket and skirt plays a zither, the man in a bicorn hat holds a flageolet and beats a tall drum. Freeman pl. 233 (scrolled bases); author's collection (mound bases). *See Plate 148, Col. Plate XI.*

DANCERS

B105   *Dancers* (group), 9½in (24.1cm). The man, clad in a brimmed hat, jacket and breeches, stands with right arm upraised, the girl wears a hat and holds out her skirt in a fan. Fitzwilliam Museum; King fig. 9; Sotheby's (as illustrated). *See Plate 149.*

B106   *Dancers* (pair), 6in (15.2cm). The man wears a tricorn hat and dances left hand on hip and right elevated, the girl clad in a tall head-dress and gown stands in a shadow position. Sotheby's 26.2.80, lot 200. *See Plate 150.*

B107   *Dutch Dancers* (pair), 7½ and 7¾in (19.1 and 20.3cm). Both stand with one foot advanced and arms akimbo, the woman clad in a linen cap, laced bodice, apron and skirt, the man in a bicorn hat, jacket and breeches. Schreiber pl. 2, no. 15 (new no. 90). Candlestick versions 9¼in (12.8cm). Stoner pl. 83. *See Plate 151.*

B108   *New Dancers* (pair), 7½in (19.1cm). Standing adolescents in wide-brimmed plumed hats with both hands raised before them. Hurlbutt pl. 45; Bradshaw pl. 66. See also C49–51. *See Plates 90 and 152, Col. Plate XIII.*

SPORTING AND PASTORAL

B109   *French Shepherds* (pair), 6½in (16.5cm). Standing bareheaded adolescents, the boy holding aloft a ball in his left hand, supporting with his right a puppy that has leapt up on to his chest; the girl clasping a lamb. Cushion pl. 24.

B110   *Huntsman and Lady Falconer* (pair), 7½in (19.1cm). Both stand, the man wearing a peaked cap, jacket, breeches and boots holding dead game in his right hand and a gun in his left; the lady, in a tricorn hat, jacket and dress, holds a hooded falcon upon her left gloved wrist. Bradshaw pl. 71; Freeman pl. 211 (white, male only). See also C54a–b for late models and group. *See Plate 153, Col. Plate V.*

B111   *Huntsman and Lady* (pair), 6¼in (15.9cm). Both wear brimmed hats and stand beside hounds holding guns. Hurlbutt pl. 46 (male only); Freeman pl. 212. Versions of 8in (20.3cm). Adams and Redstone pls 128a–b.

B112   *Huntsman and Lady* (pair), 5½in (14cm). Both stand clad in tricorn hats, the man holding a gun at the trail, the lady pistol in hand. Sotheby's 22.10.68, lot 64; Bradshaw col. pl. G. (male only). *See Plates 154 and 155.*

B113   *Liberty and Matrimony* (pair), 7½in (19.1cm). Both stand wearing hats, the youth holding before him a nest of fledglings, the girl a lantern-like bird-cage. Savage pl. 63; Sotheby's 10.12.73, lot 162. *See Plate 156.*

B114   *Liberty and Matrimony* (group), 6¼in (15.9cm). A youth sits beside a girl who holds a large bird-cage, his left arm about her shoulders, mounted on an oval flower-encrusted base. Courtesy of George Savage (as illustrated). *See Plate 157.*

B115   *Shepherd Boy Piper and Dancing Shepherdess* (pair), 5¾in (14.6cm). The youth stands with head turned to the left, wearing a brimmed hat, playing bagpipes, a dog at his side; the shepherdess in a brimmed hat over a mob-cap, raises the skirt of her fine dress with her right hand, as if about to dance, a lamb at her side. Author's collection (as illustrated). Versions in Scottish dress, Christie's 18.6.84, lot 291. *See Plate 158, Col. Plate X.*

B116   *Shepherd playing a Recorder and Shepherdess with Flowers* (pair), 7½in (19.1cm). He wears a brimmed hat and stands cross-legged playing a recorder, a dog at his side; the shepherdess in hat and dress, holds flowers in her apron and proffers a posy, a lamb at her feet. Sotheby's 12.5.81, lot 5. *See Plate 159.*

B117   *Shepherd Bagpiper and Shepherdess* (pair), 10½in (26.7cm). Both stand clad in tricorn hats beside a dog and a sheep, the man playing bagpipes, the woman holding flowers in her apron, proffering a nosegay. Lane pls 46–7; Freeman pl. 225 (female only); Bow Special Ex. Cat. nos 31 and 150. *See Plate 160.*

GALLANTS AND NOTABLES

B118   *The Blown Kiss* (pair), 7in (17.8cm). Early examples without bases: a bareheaded gallant in a tie-wig, wearing a long dressing-gown, stoops forwards to blow a kiss. The lady is bareheaded and wears a bodice and hooped skirt, and holds an open fan. Adams and Redstone, pl. 120 (male only); Egan Mew pl. xv (pair). See C64 for later versions. *See Plate 161.*

B119   *Frederick the Great*, 9¾in (24.8cm). He stands bareheaded, wearing a jacket, sash, breeches and top-boots, left hand on hip, holding a scroll in his right, amid trophies of war. Stoner pl. 80. *See Plate 162.*

B120   *Gallant and Lady Topers* (pair), 6½in (16.5cm). They recline against hampers, in mirror poses, he holding a bottle to his lips, she a goblet. Stoner pl. 81.

B121   *Gallant and Lady*, or *Squire of Alsatia and a courtesan* (pair), 6¾in (17.1cm). The man stands, his hat beneath his left arm, fashionably attired in cravat, long waistcoat, jacket and breeches. The lady is bareheaded, and is dressed in a blouse with pagoda-sleeves, and hooped skirt, holding a fan. Stoner pl. 75; Christie's 1.6.87, lot 246 (male only); Bradshaw pl. 77 (female only). *See Plate 163.*

B122   *Gallant and Lady* (pair), 7½in (19.1cm). A fashionably attired man in a tricorn hat stands with his left hand in his pocket and right outstretched. The lady wears a brimmed hat, laced bodice and flounced hooped skirt, and stands with her right hand extended before her. Possibly an actor and actress. Venner's Antiques, late stock; private collection (as illustrated). *See Plate 164.*

B123   *Price the Trick Horseman* (2 groups), size not known. Two bocaged groups, each depicting Price with paired horses; upon one pair he stands and on the other kneels. Sotheby's 16.5.47, lot 81; ibid. 28.2.51, lot 146.

B124   *Marquis of Granby*, 14in (36cm). Bereft of hat and wig, his bald pate exposed, he stands wearing the uniform of Colonel-in-Chief of the Blues, holding a scroll in his right hand and resting his left upon the pommel of his sword. Schreiber pl. 4, no. 6 (new no. 54a); Hughes pl. 6a; Sotheby's 22.10.85, lot 127. *See Plate 165.*

B125   *Hussars* (pair), 4in (10.2cm). Clad in tunic, dolman and pelisse they stand in arrogant poses. Schreiber pl. 33, no. 199 (new no. 92); Sotheby's 25.3.74, lot 211; ibid. 6.11.77, lot 13. *See Plate 166.*

B126   *Hussar on Horseback*, 4½in (11.4cm). He sits, with right arm raised, astride a dapple grey charger. Freeman pl. 218; Christie's 16.6.75, lot 40; ibid. 23.3.64, lot 124.

B127   *Tea Party* (group), 9½in (24.1cm) long. A seated bareheaded lady sits in a garden holding a cup of tea, approached by a gallant carrying his hat beneath his left arm, and a Negro Page carrying a tray of refreshments. Godden's Encyclopaedia p. 37, pl. 69; Freeman pl. 232; Phillips (as illustrated). *See Plate 167.*

B128   *Major-General James Wolfe*, 13in (33cm). He wears a cocked-hat, uniform jacket, breeches and boots, and stands with a musket slung across his back, holding in his hand a rolled map of Quebec. Lane pl. 53; Schreiber pl. 4, no. 5 (new no. 54); Hughes pl. 6d. *See Plate 168.*

Putti

B129   *Putti* (pairs), 4¾–5in (12.1–12.7cm). Male and female pairs, bedecked in chaplets and diagonal belts of flowers, stand scantily draped. Each holds a pot-plant, a basket of flowers or a puppy. Savage pl. 56a; Freeman pl. 236; Scott and Scott pl. 171. *See Plate 169.*

B130   *Putti Musicians* (pair), 4¼in (10.8cm). Each sits on a V-shaped branch, one playing a violin, the other a mandoline. Christie's 9.10.89, lot 205.

B131   *Putti as Arts* (pair), 7½in (19.1cm). Both sit on shaped plinths, *Astrology* with a celestial globe, *Music* with a lyre. Christie's 13.2.84, lot 172. *See Plate 170.*

B132   *Putti* (pair), 6in (15.2cm). One attired as the *Infant Bacchus* feeds grapes to a recumbent leopard, the other, as a scantily draped *Girl* sits on a recumbent lion. Freeman pl. 215; Fitzwilliam Museum. *See Plate 171.*

B133   *Putti garlanding a Goat* (2 groups), 7in (17.8cm). In one group, three putti garland a male goat, in the other two putti do likewise to a female goat suckling a kid. Bradshaw col. pl. H, from a private collection.

B134   *Putti with Vases* (pair), 3½in (8.9cm). Two nude putti sit in mirror poses holding a vase upon one knee. Sotheby's 27.5.86, lot 48; ibid. 17.10.89, lot 438. *See Plate 172.*

B135   *Putti Candlesticks* (pair), 7½in (19.1cm). Each sits in a mirror pose with one arm encircling a candle sconce. Bradshaw pl. 80; Sotheby's 26.11.74, lot 7. *See Plate 173.*

B136   *Putti as Pugilists* (pair), 5¾in (14.6cm). Each stripped to the waist, with discarded clothes behind them upon the ground, stands barefisted, leading with the left hand. Freeman pl. 214. *See Plate 174.*

Miscellaneous Items

B137   *Decorative Rococo Clock Cases*, about 12¼in (31.1cm).

(1) Surmounted by *Father Time*, flanked by *Putti Musicians*, with painted decoration including fanciful musical scores; inscribed in front 'Tempus Fugit', and 'To Great Handle [sic] god of Music'. Adams and Redstone pl. 106.

(2) Similar but Father Time has one arm outstretched and Putti are devoid of instruments. Inscribed '5th November 1759' *E.C.C.* 1977 Ex. Cat. pl. 132.

(3) Others less elaborate, described by Hugh Tait in *Apollo*, July 1962, 384–90, 'Handel and Bow'.

B138 *Handel Vase*, 7in (17.8cm). Twin-handled vase of double ogee shape, with three standing Putti, representing *Music*, *Drama* and *Dance*, mounted upon a projecting foot rim. The front decorated with a musical score inscribed 'Minuette', and sides showing two further scores labelled 'A Song' and 'A Waltz'. Freeman pl. 138; Bow Special Ex. Cat. no. 104, fig. 36.

B139 *Singerie Sweetmeat Containers* (pair), 6¼in (15.9cm). One monkey attired as a gallant, the other as a lady, sit beside rococo receptacles. Stoner pl. 106. *See Plate 175.*

B140 *Shepherd Sweetmeat Containers* (pair), 8in (20.3cm). A shepherd and shepherdess each stand bareheaded with one hand upon rectangular receptacles, a dog and sheep at their feet. Private collection.

B141 *Gallant and Lady Sweetmeat Containers* (pair), 7½in (19.1cm). A gallant and lady each stand with one hand upon the lid of oval receptacles. *Country Life*, June 1970, 1138.

BIRDS

B142 *Barnyard Group*, 5¼in (13.3cm). A cockerel, a begging pug dog and a recumbent hound. Untermyer pl. 75, fig. 25; Sotheby's 14.6.88, lot 562.

B143 *Bullfinches* (pair), 3¾in (9.5cm). Lady Ludlow pl. 47, no 109.

B144 *Buntings* (pair), 3¾in (9.5cm). Untermyer pl. 87, fig. 25. *See Plate 176.*

B145 *Buntings* (pair), 2½in (6.4cm). Untermyer pl. 87, fig. 258; Freeman pl. 268. *See Plate 177.*

B146 *Buntings in Bocaged Candlesticks* (group), 7in (17.8cm). A pair perch in a bocage, watched by a dog. Lady Ludlow pl. 46, no. 105: Sotheby's 14.6.88, lot 566. *See Plate 178.*

B147 *Buntings in a cherry branch* (group), 9½in (24.1cm). A pair with a nest in a bocage. Sotheby's 18.6.71, lot 115.

B148 *Cockerel and Hen* (pair), 6½ and 5¾in (16.5 and 15.2cm). Untermyer pl. 92, fig. 256; Christie's 14.10.85, lot 238. Examples 4½ and 3¾in (11.4 and 9.5 cm). Freeman pl. 266.

B149 *Cockerel and Hen* (group), 4½in (11.4cm). Christie's 1.6.87, lot 248; Adams and Redstone pl. 131. *See Plate 179.*

B150 *Cockerel and Hen with 3 Chicks* (pair), 4½in (11.4cm). Schreiber no. 226 (new no. 60).

B151 *Cormorant*, 3½in (8.9cm). Freeman pl. 263. *See Plate 180.*

B152 *Fledgling*, 4½in (11.4cm). Perched with beak open on a rocky mound. Christie's 10.10.88, lot 257.

B153 *Goldfinches* (pair), 3¾in (9.5cm). E.C.C. 1948 Ex. Cat. nos 191–2; Sotheby's 4.2.75, lot 137 (one only). *See Plate 181.*

B154 *Goldfinch*, 3¾in (9.5cm). Mounted before a small bocage. Freeman pl. 269.

B155 *Goldfinch*, 6in (15.2cm). With wing displayed. Sotheby's 2.4.68, lot 14.

B156 *Goldfinch*, 6in (15.2cm). Before a small bocage. Sotheby's 14.6.88, lot 570.

B157 *Goldfinch* (group), 8¾in (22.2cm). Two bocaged groups each with a pair with a nest. Christie's 17.12.84, lot 167.

B158 *Goldfinch* (group), 9¼in (23.5cm). A pair nesting in a cherry tree. Sotheby's 22.2.88, lot 632.

B159 *Kestrel*, 6in (15.2cm). Sotheby's 14.5.74, lot 60.

B160 *Kestrels* (pair), 3½in (8.9cm). Freeman pl. 265.

B161   *Owls* (pair), 9½in (24.1cm). Stoner pl. 105. In opposite directions. Freeman pl. 265.

B162   *Owls, Tawny* (pair), 8¼in (21cm). Sotheby's 19.2.52, lot 154; ibid. 2.10.84, lot 70; Christie's 2.6.86, lot 314. Smaller examples, 7¼in (18.4cm). Untermyer pl. 78, fig. 259.

B163   *Parrots eating Nuts* (pair), 7in (17.8cm). Perched eating nuts. Untermyer pl. 92, fig. 260; Schreiber pl. 1, no. 34 (new no. 67); Sotheby's 14.6.88, lot 564. *See Plate 182.*

B164   *Parrots in a Bocage* (group), 8in (20.3cm). Two parrots perched in a bocage, surmounted by a candle tulip. Sotheby's 14.6.88, lot 561.

B165   *Peacock and Peahen* (pair), 6½in (16.5cm). Stoner pl. 108. *See Plate 183.*

B166   *Peacock*, 4in (10.2cm). Hurlbutt pl. 29.

B167   *Pheasants, Cock and Hen* (pair), 6in (15.2cm). Untermyer pl. 87, fig. 262.

B168   *Pheasants* (pair), 10¼in (26cm). Sotheby's 23.2.64, lot 120.

B169   *Pheasant Candlesticks* (pair), 10in (25.4cm). Each bird perched in a flowering bocage, surmounted by a candle tulip. Sotheby's 23.2.64, lot 76.

B170   *Pigeon*, 1¼in (3.2cm). Untermyer pl. 49, fig. 114. *See Plate 176.*

B171   *Song Birds* (group), 8½in (21.6cm). A pair with a nest of eggs, in a flowering bocage, surmounted by a candle tulip. Untermyer pl. 86, fig. 253.

B172   *Unidentified Birds* (pair), 4in (10.2cm). Probably Buntings. Hurlbutt pl. 29.

B173   *Warblers* (pair), 5in (12.7cm). Lady Ludlow pl. 47, no. 107.

ANIMALS

B174   *Cats*, seated (pair), 2½in (6.4cm). Freeman pl. 253; Christie's 18.3.85, lot 21c. *See Plate 184.*

B175a   *Cats*, seated with Prey (pair), 3 and 3½in (7.6 and 8.9cm). Schreiber no. 33 (new no. 99); Sotheby's 29.9.87, lot 106. *See Plate 185.*

B175b   *Cat*, seated with Prey, its left paw upon a sack into which a second mouse creeps, 3in (7.6cm). Ex. Bow Porcelain 1981 held at Stoke-on-Trent Museum, cat. no. 174. *See Plate 185,193.*

B176   *Cow and Bull*, standing (pair), before leafing tree-stumps, 8¼in (21cm). Stoner pl. 104; without tree-stumps, 5¾in (14.6cm). Sotheby's 8.7.80, lot 104. *See Plate 186.*

B177   *Cow and Bull*, recumbent (pair), 3¼in (8.3cm). Freeman pl. 257 (one only).

B178   *Dog, Goat and Squirrel* (group), 7½in (19.1cm). Sotheby's 26.11.74, lot 138.

B179   *Ewe and Ram* (pair), 3¾in (9.5cm). Standing with heads turned in opposite directions. B. & T. Thorn late stock.

B180   *Ewe and Ram* (pair), 2¾in (7cm). Recumbent. Thornton's of Harrogate late stock.

B181   *Fox*, seated, 1½in (3.8cm). Freeman pl. 259.

B182   *Goats* (pair), 3¼in (8.3cm). Both standing, the female suckling a Kid. Private collection.

B183   *Hare*, 5½in (14cm). Seated scratching itself. Freeman pl. 256; Christie's 10.10.88, lot 260. *See Plate 187.*

B184   *Hares*, seated (pair), 5¾in (14.6cm). Christie's 1.6.87, lot 249. *See Plates 179 and 234.*

B185   *Hounds, Dog and Bitch*, seated (pair), 2¼in (5.7cm). Temple Newsam House, Leeds; David Thorn collection; Freeman pl. 255 (one only). *See Plate 188.*

B186   *Lion and Lioness* (pair), 4 and 4½in (10.2 and 11.4cm). Recumbent one paw upon a globe, in mirror positions. Sotheby's 25.2.86, lot 139. *See Plates 189 and 193.*

B187   *Lion and Lioness* (pair), 10¾in (27.3cm) long. Recumbent on platform bases. Ex. Bow Porcelain 1981 held at Stoke-on-Trent Museum, cat. no. 161; Museum of London.

B188   *Monkeys* (pair), 3½in (8.9cm). Seated eating nuts, the female carrying a baby on her back. Schreiber no. 31 (new no. 58); Freeman pl. 260 (one only).

B189   *Monkey and Squirrel* (group), 7in (17.8cm). Two monkeys with a squirrel in a bocage. Sotheby's 3.6.85, lot 152.

B190   *Pug Dog, begging*, 3¾in (9.5cm). Christie's 23.2.87, lot 206. *See Plate 190.*

B191   *Pug Dogs*, standing (pair), 3¾in (9.5cm). On oval bases edged with scrolls. Christie's 3.6.85, lot 152; Freeman pl. 261. *See Plate 191.*

B192   *Pug Dogs*, seated (pair), 2¾in (7cm). Wearing studded collars. Sotheby's 25.2.86, lot 142 (one only). *See Plate 190.*

B193   *Pug Dogs*, recumbent on cushions (pair), 2¼in (5.7cm). Sotheby's 29.9.87, lot 107; David Thorn collection. *See Plate 192.*

B194   *Puppy*, recumbent, 2¼in (5.7cm). David Thorn collection.

B195   *Putto and Monkey* (group), 3½in (8.9cm). Adapted from B53, a Putto stoops to feed nuts to a monkey. Freeman pl. 217. *See Plate 193.*

B196   *Stag and Doe*, at lodge (pair), 3½in (8.9cm). Stag lacks its antlers. Christie's 20.10.88, lot 259; Freeman pl. 250.

B197   *Squirrels* (pair), 8in (20.3cm). Red squirrels with long ear-tufts, eating nuts, on four-footed bases. Stoner pl. 110.

14 BOW PORCELAIN MODELS C.1765–74

MODELLING

THE PAUCITY OF FRESH MODELS ISSUED AFTER c.1764, together with the poor quality of many of them, point to a dearth of talent in the figure department. Replicas of ancient *Divinities* (C16 and C20, Plate 200) often have absurdly small heads and thin spidery limbs, while human subjects in contemporary dress (C31, C63 and C68, Plates 228 and 233) may have blown cheeks, ill-fitting garments and stand woodenly, lacking any semblance of animation. There are, however, a few finely sculpted figures incorporating two pairs of *Musicians* (C46–7) and *Arlecchino with Columbina* (C2, Plate 194).

A pair of models emblematic of *Spring and Autumn* (C30, Plates 214–15), the muse *Clio* (C14), and possibly a *Fortune Telling Group* (C65, Plate 230) appear to have been plagiarised from Chelsea with only minor modifications. The vast majority of figures were cast from old moulds and comprise degraded and often also smaller versions of earlier work.

BASES

THE FOUR-FOOTED BASES, first introduced c.1756, became more elaborate (C24, Plate 203) and were decorated in polychrome accented with gilding. In a few examples an additional upper tier was provided consisting of C- and S-shaped scrolls about round or oval fenestrations. More popular were bases resembling ormolu mounts (C10, Plate 198), some of which are circular in plan, with deeply moulded scrolls between concave and convex surfaces bearing comma-shaped windows (C23, Plate 202). These were decorated with turquoise or, rarely, pale pink, underglaze dark blue and gilding. Other forms include round bases with three or four short legs (C5, Plate 196), pierced pedestals (C25, Plate 205), cube-shaped with vertical slot-like apertures (C2, Plate 194), or wide flat platforms edged with small shallow scrolls (B45, Plate 103). A pair of *Musicians* (C46) in the Untermyer collection are mounted on bases which, when viewed from the front, resemble a double inverted U. The upper surface was either left white or coloured green and sprigged with enamelled leaves and flowers. Bases were concave underneath, glazed and pierced by a small ventilation hole, with points of contact with the table-top ground to ensure level and stable stance.

MOULDED LEAVES, FLOWERS AND BOCAGE

MOULDED LEAVES REMAIN large in scale, and are mostly yellow-green with moulded mid-ribs and serrated edges in place of their earlier spiky contours. Flowers with long pointed petals are less often seen and in their place are others resembling miniature saucers with raised centres that have between eight and ten short petals protruding like the teeth of a cog-wheel.

Perhaps the most attractive bocages are composed of discrete aggregations of foliage leaving gaps through which the white supporting tree-trunk and its branches are visible. Some were adapted as chamber candlesticks by the attachment of a candle holder, a loop handle and floral thumb-rest. Less pleasing are bocages consisting of dense arbours of flowers and leaves that may be surmounted by a candle tulip or flanked by swan-necked candle sconces. These are sometimes enlarged to overhang and envelop the subject on either side. Semi-miniature figures usually have proportionally small leafed bocages seldom extending above waist height, and a few late models have leaves backed by a flat plate of paste resembling those commonly found on Walton's pottery models. Lastly, some figures are mounted before flower-encrusted candlesticks.

ENAMEL DECORATION

BOTH THE ENAMEL palette and the style in which models were decorated altered c.1762–4. The pink became paler but more glossy and the former opaque turquoise was replaced by a clear but watery substitute. The brilliance of the vermilion was muted, the lovely emerald gave place to an inferior opaque yellow-green, while the sparkling dark blue enamel was abandoned for an inky underglaze colour of uneven texture. A spectrum of opaque pale mauves and purples also made their debut.

Flesh tints deepened although the orange blush became less conspicuous. The lips, now stylised, were pencilled in dark vermilion and their upturned corners frequently create the semblance of a smirk. Often a lack of neatness and precision affects the pencilling of eyelashes, lids and nostrils, but the manner in which these and other features were depicted remains essentially the same.

The decoration of garments increasingly aped the flamboyant gold-anchor Chelsea style but lacks its nobility of design and execution. Little of the surface was left white and ground colours are usually broken by large reserves containing diaper patterns embellished with gilt. When occasionally floral sprays appear, they are most often small in scale after the manner of *indianische Blumen* and rare examples of *deutsche Blumen* are invariably of poor quality. Alternatively, scale patterns in blue, mauve or peacock colours may appear, or designs composed of geometrical symbols that may incorporate the *œil de perdrix*.

Gilding may have a coppery aspect and was used lavishly upon the edges of garments, buttons, shoe-buckles, garters, appropriate accessories such as musical instruments, and to accent scrolls upon bases. Bands of gold laid on hat brims and jackets often have an inner border of dentil form that would seem peculiar to Bow models.

THE MODELS

THE VAST MAJORITY of models issued after c.1764 were cast from old moulds but were mounted upon restyled bases and decorated in the current flamboyant manner with the new enamel palette of which the following serve as examples: *Diana* (B19 and C15, Plate 78), *Flora Farnese* (B21 and C17, Plates 80 and 201), *Mars* (B25 and C20, Plates 84 and 200), *Seated Rustic Seasons* (B46 and C27, Plates 105, 106 and 208), *Turks* standing (B59 and C35, Plates 117–18, Col. Plate XII), *Turks* seated (B60 and C34, Plates 119–20), *Cooks* with platters (B69 and C37, Plates 127 and 217, Col. Plate III), *Boy Singer* (B5 and C43), *Shepherd Boy Piper and Dancing Shepherdess* (B115 and C52, Plates 158 and 223, Col. Plate X), *Shepherd Bagpiper and Shepherdess* (B117 and C60, Plate 160), *Liberty and Matrimony* (B113 and C57, Plate 156), *Gardener* and *Companion* (B73 and C39, Plate 218).

When pairs of figures were remounted upon tall plinths, the rapport that had often earlier existed between them was replaced by an air of isolated detachment. In many a bocage was also added: *Sir John Falstaff* (A3 and C10, Plates 3 and 198), *Huntsman and Lady* (B110 and C56, Plates 153 and 226, Col. Plate V), *Hussars* (pair) (B125 and C67, Plates 166 and 232), *New Dancers* (B108 and C49, Plates 90 and 152, Col. Plate XIII), *Idyllic Musicians* (B103 and C45, Plates 147 and 221), *Shepherd and Shepherdess* (B116 and C61, Plate 159).

Several models originally issued as pairs were now married on a single four-footed base before a bocage to form a group: *Arlecchino and Columbina* dancing with slap-sticks (B4 and C3, Plate 71, Col. Plate VII), *Arlecchino and Columbina* seated playing music (B2 and C4, Plates 70 and 195), *Turkish Children* (B55 and C31), *Huntsman and Lady Falconer* (B110 and C54b, Plate 153, Col. Plate V).

The use of earlier models in freshly contrived groups was sometimes accompanied by alteration of accessories so that, for example, the seated figure of *Columbina* (B2, Plate 70) in some versions may exchange her hurdy-gurdy for either a triangle (C7), a zither (C8, Plate 197) or a bouquet (C9). Sometimes minor postural adjustments were effected when, for example, in the *Gardener and Companion* (B73), the man's right arm was repositioned to encircle his companion's waist (C40, Plate 219), while in the *Sailor and Lass* (B82) the man's right hand was placed upon the girl's shoulders (C59). In some other examples models previously unrelated were brought together as a group. Thus *Columbina*'s traditional partner *Arlecchino* playing bagpipes (B2, Plate 70) was sometimes displaced by a *Boy Singer* (B5) in a new association (C8, Plate 197), or by a *Violinist* (B95) as a duet group (C7) when, in one absurd grouping, a begging pug dog separates the two musicians. Only one example is known to the author of models originally issued as a group, namely two *Dancers* (B105, Plate 149) reappearing subsequently as a pair, *Dancing Man and Girl* (C44, Plate 220).

The *Huntsman and Lady Falconer* (B110, Plate 153, Col. Plate V) were reissued on four-footed bases without other alteration, (C54a) or as a bocaged candlestick group (C54b). They were also made as a pair standing before a low bocage, each with a large standing hunting-dog, and with a dead hare attached to the man's belt. The *Idyllic Musicians* (B103, Plate 147) were adapted to provide a bocaged candlestick group (C45, Plate 221), while the early group known as the *Italian Musicians* (A14, Plate 12) prompted a pair of identical flower-encrusted candlesticks (C11, Plate 199). The rare set of the four *Adolescent Seasons* (B46, Plates 105 and 106) were refurbished to provide two bocaged groups (C28, Plates 211 and 212), which in some examples are flanked by swan-necked rococo candle sconces.

Mention has been made of the *Chinese Magician's Family* group reduced from five (B53, Plate 115) to three figures (B54). The depleted version was now reissued and mounted in a chinoiserie gazebo beneath a cupola (C32). The *New Dancers* (B108, Plates 90 and 152, Col. Plate XIII) too, re-emerged either as a bocaged pair or group (C49), alternatively mounted before candlesticks (C50) or adapted to stand in mirror poses with one hand upon the lid of decorative sweetmeat containers (C51), while the simple charm of two groups portraying *Putti garlanding Goats* (B133) was sadly lost in later more elaborate replacements (C69).

Many late Bow figures are smaller than their prototypes and lack their crispness of modelling, having been cast from secondary, or replacement, moulds. The *Four Quarters of the Globe* (B42–3, Plates 96 and 97) reappear as a set of four semi-miniatures (C25, Plate 205) mounted upon pierced pedestals before waist-tall bocages. The unattractive *Fountain Group* (C66, Plate 231) appears to have been compiled from reduced and debased versions of a *Huntsman and Lady* (B111). Late examples of the *Antique Seasons* (B45 and C26, Plates 103, 104, 206 and 207) include small examples of *Flora*, *Ceres*, *Bacchus* and *Vulcan*, each standing beside a vase or urn, but now acquire an attendant putto after the manner of the *Classical Seasons* (B48, Plates 108–10). Another set of models representing the *Four Seasons* (C29, Plate 213) provides a strange mixture of the sacred and the profane, for *Spring* and *Summer* are both represented by scantily clad goddesses, whilst *Autumn* and *Winter* are depicted as men wearing contemporary dress bearing respectively grapes and holly.

A large model of *Clio* (C14), stands upon a cylindrical base provided with a detachable four-footed plinth and was evidently copied from the gold-anchor Chelsea model[1] by Joseph Willems taken from his set of *Apollo* and the nine *Muses*. Another pair comprising a lady with flowers, representing *Spring*, and a gardener with fruits, representing *Autumn* (both C30, Plates 214 and 215) are elaborately decorated and were based on figures included in two Chelsea groups, known as the *Allegorical Seasons*.[2] They were, by reason of dissimilarities, cast from fresh moulds constructed at the Bow factory. A pair of *Harvesters* (C53, Plate 224) are lavishly decorated and are known in similar gold-anchor Chelsea[3] as well as Chelsea-Derby versions incised No. 296 (Plate 225) with a different male figure. All five of these Bow models range between $10\frac{1}{4}$ and 15in (26–38cm) in height. It is possible that the *Fortune Telling Group* (C65, Plate 230) was plagiarised from Chelsea[4] for it is mentioned in the Chelsea Sale Catalogue of 1 May 1761: 'A fine group of a gipsy telling a lady's fortune under a tree, upon a richly ornamented floor'. This, unlike an earlier representation of the subject (A48, Plate 41) after Boucher, was based on Antoine Watteau's 'La Diseuse d'Aventure', engraved by Laurent Cars, although English modellers most likely referred to Robert Hancock's engraving of a design by Louis-Philippe Boitard. It will be recalled that the figure of the Gipsy earlier prompted two *Pedlars* (B77, Plate 133 and B78, Plate 134) and reappears in Hancock's 'Tea Party'.[5]

Amongst the finest of the late Bow models are a dancing *Arlecchino and Columbina*, issued both as a pair (C1) and as a group (C2, Plate 194), which have strangely pointed heads. They engender an admirable sense of movement suggesting Meissen prototypes, although none have so far been identified. A seated *Bagpiper and Tambourine Player* (C46) are nobly conceived but over-large to appeal to most collectors. Another pair of *Musicians* (C47) sit barefoot with one leg flexed and knees separated, the youth in a tricorn hat holding a reed pipe, the girl wearing a head-scarf, playing a triangle. Major Tapp discovered a brass fender decorated with four human and two monkey instrumentalists that included similar musicians to the Bow pair.[6]

Replicas of ancient deities are artistically far less successful. *Apollo* (C12) is loosely based on an earlier model (B14, Plate 76), And *Jupiter* (C19) astride an eagle and *Neptune* riding a dolphin (C22) lack the brilliant exploitation of mass and form evident in their precursors. There is also a rather ugly *Flora* (C18) depicted reclining and holding aloft one end of a U-shaped garland. *Father Time* (C16, Plate 200) with the traditional scythe and hour-glass was first issued as the finial of a decorative clock case (B137) made to commemorate the death of Handel. The model closely resembles the Chelsea-Derby *Winged Time* which Timothy Clifford once suggested might have been a transposed adaptation of Giovanni da Bologna's marble *Venus* in the Boboli Grotto.[7] However, it would seem more likely that both the Derby and Bow models were based on the Meissen *Cronus*.[8]

Putti as *Pugilists* (B136, Plate 174) were reissued on fenestrated bases (C58, Plate 227), and were most likely inspired by sporting prints. A *Shepherdess* with a lamb (C62) appears to have become separated from her companion, but a *Dancing Shepherdess* (C63, Plate 228), who holds aloft a floral chaplet, is sometimes paired with a refurbished version of the *Shepherd playing a recorder* (B116, Plate 159). A *Negress* (C33, Plate 216) carrying a pierced basket upon her head doubtless represents one of a pair known as 'Slave Figures' mentioned in the Memorandum Book. Two bocaged groups show *Cupid* in mirror poses, stretching upwards to grasp a bird, his longbow and quiver at his feet and a hound beside him (C68, Plate 233).

Only a small representative sample of animal and bird models issued after c.1762–4 is here presented. A pair of horned *Ewe and Ram* (C70, Plate 234), and three groups portraying a *Ewe Standing beside her Sleeping Lamb* (C71), a similar *Goat and Kid* (C72, Plate 235), and a female *Goat suckling a Kid* (C73), are all mounted upon oval scrolled bases before low bocages. There is a *Retriever* regarding two partridges perched in a tree (C74), and candlestick adaptations of the *Stag and Doe* at lodge (C77, Plate 237), which are little more than decorative ensembles.

Two bocaged *Fable Groups* (C75–6, Plate 237) illustrate Aesop's tale of the 'Fox and Stork' who each hosted a dinner for the other. One portrays the Stork drinking from a tall narrow-necked bottle, watched by the Fox; the other shows the Fox devouring a plate of game regarded by the Stork. Neither guest was able to eat or drink anything! The first mentioned, when stripped of superfluous ornament, resembles a Girl-in-a-Swing group based on an engraving that appeared in the *Weekly Apollo* of 1752.[9] Bow also based a pair of flower-encrusted candlesticks on the same subject, and the Chelsea factory issued two large bocaged groups in natural colouring, mounted upon four-footed bases.

Between c.1764 and 1774 only a handful of ornithological models seem to have been made at Bow, limited to a few *Finches* (C78, C79, Plate 176), a *Green Parrot* (C80) and a *Bird* of undetermined nature perched in a bocage (C81). A similar dearth of bird models at both Chelsea and Derby during the same period would suggest they were no longer in fashion. However, most will agree that porcelain models of birds look their best when mounted upon either white tree-stumps, or truncated cones with spreading base, encrusted sparsely with leaves, flowers and insects, sometimes with nuts, fruit and fungi. Should craftsmen in the Bow modelling shop have shared this appraisal, they may have opted to continue to mount their work on the old-style bases, which would necessitate reconsideration of their dates of first issue.

194

195

194 (C2) *Arlecchino and Columbina* dancing
6½in (16.5cm) c.1765

195 (C4) *Arlecchino and Columbina* seated
with bagpipes and a hurdy-gurdy (after B1)
8in (20.3cm) c.1765

196

197

196 (C5) *Children* in masquerade as *Arlecchino and Columbina* 7½in (19.1cm) c.1765

197 (C8) *Columbina and Boy Singer* playing a zither 8in (20.3cm) c.1765

198 (C10) *David Garrick as Sir John Falstaff* 7½in (19.1cm) c.1765

199 (C11) *Candlestick* version of the *Italian Musicians* 12in (30.5cm) c.1765

200 *Left*, (C22) *Neptune* riding a dolphin 6½in (16.5cm) excluding the metal trident c.1765; *Right*, (C16) *Father Time*, seated upon a globe, holding an hour-glass and a scythe 6½in (16.5cm) c.1765

198

199

200

201

201 (C17) *Flora* reclining with a garland 11in (22.9cm) c.1765

202 (C23) Seated *Monk and Nun* holding books, on pierced and scrolled bases 7¾in (14.6cm) c.1765

203 (C24) *Neptune* and *Juno*, representing *Water* and *Air*, from a set of the *Four Elements*, after B41 7in (17.8cm) c.1765

204 (C24) Companion models of *Vulcan* and *Ceres*, representing *Fire and Earth*, idem.

202

203

204

205

205 (C25) *The Four Quarters of the Globe*, mounted on pierced pedestals 5½in (14cm) c.1768

206 (C26) *Vulcan with a Putto* beside a flaming urn, representing *Winter*, and *Flora* likewise before a flower vase, emblematic of *Spring* 7½in (19.1cm) c.1768

207 *Left*, (C26) Reduced and debased reissue of *Spring*, with an added *Putto* 6¾in (17.1cm) c.1768; *Right*, (B45) *Spring*, from the *Antique Seasons* 9½in (24.1cm) c.1762

208 (C27) The *Seated Rustic Seasons* after B46 6in (15.2cm) c.1765

206

207

208

209

211

209 (C28) *Spring and Winter*, in a bocaged group, from the *Adolescent Seasons*, after B47 9½in (21.1cm) c.1765

210 (C28) Companion to Plate **209**, a bocaged group of *Summer and Autumn*, ibid.

210

211 (C28) Slightly
different group of
Spring and Winter to
Plates 209 and 210.

212 (C28) Companion
group to Plate 211, of
Summer and Autumn,
ibid.

212

213

214

215

213 (C29) *Standing Peasant Seasons*, represented by *Flora*, *Ceres* and two men in contemporary dress 7in (17.8cm) c.1770

214 (C30) *Lady* with flowers, emblematic of *Spring* 10in (25.4cm) c.1770

215 (C30) Companion *Gardener* with fruits, emblematic of *Autumn*, ibid.

216 (C33) One of a pair of *Slave Figures* 7in (17.8cm) c.1765

217 (C37) Pair of *Cooks*, after B69, on four-footed bases 7in/6½in (17.8cm/15.9cm) c.1765

216

217

218

219

220

218 (C39) *Gardener's Companion* 7¼in (18.5cm) c.1765

219 (C40) Group showing a *Gardener and Flower Seller* 10in (25.4cm) c.1765

220 (C44) *Pair of Dancers*, after B106 7¾in (19.7cm) c.1765

221 (C45) Group of the *Idyllic Musicians*, after B104 9¼in (23.5cm) c.1765

222 (C50) Bocaged candlestick versions of the *New Dancers*, after B109 6¾in (17.1cm) c.1765

221

222

223 (C52) *Boy Shepherd Piper* and *Dancing Shepherdess*, after B115 6¾in (17.1cm) c.1765

224 (C53) Pair of *Harvesters*, about 10¼in (26cm) c.1768

223

224

225

225 Pair of Chelsea-Derby
Harvesters, incised *No. 198*
c.1780. The female figure
resembles the earlier Bow
version.

226 (C56) Bocaged
candlestick version of the
Huntsman and Lady, after
B112 8½in (21.6cm) c.1765

226

227

228

227 (C58) Pair of *Putti as Pugilists*, after B136 6½in (16.5cm) c.1765

228 (C63) *Shepherdess* dancing with a wreath 6¾in (17.1cm) c.1770

229 (C64) *Gallant and Lady*, representing the *Blown Kiss*, after B118 8¼in (21cm) c.1768

230 (C65) *Fortune Telling Group*, after Watteau 10¾in (27.3cm) c.1765

231 (C66) *Fountain Group* 9in (22.9cm) c.1770

229

230

231

232

232 (C67) Pair of *Hussars*, after B125 6½in (16.5cm) c.1768

233 (C68) Paired *Bocaged Candlesticks* showing *Cupid catching a Bird* 10in (26.5cm) c.1770; (C31) Group of *Children in Turkish Costumes* 7in (17.8cm) c.1768

233

234

234 (C70) Pair of *Ewe* grazing and a horned *Ram* 6in (15.2cm) c.1768; (B183) Seated *Hare* scratching itself 3½in (8.9cm) c.1760

235 (C72) *Goat* beside her recumbent *Kid* 5in (12.5cm) c.1765

235

236

236 (C75, C76) Pair of *Bocaged Fable Candlesticks*, illustrating the tale of the 'Fox and Stork' 9½in (21.1cm) c.1765

237 (C77) Candlestick versions of the *Stag and Doe* at lodge, after B196 9¼in (23.5cm) c.1765

237

Bow Porcelain Models c.1765–74

Italian Comedy

C1   *Arlecchino and Columbina* (pair), 6½in (16.5cm). Arlecchino in motley and Columbina in falling ruffle, bodice and skirt, are shown bareheaded, one arm outstretched, dancing. Mounted on cube-shaped bases with vertical fenestrations. Untermyer pl. 90, fig. 249; Hurlbutt pl. 61.

C2   *Arlecchino and Columbina* (group), 6½in (16.5cm). Same as C1 married on a single flat base edged with scrolls. Stoner pl. 101; Christie's 6.6.88, lot 144. *See Plate 194.*

C3   *Arlecchino and Columbina* (group), 9¼in (23.5cm). Standing models from B4 married on a scrolled base before a bocage surmounted by a candle tulip. Morley-Fletcher col. pl. facing p. 91; Sotheby's 22.10.85, lot 120.

C4   *Arlecchino and Columbina* (group), 8in (20.3cm). Seated respectively with bagpipes and hurdy-gurdy from B2, married on a four-footed base before a sparse bocage. Sotheby's 22.10.85, lot 116; private collection. *See Plate 195.*

C5   *Children attired as Arlecchino and Columbina* (pair), 7½in (19.1cm). Standing models from B6, each mounted on a four-footed base before a sparse bocage. Freeman pl. 240. *See Plate 196.*

C6   *Columbina and Male Dancer* (group), 9½in (24.1cm). Standing models from B106 married on a four-footed base before a sparse bocage. Sotheby's 21.5.85, lot 346.

C7   *Columbina and Male Fiddler* (group), 8¼in (21cm). Seated Columbina from B2, with a triangle in place of a hurdy-gurdy, and a male fiddler, mounted on a four-footed base before a sparse bocage. Private collection.

C8   *Columbina and Boy Singer* (group), 7¾in (19.7cm). Columbina from B2, with a zither in place of a hurdy-gurdy, and a boy singer holding a song-sheet from B5, mounted on a four-footed base before a sparse bocage. Sotheby's 22.10.85, lot 116; Stoner pl. 91, with a begging Pug between the musicians. *See Plate 197.*

C9   *Columbina seated with Flowers*, 6in (15.2cm). Adapted from B2, with flowers replacing the hurdy-gurdy. Private collection.

C10   *David Garrick as Sir John Falstaff*, 7½in (19.1cm). Reissue of A3, on a scrolled base with a low bocage. Private collection. *See Plate 198.*

C11   *Italian Musicians* (candlestick group), 12in (30.5cm). Adapted from A14, showing Isabella playing a guitar and Scaramuzzi singing, placed before a flower-encrusted candlestick. Sotheby's 22.10.85, lot 119; Lucy Aldridge Collection, Rhode Island, cat. figs 90–1. *See Plate 199.*

Mythology

C12   *Apollo*, 7¾in (19.7cm). Reissue of B14, on a four-footed base. Sotheby's 23.10.79, lot 192.

C13   *Bacchus*, 10½in (26.7cm). Adapted from standing model B44, emblematic of *Autumn*, standing beside an urn, holding aloft a bunch of grapes and with a goblet. Freeman pls 237–8.

C14 *Clio*, 15in (38.1cm). She stands bareheaded holding a scroll in her left hand to which she points. Mounted on a cylindrical base with detachable four-footed plinth. Stoner pl. 102.

C15 *Diana*, 7¾in (19.7cm). Reissue of B18, mounted on a scrolled base, with garments decorated to simulate brocades. Hurlbutt pl. 63b.

C16 *Father Time*, 6½in (16.5cm). An elderly bearded man with wings, scantily draped, leaning on a scythe supporting an hour-glass in his right hand. Sotheby's 21.5.85, lot 350. *See Plate 200.*

C17 *Flora Farnese*, 11in (28cm). Reissue of B22 upon a legged and scrolled base. Christie's 5.4.83, lot 252. *See Plate 201.*

C18 *Flora*, 9in (22.9cm). A scantily draped goddess reclines against a tree-trunk, holding aloft in her right hand the end of a long garland. Stockspring Antiques, late stock.

C19 *Jupiter*, 7¾in (19.7cm). Adapted from B24 showing the god astride an eagle. Sotheby's 24.2.87, lot 104.

C20 *Mars*, 9in (22.9cm). Adapted from B25 showing the god clad in a helmet and Roman armour holding a shield and spear. Sotheby's 14.2.84, lot 64; B. & T. Thorn, late stock. *See Plate 200.*

C21 *Mercury*, 7¾in (19.7cm). Reissue of B28 on a legged and scrolled base. Sotheby's 23.10.79, lot 192.

C22 *Neptune*, 7½in (19.1cm). Adapted from B29 showing the god riding a dolphin, holding out his cloak in either hand, on a scrolled base. Sotheby's 25.2.86, lot 148.

RELIGIOUS

C23 *Monk and Nun* (pair), 7¾in (19.7cm). Both wearing habits, seated reading books, the nun in a veil, the monk with tonsured pate exposed. Adapted from B46, mounted on fenestrated plinths. Christie's 23.2.87, lot 241. *See Plate 202.*

ALLEGORICAL

C24 *Four Elements* (4 models), 11in (27.9cm). Reissue of B41, comprising standing models of Neptune, Ceres, Bacchus and Vulcan, mounted on tall fenestrated and scrolled bases. Sotheby's 22.10.85, lot 121. Examples 9¾in (25cm). Freeman pl. 245. *See Plates 203–4.*

C25 *Four Quarters of the Globe* (4 models), 5½in (14cm). Reissue of semi-miniature versions of B42 or 43, each mounted on a pierced pedestal before a waist-tall bocage. Freeman pl. 239; Bradshaw pl. 84. *See Plate 205.*

C26 *Antique Seasons*, 8in (20.3cm). *Spring*, Flora, scantily draped, standing and supporting a vase of flowers upon a plinth, with a seated putto with a basket of blossoms. *Winter*, a bearded man, possibly Vulcan, warming his hands over a brazier resting on a pedestal, with a seated putto wrapped in a cloak beside him. *Summer* and *Autumn* unknown to author. Groups seem loosely based on B19. Sotheby's 22.10.85, lot 112. *See Plates 206–7.*

C27   *Seated Rustic Seasons* (set of 4 models), 6¾in (17.1cm). Reissue of B46 on tall scrolled bases. Sotheby's 27.5.80, lots 56–7. *See Plate 208.*

C28   *Adolescent Seasons* (2 groups), 9½in (24.1cm). The two groups are mounted on scrolled bases, before bocages, some examples of which are flanked with sconces, including figures first issued separately in B46. *Spring and Winter, Autumn and Summer.* Untermyer pl. 84, fig. 252; Sotheby's 22.10.85, lot 118; Freeman pl. 244 (Autumn and Summer only). *See Plates 209–12.*

C29   *Standing Peasant Seasons* (4 figures), 7in (17.8cm). *Spring,* a bareheaded, scantily clad woman, holding a mass of blossoms in her apron. *Summer,* a scantily clad woman standing bareheaded with corn and a reaping-hook in either hand. *Autumn,* a bareheaded man in contemporary street attire, holding a fruiting vine and a reaping-hook in either hand. *Winter,* a man wearing a soft cap, fur-trimmed jacket and breeches, holding a bunch of holly and warming his right hand over a brazier. Bradshaw pl. 82. *See Plate 213.*

C30   *Chelsea Seasons* (2 of a set of 4 identified), 13in (33cm). Standing models mounted on cylindrical bases. *Spring,* a lady wearing a wide-brimmed hat, bodice and skirt, a basket of flowers over her arm, proffering a posy held in her right hand. *Autumn,* a bareheaded gardener holding his hat in his dependent left hand and with his right securing fruits in his apron. Stoner pl. 103; Bradshaw pl. 87 (Autumn only). *See Plates 214–15.*

Foreign personages

C31   *Children in Turkish Costumes* (pair), 6in (15.2cm). Reissue of B55, mounted on fenestrated bases before bocages. Sotheby's 25.9.79, lot 185 (male only). Larger versions, 7½in (19.1cm). Freeman pl. 242. *See Plate 233.*

C32   *Chinese Magician's Family* (group), 11¼in (29.8cm). Adapted from B53, omitting female assistant and one child, the second child is rotated to look the opposite way and the monkey replaced by a bear, the whole placed in a gazebo surmounted by a chinoiserie cupola. Stoner pl. 73.

C33   *Slave Figures* (pair), 7in (17.8cm). Kneeling models of a negro and negress wearing veil and dress secured by a sash, each supporting upon their head a pierced circular basket. Sotheby's 14.2.84, lot 62 (female figure only). *See Plate 216.*

C34   *Turk and Levantine Lady* (pair), 8in (20.3cm). Seated models adapted from B61, each holding a shell container, mounted on scrolled bases. Untermyer pl. 80, fig. 245.

C35   *Turk and Levantine Lady* (pair), 7in (17.8cm). Reissue of standing models B60, mounted on fenestrated bases. Christie's 13.2.84, lot 137.

C36   *Turk and Levantine Lady* (pair), 8½in (2.6cm). Adapted from B63, mounted before flower-encrusted candlesticks on scrolled bases. Rhode Island School of Design, pl. 40, figs 94–5.

PEASANTS AND ARTISANS

C37   *Cooks* (pair), 8½in (21.6cm). Reissue of B69 on four-footed bases. Christie's 18.6.84, lot 290. *See Plate 217.*

C38   *Gardener and Companion* (pair), 10in (25.4cm). Both stand; the man clad in hat, jacket, apron and breeches dances spade in hand; the woman in a head-scarf, blouse and skirt in mirror pose. On large mound bases decorated with scrolls. Albert Amor Bow Ex. Cat. no. 78.

C39   *Gardener and Companion* (pair), 9¾in (24.8cm). Large versions of B73, on scrolled bases. Christie's 13.2.84, lot 136. *See Plate 218.*

C40   *Gardener and Flower Seller* (group), 9½in (24.1cm). Adapted from B37 Sotheby's 14.6.88, lot 535. *See Plate 219.*

C41   *Lady with Flowers*, 9¾in (24.7cm). She stands in hat, bodice, apron and skirt, her left arm encircling a flowering bush. Sotheby's 25.2.85, lot 146.

MUSICIANS AND DANCERS

C42   *Boys with Drum and Fife* (pair), 11in (27.9cm). Adapted from B90, on four-footed bases. Sotheby's 1.2.82, lot 135.

C43   *Boy Singer*, 6in (15.2cm). Reissue of B5, on fenestrated plinth. Hurlbutt pl. 46a.

C44   *Dancing Man and Girl* (pair), 7¼in (18.4cm). Adaptation from B106 and reduced. Private collection, as shown. *See Plate 220.*

C45   *Triangle Player and Man with flageolet and tabor* (pair), 9½in (24.1cm). Reissue of B104, each on a scrolled base before a large bocage. Known as the *Idyllic Musicians*. Freeman pl. 241. Also, as a group, 9in (22.9cm). Untermyer pl. 83, fig. 246. *See Plate 221.*

C46   *Bagpiper and Tambourine Player* (pair), 8¾in (22.2cm). Both seated, the man in a soft cap plays bagpipes, the lady in a brimmed hat holds a tambourine. Mounted on bases shaped like a double inverted U. Untermyer pl. 89, fig. 248.

C47   *Lady playing a Triangle and Boy with a Reed Pipe* (pair), 9½in (24.1cm). They sit with one knee bent and legs separated, barefoot in mirror poses, the boy in a tricorn hat holding a reed pipe, the girl in a head-scarf playing a triangle. *Trans. E.C.C.*, 1975, Vol. 9, pt. 3, pls 180a–b; Adams and Redstone 1991, col. pl. M, pl. 10a, similar figures on a brass fender.

C48   *Lady with a Zither*, 5¾in (14.6cm). Adapted from Columbina with a hurdy-gurdy B2, mounted on a scrolled base with comma-shaped fenestrations. Phillips 11.6.86, lot 202. *See Plate 222.*

C49   *New Dancers* (pair), 9½in (24.1cm). Reissue of B109, each mounted on a scrolled base before a large bocage. Hurlbutt pl. 90; Sotheby's 24.7.84, lot 178. Also as a bocaged group, 9¼in (23.5cm). Sotheby's 30.9.80, lot 146.

C50   *New Dancers* (pair of candlesticks), 9¾in (24.5cm). Reissue of B109 before bocaged candlesticks. Christie's 12.10.87, lot 237.

C51   *New Dancers* (pair of sweetmeat containers), 6¼in (15.9cm). Adapted from B109. Each stands in mirror pose with one hand resting on the open lid of a rococo receptacle. Christie's 23.2.87, lot 24; Sotheby's 2.2.82, lot 158.

PASTORAL AND SPORTING

C52 *Boy Shepherd Piper and Dancing Shepherdess* (pair), 6¾in (17.1cm). Reissue of B115, mounted on scrolled bases with comma-shaped fenestrations. Sotheby's 5.10.82, lot 37. *See Plate 223.*

C53 *Harvesters* (pair), about 10¼in (26cm). Both stand and wear hats, the man holding a wine-keg, the woman with a flask hanging from her waistband. Tullie House, W. H. Williamson Bequest. *See Plate 224.*

C54a *Huntsman and Lady Falconer* (pair), 8¼in (20.9cm). Reissue of B110 on scrolled base. Sotheby's 22.10.85, lot 114. Similar models 6in (15.2cm) on fenestrated bases. Hurlbutt pl. 46b (male only).

C54b *Huntsman and Lady Falconer* (group) on scrolled base before a bocaged candlestick, 12½in (31.75cm). Stoner col. pl. 3; Williams College Museum, Williamstown, Mass.

C55 *Huntsman and Lady Falconer* (pair), 7½in (19.1cm). As B110 each with a standing hound, before a bocage. Stoner pl. 96; Untermyer pl. 96, fig. 251.

C56 *Huntsman and Lady* (group), 8½in (21.6cm). Adapted from B112, on a scrolled base before a bocage. Sotheby's 28.10.80, lot 79. *See Plate 226.*

C57 *Liberty and Matrimony* (pair), 8½in (21.6cm). Adapted from B113, on scrolled bases before bocages. Sotheby's 25.2.8, lot 144.

C58 *Putti as Pugilists* (pair), 6½in (16.5cm). Adapted from B136, mounted on fenestrated bases. Stoner pl. 98; Freeman pl. 235 (one only); for versions 5¾in (14.6cm). Freeman pl. 214. *See Plate 227.*

C59 *Sailor and Lass* (group), 7½in (19.1cm). Adapted from B82, with sailor's right arm repositioned to lie upon his lass's shoulders, mounted before a bocage on a scrolled base. Harris p. 52.

C60 *Shepherd Bagpiper and Shepherdess* (pair), 11¼in (28.6cm). Reissue of B117 on a four-footed base. Phillips 11.6.86, lot 213.

C61 *Shepherd playing a Recorder and Shepherdess with Flowers* (pair), 9in (22.9cm). Reissue of B116 upon four-footed bases before bocages. Stoner pl. 97.

C62 *Shepherdess* (probably one of a pair of models), 9½in (24.1cm). She stands clad in a brimmed hat, jacket and dress, holding flowers in her apron and in her right upraised hand, a lamb at her feet. Private collection.

C63 *Dancing Shepherdess* (probably one of a pair of figures), 6¾in (17.1cm). She stands clad in a brimmed hat, laced bodice, apron and skirt that she holds out with her right hand while holding in her upraised left a floral wreath; a lamb lies at her feet. Sotheby's 21.2.89, lot 438. *See Plate 228.*

GALLANTS AND LADIES

C64 *The Blown Kiss* (pair), 7¾in (19.7cm). Both figures stand on scrolled and fenestrated plinths. The male is identical to B118. The female may wear a brimmed hat, mantua with pagoda sleeves, a hooped skirt and flounced underskirt. Stoner pl. 89; Untermyer pl. 99, fig. 250; Luton Hoo. *See Plate 229.*

C65   *Fortune Telling Group*, 10¾in (27.3cm). A bareheaded lady, in a fine gown, stands beneath a tree before a gipsy woman who has a baby upon her back, a child and a dog at her side. Stoner pl. 92. *See Plate 230.*

C66   *Fountain Group*, 9in (22.9cm). A huntsman and lady, wearing tricorn hats bearing guns, stand before a putto's-mask fountain, on a scrolled base in front of a huge bocage. Freeman pl. 243; Sotheby's 3.11.81, lot 78. *See Plate 231.*

C67   *Hussars* (pair), 6½in (16.5cm). Reissue of B125 in arrogant poses, mounted on scrolled bases before large bocages. Sotheby's 22.10.85, lot 128. *See Plate 232.*

PUTTI

C68   *Cupid with a Bird in bocaged Candlesticks* (paired groups), 10¼in (26cm). Mirror image groups each of Cupid, his bow and quiver with a dog at his feet, reaching up to capture a bird in a bocage. Christie's 20.10.86, lot 106 and 2.6.86, lot 310. *See Plate 233.*

C69   *Putti garlanding a Goat* (paired groups), 13in (33cm). One depicts three putti decking a goat with flowers; the other two putti garlanding a female goat suckling a kid. Reissue of B134 on scrolled base with metal fitments. Stoner pl. 94.

ANIMALS

C70   *Ewe and Ram* (pair), 5½in (14cm). A ewe grazes and a horned ram stands with head turned, each before a flowering shrub, on a flat base edged with scrolls. Sotheby's 8.7.80, lot 92. Candlestick versions, 7¾in (19.8cm). Christie's 20.10.86, lot 198. *See Plate 234.*

C71   *Ewe standing beside her sleeping Lamb* (group), 5¼in (13.3cm). A ewe stands with a lamb curled up at her feet, before a flowering shrub. Sotheby's 18.5.82, lot 66.

C72   *Goat and Kid* (group), 5½in (14cm). A female goat stands with a kid curled up at her feet, before a flowering shrub. Sotheby's 18.5.82, lot 64. *See Plate 235.*

C73   *Goat suckling a Kid* (group), 5½in (14cm). A female goat stands suckling her kid, mounted on an oval base before a small bocage. Private collection.

C74   *Retriever with Game* (group), 11¼in (28.6cm). A retriever stands regarding two partridges in a flowering bocage surmounted by a candle tulip. Sotheby's 22.10.85, lot 125. An example 8in (20.3cm). Christie's 23.2.87, lot 242.

C75   *Fable Group of Stork and Fox*, 9½in (24.1cm). A bocaged group of a fox regarding a stork as it drinks from a narrow-necked bottle, unable to share the repast. Grosvenor Antiques, Northern Antique Dealers' Fair, September 1971. *See Plate 236.*

C76   *Fable Group of Fox and Stork*, 9½in (24.1cm). A fox devours raw meat from a platter watched by the stork, unable to share the meal. Reference as C75. *See Plate 236.*

C77   *Stag and Doe* (pair of candlesticks), 9¼in (23.5cm). Adapted from B196, mounted on four-footed scrolled bases before flower-encrusted candlesticks. Christie's 12.10.87, lot 236. *See Plate 237.*

BIRDS

C78   *Goldfinch*, 4¾in (12.1cm). Possibly one of a pair, perched on a flowering branch on a pierced base with three feet. Freeman pl. 269. On different base, 5in (12.7cm). Adams and Redstone pl. 134.

C79   *Goldfinch* (pair), 5¼in (13.3cm). Mounted on pierced pedestals. Freeman pl. 170. *See Plate 176.*

C80   *Green Parrots* (pair), 7¼in (18.4cm). Perched on three-footed scrolled bases eating nuts. Schreiber pl. 1, no. 227 (new no. 67). Similar models 7½in (19.1cm). Stoner pl. 111.

C81   *Unidentified Bird*, probably a finch, perched in a bocage, on a scrolled base, 7¾in (19.7cm). Hurlbutt pl. 30.

---

15 ADDENDUM

TWO ITEMS WERE drawn to the author's notice after completion of the manuscript:

A Puppet Showman, 7in (17.8cm). He stands clad in a brimmed hat and contemporary clothes, holding the strings that control a dog puppet, with a pair of others representing a dancing couple at his feet. Private collection. Middle period, c.1760.

Putti with a Goat (paired groups), 9in (23cm). Each group includes a putti astride a goat and seated companion, decked either in flowers or grapes, emblematic of spring and autumn. Phillips 6.6.91, lot 417.

APPENDICES

A The Commedia dell'Arte

THE ORIGINS OF THE COMMEDIA DELL'ARTE most probably lie in those un-scripted farces and satires performed by masked actors in the ancient city of Atella (now Aversa), known as the *Fabulae Atellanae*. These were brought to Rome in the first century BC to amuse a populace that had grown weary of the frequent revivals of classical Greek drama. During the 'Dark Ages' the theatre, together with most of the other arts, was temporarily eclipsed but during the ensuing Renaissance troupes of strolling players formed throughout the Italian peninsula to provide light entertainment. Those who provided orthodox scripted performances became known as the *Commedia Sostenuta*, others who adhered to the traditions of the *Fabulae Atellanae* comprised the *Commedia dell'Arte*.

Early troupes included between eight and fifteen players, drawn from the educated class, and were usually based upon a great city under the protection of a nobleman or prelate. They toured the surrounding countryside and, where no permanent theatre existed, set up stage upon a farm cart in the market square. A backdrop, usually painted as a street scene in perspective, and drapery were erected, with ladders providing access through slits cut in the hangings, while underneath an area was curtained off to afford a dressing-room.

Each actor was allotted a specific role, costume and mask, which he retained until death or retirement. The scenario was often posted up barely an hour before the curtain rose and the impromptu dialogue evolved as the drama unfolded, although it might include short memorised speeches suitable for particular scenes or to fulfil a special need. Luigi Riccoboni, who had frequently himself played the role of *Lelio* (the 'Lover'), wrote in his *Histoire du Théâtre Italien*, published in 1728:

> Impromptu Comedy throws the whole weight of the performance on the acting with the result that the same scenario may be treated in various ways and seem a different play each time. The actor who improvises plays in a more natural manner than one who learns the role by heart. People feel better, and therefore say better, what they invent than what they borrow from others with the aid of memory . . . The drawback of improvisation is that the success of even the best actor depends upon his partner in the dialogue . . . .

Certainly the qualities required in a Comedy actor were vastly dissimilar from those demanded of an orthodox thespian, for he had not only to speak and behave in accordance with the character role within the ambit of the scenario, but also promote dialogue with appropriate cues and refrain from interruptions that would prevent his partner from developing a theme. The wearing of a face-mask necessitated recourse to *saltatio* (gesture) and, when the action faltered, to *lazzi* (stage tricks) that included slapstick, mime, acrobatics, song and dance. Most actors were accomplished acrobats and could play at least one musical instrument. Humour was decidedly earthy, much enjoyed by the nobility and peasantry but often causing offence to the less robust sensibilities of the *bourgeoisie*. Crude stage machinery enabled transportation of a player through the air by means of ropes and pulleys, the creation of jets of water and the release of smoke or fireworks.

Many of the *dramatis personae* were shared by several troupes, but as need arose might be modified for a particular scenario or for a regional audience. The major character roles were as follows.

Pantalone (*Pantaloon*) was usually an elderly retired Venetian merchant, evolved from the character of *Pappus* in the *Fabulae*. Notoriously mean, it was said he would engage a servant after the mid-day meal and dismiss him before supper. Sometimes cast as a lecherous bachelor, he would be mocked by *innamorate* for his impotence and defrauded by his varlets. Alternatively, he might have a pretty, flirtatious young wife, or be the respected husband of *Dame Ragonda* and the father of a daughter, Isabella, for whom he strove to arrange an advantageous marriage. She, however, preferred another to the suitor favoured by her parents and followed the cause of true love aided and abetted by the rascally servants. Pantalone wore either a skull-cap or a toque, a white falling ruffle, jacket, breeches and hose of well-worn red material, slippers and a long black *zimara* (cloak); in the Roman troupe he was portrayed as a dandy. His brown mask has a hooked nose, grey wispy moustache and long pointed beard, and he sometimes also wore spectacles.

Il Dottore (the *Doctor*) was supposedly a professor of medicine from Bologna, named Boloardo, Hippocrasio, Grazian Violino Scatalone etc. He was the friend of

Pantalone whose niggardly nature he shared, and having been deserted by his bride upon his wedding night he became a womaniser. A pompous ignoramus, he had a bent for misquoting Latin phrases and was sometimes cast as the father of *Il Capitano*. His costume included a white ruffle but was otherwise all black and included a velvet academic hat, doublet, gown and zimara. The mask, also black, covered only his forehead and nose and may possibly have originally represented a naevus upon the face of an actor who took the role.

Il Capitano (the *Captain*) evolved from the ogre *Manducis* in the *Fabulae* and the *Miles Gloriosus* of Plautus, and went by such names as Cocodrillo, Rinoceronte, Rodomondo, or Spavento della Valle Inferna. He was a braggart, a bully and a coward and could have been no stranger in a land ravaged by *condottieri*. Initially depicted as a mercenary bearing a huge sword, wearing a metal helmet and leather armour, he was later portrayed in Spanish dress with a starched white ruffle, hat, doublet and hose all of black; during the eighteenth century he was transformed into a courtier with a tricorn hat, tight-fitting jacket and breeches, and tabarro (cape), carrying a rapier in a sword-belt. Sometimes he was the suitor for the hand of Isabella most favoured by Pantalone. His mask was pale, to match his craven nature, with upturned moustache, protuberant short beard and a long nose.

Innamorati, primo e secundo (Lovers), went by such names as Lelio, Octavio, Mario and Cinthio del Sole. The roles were played by passionate, handsome and smartly-dressed young men without masks.

Innamorate, prima e secunda (Loved Ones), might be called Celia, Isabella, Lavinia and Lydia. Until the fifteenth century women were forbidden by Canon Law from appearing upon the boards and their roles were taken by boys or clean-shaven youths. Later, women wore fashionable gowns with a velvet mask covering the upper part of their faces called a *Loup* which was designed to protect their milk-white complexion from the sun. They represented both high-born ladies and coquettes.

Servette (Maids) might be called Columbina, Franceschina, Nespola, Olivetta and Violetta. Until c.1700 they could be distinguished from *innamorate* by their simpler attire and an apron, but subsequently discarded the apron and, instead, wore a large bow on the top of their heads. They were classified according to their attributes as *Cantarinas* and *Ballerinas*. An elderly gossip, or go-between, was named *La Ruffina*.

Arlecchino (*Harlequin*) was evolved from the *Funambuli* (clowns) of the *Fabulae*. Possibly the son of Trivelino, he was born in the lower town of Bergamo, a dimwit but with rare flashes of brilliance. Other Zanni (clownish) characters including Brighella and Scapino originated from the upper town and were highly intelligent. Most of Arlecchino's time on stage was spent plotting mischief, performing slapstick, comic mime and acrobatics, or engaged in romantic dalliance. Originally he wore a brimmed hat adorned with a hare's scut, the badge of a fool, a loose jacket and trousers of light-coloured material on which irregular patches of a darker hue were sewn, after the manner of *Tatterdemalia*. Early in the seventeenth century his costume became tighter fitting, the jacket shorter, and the ensemble adorned with multicoloured triangles sewn between strips of yellow braid. Around 1750, a falling ruffle about the neck was added, and the triangles replaced by lozenges. The rounded crown of his hat also became conical in shape. A black leather mask covered the whole face with small round apertures for the eyes, a deeply furrowed forehead, bushy eyebrows and short bristly beard. Latterly only the upper three-quarters of the face was covered although a separate chin-piece was often worn.

Pulcinella (*Punch*), the hunchback, seems to have been evolved both from *Bucco*, a fawning, shy yet boastful character, and from *Maccus Mimus Albus* (the White Mime), who was quick, witty but cruel, from the *Fabulae*. He was supposedly born in the upper town of Benevento, although he was adopted by Naples. Like Arlecchino, he was for ever plotting mischief but underlying his pranks there was a cruel streak and he readily turned to violence. He sought to avoid punishment by feigning stupidity, when he would walk like a frightened chicken peeping sideways, his proboscis balanced by his prominent belly. He wore a grey toque or white skull-cap, blouse of the same gathered by a leather belt, and trousers either grey or red. A wallet hung from his waist and he carried a wooden sword. About his neck he usually wore a green-edged wide scarf in lieu of a tabarro. His black leather mask with wispy beard and moustache was dominated by a hooked nose and covered the whole face.

Pedrolino (*Pierrot*) has affinities with the slave who appears in the plays of both Titus Plautus (250–184 BC) and Publius Terentius (190–159 BC) but made his debut in the *Commedia* during the second half of the sixteenth century as a loyal dependable servant, a simpleton eager to defend the honour of the fair sex. When he was drawn reluctantly into the mischief of the other varlets, he was invariably the one to be caught when their schemes misfired, and although he was a charming lover his romances with the *servette* usually ended unhappily. In the seventeenth century he was adopted as *Pierrot* by the Comédie-Française and, in that role, was immortalised in a painting of 'Gilles' by Antoine Watteau. He wore a white costume comprising a brimmed hat, falling ruffle, a jacket with over-long sleeves and trousers that were too short; his face was heavily powdered and he had no mask. A Sicilian version, called *Peppe Nappa*, wore a white mask over his upper face and was clad in an altogether neater costume.

Brighella, supposedly born in the upper town of Bergamo, was the epitome of evil and his appearance sent a cold shiver down the spines of his audience. He was self-centred, indolent, a cheat and a liar entirely without scruples, and would bury his stiletto in the back of his unsuspecting victim to gain the slightest personal advantage, yet played a guitar and sang in a mellifluous voice. He was the forefather of numerous lesser knaves and rascals. His costume consisted of a soft cap, tabarro, loose jacket adorned with green braid and trousers secured by a belt from which a purse hung and into which a dagger was thrust. The mask was olive green with sloe eyes, thick sensual lips, hook nose, menacing chin covered by a wispy beard, and with a moustache.

Scapino (*Scapin*) was a varlet who evolved from Brighella but lacked his capacity for evil. Although he too would lie and cheat, pick pockets and defraud, he usually ran away when trouble threatened him and stopped short of murder. His double, *Mezzetino* (*Mezetin*) was an altogether more amiable character, gentle, simple, often the subject of unrequited love, who played the guitar. Both were attired after the fashion of Brighella until c.1700 when their costumes were redesigned by Angelo Constantini to afford the audience instant recognition of them. That of Scapino was decorated with vertical stripes of green and white whereas Mezzetino's had stripes of red and white. A third servant, *Beltrame*, a pious but wilfully blind husband, was also based on the character of Brighella.

Narcissino (*Narcissus*) was adopted from the Comédie-Française to fulfil the functions of a modern *compère*. He would perch on a ladder beside the stage and between acts would tell jokes, sing or play a guitar. He wore a wide-brimmed hat, linen tabs at his throat, doublet, a broad sash, baggy breeches and a zimara. His flesh-coloured mask had a prominent nose, short protruding beard and an upturned moustache.

Scaramuzzi (*Scaramouche*) first appeared in the *Commedia dell'Arte* about 1700 in place of *Il Capitano*, with whom he shared many characteristics. He buzzed about like a bee, sowing the seeds of dissent and discord, picking pockets and indulging in petty crime, often running away but returning in the expectancy of further pickings. He was attired all in black except for a white ruffle and wore a soft cap, jacket, breeches, hose, buckled shoes, and bore a rapier in his sword-belt. His mask included a short beard and a drooping moustache.

During the second half of the sixteenth century, several troupes of the *Commedia dell'Arte* left their home territory to tour Europe where they were greeted with acclaim. In 1573 the Ganassa Company played before the Court of Charles IX in Paris, later visiting Spain, while in 1574 the Gelosi troupe performed in Venice. The Duke of Modena's troupe was established c.1688 at the Palais-Royal in Paris, when Dominico Biancolelli took the role of Arlecchino to the delight of Louis XIV who referred to him as 'Mon Dominique'. One night when attendant on the king at supper, he looked hungrily at a platter of partridges upon the table. Noticing this, the king said, 'Give Dominique a plate', and the clown took it and replied, 'May I have the partridge as well?' Everybody laughed but Dominique knew the plate was of solid gold!

Some months after the death of Marie Thérèse, queen of France, in 1683 Louis XIV secretly married Madame de Maintenon, who had been governess to the royal children. An ardent Catholic, she set about correcting the morals of a licentious

Court with the zeal of a poacher turned gamekeeper and, perhaps inevitably, destroyed much of the gaiety in the process. Her actions caused deep resentment and prompted a book published in the Low Countries lampooning her as *La Fausse Prude*. In 1697 the Modena troupe was sufficiently foolhardy to stage a dramatised version of this work entitled *La Finita* and were summarily dismissed for their pains. Indeed, they were forbidden to appear within thirty leagues of Paris so that public morality might be preserved.

The death of Louis XIV in 1715 was followed by the *Régence* of the pleasure-seeking Duc d'Orléans who invited to Paris the troupe of Luigi Riccoboni. Initial success was soon followed by complaints relating to the vulgarity of Arlecchino and Pantalone, while many were unable to follow the badinage and persiflage in the Italian tongue. Riccoboni commissioned Angelo Autreau to compose scripted dramas in French and these temporarily restored the *Commedia* to favour. Sadly, however, the spontaneity of the dialogue, the rapier-like repartee, the bawdy humour and slapstick were abandoned and, in 1762, the *Commedia* was amalgamated with the Paris Opéra Comique in which performances were transformed into genteel operettas. The 'New Italian Comedy' of 1779 was renamed the 'Theatre of the Italians' in 1780 but paradoxically not a single Italian player remained in the cast. Valiant attempts by both Sacchis and Gozzi in Italy to preserve the old traditions of the *Commedia* were without any lasting success and soon emasculated revivals called 'Harlequinades', 'Punch and Judy shows', and Pierrot Minstrels provided the last vestiges of the Comedy at fairs, circuses and seaside resorts.

Amongst the first pictorial records of the *Commedia* is an oil painting by Franz Porbus of c.1574,[1] portraying members of what was probably the Ganassa Troupe mingling with personages of the Court of Charles IX of France. Later Louis XIV commissioned a folio of engravings entitled 'Recueil Fossard' depicting scenes played by the troupe of the Duke of Mantua before Henri III.[2] These include a lewd episode involving Arlecchino and Franceschina, played by a youth, and Pantalone wearing the phallus. Giocomo Calotto also made etchings of Pantalone, Il Capitano, Scapino, and several small plates of other characters drawn in the Mannerist style in his 'Balli di Sfessania' of 1621.[3] François Joullain's engravings were executed to illustrate Luigi Riccoboni's *Histoire du Théâtre Italien*, published in 1728. They were loosely based on work by Calotto, Coypel and Gillot. Finally, the works of Antoine Watteau[4] were engraved by many different artists and published in 1734 as a folio volume entitled *Recueil de Jullienne*.[5]

Most porcelain manufactories throughout the ages, including Bow, were more concerned with producing attractively decorated, and hence readily saleable, models than with providing an accurate historical record of theatrical costumes. Thus, apart from representing the motley and Arlecchino's black mask, few of the costumes are correctly coloured. The use of playing-cards, in particular, on some jackets, dresses and trousers is entirely fanciful and it is highly improbable that Pedrolino would have on his jacket gold facings and buttons to match.

B Classical Mythology and Bow Models

According to the Olympian myth of creation, *Mother Earth* arose from *Chaos* and, while she slept, gave birth to *Uranus* who coupled with her to sire the *Hundred-handed Giants*, the *One-eyed Cyclopes* and the *Titans*. When the Cyclopes rebelled against Uranus they were defeated and sent to *Tartarus*, a place of punishment in the *Underworld*. Subsequently, Mother Earth urged the Titans, led by *Saturn (Cronus)*, to free the Cyclopes and overthrow Uranus who was castrated and slain. Saturn became the 'Supreme Deity', married his sister *Rhea*, and dispatched the Cyclopes once again to Tartarus.

Uranus before he died prophesied that a child of Saturn would one day usurp his father's throne and, in a vain attempt to confound this prediction, the god proceeded to swallow each child born by Rhea immediately after birth. In this manner he disposed of *Vesta (Hestia)*, *Ceres (Demeter)*, *Juno (Hera)*, *Pluto (Hades)*, and *Neptune (Poseidon)*. This macabre event is portrayed in a painting by Peter Paul Rubens[6] which prompted a red-anchor Chelsea porcelain group.[7] When Rhea became pregnant for the sixth time she asked Mother Earth how the child might be saved. Obeying her instructions she travelled to Mount Lycaeum, where no creature casts a shadow, and gave birth to *Jupiter (Zeus)* by dead of night. The baby was smuggled away to the Cave of Dicte on Crete and there nourished on milk provided by the Goat-Nymph, *Amalthea*, and honey from wild bees. Later Jupiter placed the image of the goat, *Capricorn*, in the firmament and one of its horns became the *Cornucopia*. Meanwhile, Rhea presented her spouse with a boulder wrapped in swaddling-bands which, believing it to be his child, he swallowed.

Jupiter grew to maturity before returning to his mother and, at her suggestion, placed an emetic in his father's wine. Saturn quaffed the potion and promptly regurgitated intact the offspring that earlier he had ingested. They elected Jupiter their leader, released the Cyclopes from Tartarus, and waged war on Saturn and the Titans except for Prometheus and Epimetheus who fought on the side of Jupiter. The Cyclopes gave thunderbolts to Jupiter, a trident to Neptune and the 'Helmet of Darkness' to Pluto which rendered him invisible. These weapons ensured the defeat of Saturn and the Titans who were banished to Tartarus, except their leader, Atlas, who was condemned to carry the firmament upon his shoulders for all eternity, while the Titanesses were pardoned. Jupiter married his sister Juno and became the 'Supreme Deity', choosing the firmament for his kingdom but presiding over the feasts of the gods on Mount Olympus where he maintained decorum by the threat of his thunderbolts.

Juno bore her husband two sons, *Mars (Ares)* and *Vulcan (Hephaestus)*, and a daughter, *Hebe*. She was constantly troubled by Jupiter's amorous escapades with goddesses, nymphs, Titanesses and mortals of both sexes and, unable to punish her omnipotent spouse, instead wreaked vengeance upon the human partner or the issue of their adulterous union. Hebe served as cup-bearer to the gods and later wed *Hercules (Heracles)* following his apotheosis. Jupiter then, disguised as an eagle, chose *Ganymede*, the comely son of king *Tros* as her successor and, after seducing him, bore him off to Olympus.

When Jupiter first wooed Juno she rejected him but he returned disguised as a bedraggled cuckoo and looked so wretched that Juno pressed the creature to her bosom. Jupiter took full advantage of her vulnerability and ravished her. The legend may explain why Juno may be shown holding a sceptre with a finial shaped like a cuckoo. On one occasion when Jupiter was making amorous advances to the minor goddess *Io*, he saw Juno approaching and enveloped both his beloved and himself in a cloud. Juno, her suspicions now aroused, advanced to investigate and Jupiter hurriedly metamorphosed Io into a white heifer. Juno led the animal away and placed the hundred-eyed *Argus* to guard it but Jupiter dispatched *Mercury (Hermes)* to the rescue, who first recited a long and tedious tale that sent Argus asleep and then slew him. Juno placed the hundred eyes in the tail-feathers of a peacock which henceforth became sacred to her name. Porcelain versions often show Juno beside a peacock and Jupiter holding thunderbolts with an eagle.

Jupiter's sister, *Ceres (Demeter)* probably originated as a primitive 'Mother Goddess', the protector of crops and vines, and porcelain models often show her holding a sickle beside a corn-sheaf. Her daughter *Core*, sired by Jupiter, was her pride and joy, but one day while she was gathering flowers the earth opened up and *Pluto (Hades)*, riding a chariot drawn by coal-black steeds, emerged, seized the girl and bore her off to Tartarus to make her his queen with the title *Proserpina (Persephone)*. When she failed to return to her mother, Ceres forbade the earth to bring forth its fruits until she was restored to her. Jupiter, by now thoroughly alarmed, asked his brother Pluto to release her and this he did. However, during her captivity she had swallowed some seeds from a pomegranate which, being of a red colour, constituted food reserved for the dead. Accordingly Core had to return to Tartarus as Persephone for three months in every year. Ceres was a 'Triple Moon Goddess' and wore a crescentic ornament in her hair. Her three natures included

Core the maiden, Ceres the nubile woman and Persephone the crone, representing seed-corn, ripe corn and reaped corn. It should be recalled that the ancient calendar included only three seasons, symbolised by a lion, a bull or a goat, and a serpent, sometimes combined to form the *Chimera*. The lion accompanying Ceres in porcelain models, accordingly, denotes 'Spring' and has no African connotations. Porcelain modellers often confused Ceres with *Cybele*, the Phrygian goddess of 'Earth' as contrasted to 'Fertile Soil', who was worshipped in deep caverns among the rocks or upon the barren hilltops. Her devotees sometimes castrated themselves in orgiastic ceremonies so that their bodies might more closely resemble that of the goddess. Porcelain figures usually portray Cebele wearing the 'Turret Crown' of a 'Mother Goddess' but inappropriately provide her with a cornucopia and place her beside a lion.

Neptune (*Poseidon*) became lord of the oceans, rivers and lakes but from time to time tried unsuccessfully to extend his domain to include dry land. He courted the nereid *Thetis* but deserted her when he heard the prophecy that any child she bore him would ultimately usurp his kingdom. Next he wooed the nymph *Amphitrite*, but she took fright and fled to the Atlas mountains. *Delphinius* was sent to plead his cause and this he did so eloquently that she returned to marry the god who, in gratitude, set the image of a *Dolphin* in the firmament. When Neptune ventured forth from his watery palace he rode in a chariot drawn by hippocampi, attended by nereids, dolphins and other sea creatures. Porcelain models usually portray him as a bearded man, scantily draped, wearing a crown either of gold or seaweed, holding a trident or paddle, standing beside a dolphin, although in one rare Derby version the creature is replaced by a hippocampus.[8]

Pluto (*Hades*) was Lord of the Underworld and, since he usually wore the 'Helmet of Darkness', was rarely seen on earth. The principal entrance to his domain was guarded by the three-headed dog *Cerberus*, and it was necessary to pay one penny to *Charon*, to be taken across the river Styx in his barque. Upon the far shore lay the *Fields of Asphodel* where the souls of the recent dead awaited judgment; beyond was *Erebus* where stood the palace of Pluto and Proserpina beside the pools of *Memory* and *Lethe* ('forgetting'). From thence a single path divided into three: here sat the judges *Minos*, *Rhadamanth* and *Aeacus* who directed those ghosts deemed to have led virtuous lives to their reward in the orchards and meadows of the *Elysian Fields*, and dispatched the wicked to *Tartarus*. Others, who failed to incur sufficient blame or praise, returned to the Fields of Asphodel to continue their spiritual life in a colourless environment, twittering like bats, sustained only by drinking the blood of the dying and the slain.

Vesta (*Hestia*), the first-born child of Saturn and Rhea, was a self-effacing goddess, 'Protector of Hearth and Home', whose temple in Rome contained the eternal flame tended by the Vestal Virgins. No soft-paste English models of her are known.

The offspring of Jupiter and Juno included *Mars* (*Ares*), the god of war. Understandably he was generally disliked except by Pluto who hoped that by his actions he might increase the number of his subjects, and by *Venus* (*Aphrodite*) who shared with him a mutual passion and bore his son *Cupid* (*Eros*). Those struck by Cupid's golden arrows were filled with insatiable love. During the ascendancy of Rome, Mars was adopted as the symbol of the militaristic *State of Rome* and was often coupled with *Minerva* (*Athene*) who became a warrior goddess with the title *Bellona*. Most porcelain models of Mars show him wearing the helmet and armour of a Roman centurion, paired either with Venus and Cupid, or with Minerva.

Vulcan (*Hephaestus*) appeared to Juno his mother to be such a weakling that she threw him off Olympus and, falling into the sea, he was reared by the gentle nereids *Thetis* and *Eurinome*. He learned the art of metalwork and presented Thetis with a beautiful brooch he had made. Juno noticed it and asked who had been responsible for such fine work and was astonished to find out it was her own son. Vulcan was brought back to Olympus. Shortly afterwards, the gods and goddesses grew weary of the conceit and perpetual boasting of Jupiter, and Juno resolved to teach him a lesson. She came upon him asleep and, after binding him with thongs of raw hide, she removed his thunderbolts and mocked him. Thetis saw that if this action continued it would cause perpetual strife amongst the Olympians and sent for help to the Hundred-handed Giants who untied the knots faster than Juno and her associates could retie them. Juno was punished by being suspended by gold bracelets from the firmament with an anvil bound to her feet and, when Vulcan came to her rescue, Jupiter kicked him off Olympus. This time he fell on hard ground and sustained injuries that gave him a permanent limp. Vulcan was married to *Venus* and, suspecting her of infidelity, laid a trap to establish her guilt. He suspended a metal hunting-net above his couch and then announced he was leaving on a journey and would be away for a week. Returning secretly that same night he found his wife and Mars together naked, entrapped in the snare, and called all the other divinities to witness the adultery. He was roundly admonished by Jupiter for such folly. Vulcan was supposed to live in the volcanic islands off Sicily whose emissions of lava were thought to emanate from his furnaces. He was the patron of armourers, smiths and metalworkers. Porcelain models usually show him beside a flaming urn or before an anvil,[9] a phoenix or salamander at his feet.

The third child of Jupiter and Juno was *Hebe* but she does not appear to have been portrayed in English porcelain. The remainder of the Olympians were the issue of Jupiter by nymphs, Titanesses or mortal women. He sired *Bacchus* (*Dionysus*) on *Semele*, daughter of the king of Thebes, when he came to her by night in disguise. Juno, determined to punish the adulteress, advised Semele to withhold her favours from her mysterious lover until he revealed his true identity. This action provoked Jupiter to fury and he slew her with a thunderbolt without realising she was carrying his child. *Mercury* (*Hermes*) saved the infant Bacchus by performing a post-mortem Caesarian section and sewed him into a gash made in Jupiter's thigh until he was viable on his own account. Juno pursued Bacchus relentlessly and incited the Titans to tear him to pieces but he was miraculously reconstituted by Rhea. Then he was reared in the women's quarters in the palace of *King Athamas* in Thessaly, but Juno drove the monarch mad, and the child was placed in the care of the nymphs on Mount Nysa. There he learned to ferment the grape to make wine but Juno sent the spirit of madness upon him and he embarked with his tutor *Silenus* and a band of *Satyrs* on his peregrinations, introducing all nations to the wine cult and debauchery. He found *Ariadne*, daughter of *Minos* king of Crete, on the island of Naxos where she had been deserted by *Theseus*, and married her. By this time Juno had forgiven Bacchus and he was admitted to Olympus where he sat at the right hand of Jupiter. Porcelain models show Bacchus crowned and bedecked with vine leaves and grapes, drinking wine from a goblet or eating a bunch of grapes.

Apollo (*Phoebus*) was the son of Jupiter and the Titaness, *Leto*. Originally he was a primitive 'Sun God' but became the patron of Archery, Mathematics, Medicine and the Arts. He obtained his lyre in exchange for a herd of cattle stolen from him by Mercury and its seven strings represent the seven vowels of the Greek tongue. His association with the Arts afforded him the title of *Musagetes* or leader of the Muses, and he sired the Corybantes on *Calliope*. One day Minerva was playing an end-flute and was irritated to see Juno was laughing at her, but looking at her reflection in a pool she appreciated that she did indeed appear ridiculous. Throwing the instrument away, she placed a curse on anyone who played it. The shepherd *Marsyas* picked it up and discovered he could play most beautifully upon it and challenged Apollo to a musical contest with the Muses as the judges. They adjudged the two performances to be of equal merit but ordered the contestants to play again with their instruments reversed. This was possible, though difficult, with the lyre but impossible with an end-flute, and the wretched shepherd was flayed alive for presuming to challenge a god. Most porcelain models of Apollo show him wearing a laurel chaplet and loose robe with a lyre.

Diana (*Artemis*) was also sired by Jupiter of Leto and, when her father asked what she wanted the most, she replied a longbow to hunt like her brother, and perpetual virginity. She became the virgin huntress of the forests and the patron of women in childbirth. Her silver longbow was made by the Cyclopes, her three hunting-dogs were a present from *Pan*, the ancient woodland deity, and her gilded chariot was drawn by three horned hinds watered from golden troughs and fed on clover from Juno's pastures. She demanded absolute chastity from her adherents and when an attendant nymph became pregnant by Jupiter, Diana transformed the girl into a bear that would have been torn to pieces by the hounds had not Jupiter intervened. The unfortunate *Actaeon*, who accidentally came upon the goddess bathing in the nude, was metamorphosed into a stag and hunted to death by his own pack of hounds. Most porcelain models show Diana with the crescent of a Triple Moon Goddess in her hair, wearing a loose robe, holding a longbow and quiver, standing or running with a hunting-dog.

The birth of *Minerva* (*Athene*) was miraculous. When Jupiter impregnated the Titaness *Metis* he learned that if she bore him a son he would usurp his kingdom, so he swallowed Metis with the unborn child. When subsequently he complained of a headache, Mercury borrowed a mallet and wedges from Vulcan and split open Jupiter's skull. Minerva stepped out of the wound and the headache resolved. She was initially a peace-loving deity who would only borrow arms when need arose. She became the protector of the Argonauts when under *Jason* they set off on a hazardous journey in their ship Argo to bring back the Golden Fleece from Colchis. She also gave much help to *Perseus* in his quest to kill one of the three Gorgons, showing him how to identify *Medusa*, who alone was mortal, from *Steno* and *Euryale*. She warned him that if he looked directly at Medusa he would be turned to stone and suggested he watched only her reflection in his burnished shield. Also, she gave him the adamantine sickle with which to decapitate the monster, a magic wallet to contain the severed head and winged sandals to speed him on his way, and told him how the *Stygian Nymphs* might loan him the helmet of darkness. Perseus located the *Graeae*, who had only one eye and one tooth between the three of them, on the slopes of Mount Atlas and tricked them into revealing where the Stygian Nymphs might be found, and having obtained the helmet slew Medusa. He presented the head to Minerva, who placed it upon the centre of her shield, and also the creature's bile, which had medicinal properties that earned for Minerva the title of 'Hygieia'. Porcelain models of Minerva show her wearing a crested helmet, cuirass, thonged skirt and sandals, holding a spear and a shield upon the centre of which is the head of Medusa.

Some hold that *Venus* (*Aphrodite*) was sired by Jupiter on the Titaness *Dione*, others that she arose from the ocean foam after the waters had been fertilised when the severed genitals of Uranus had been cast into the deep. She married Vulcan but became notorious for her promiscuity and was the 'Goddess of Love'. Her child *Cupid* fired golden arrows from his longbow and whoever they struck was filled with sexual desire. Once Venus was herself accidentally scratched by one of her son's arrows while in the company of *Adonis* and became besotted with him until he was killed by a wild boar. Her other children included *Rhodus* and *Hermophilus* by Neptune, a creature of intermediate sex named *Hermaphroditus* by Mercury, an ugly boy with huge genitalia called *Priapus* by Bacchus, and *Phobus*, *Deimus* and *Harmonia* by Mars. Jupiter, rather surprisingly, never slept with Venus but he filled her with a lust for mortal men. One night, disguised as a Phrygian princess, she came to the couch of *Anchises*, king of the Dardanians, and at dawn next day revealed her true identity. He, terrified that he had coupled with the goddess, begged that his life should be spared. Venus told him provided he kept their secret he would not be harmed. The child of their union was *Aeneas*, ancestor of the Romans. Some time after, when Anchises was deep in his cups, a friend asked whether he would rather sleep with the daughter of a particular acquaintance or with Venus. He replied that since he had enjoyed them both he found the question inept. Jupiter hearing the boast hurled a thunderbolt at him, which Venus deflected with her magic girdle, but he was never the same man again. Porcelain models show Venus scantily draped, often with one breast exposed, with either doves, or sparrows emblematic of 'Lechery', at her feet.

Mercury (*Hermes*) was the son of Jupiter and Maia, a nymph descended from the Titans. While yet in his cradle, he greatly amused Jupiter by stealing a herd of cattle from Apollo and cunningly concealing the evidence. His father admonished him that he must in future respect private property and refrain from lying although, he added, this was not the same thing as always telling the truth. Mercury informed him that he had sacrificed two of the cattle which he had cut into twelve portions, one for each divinity. Jupiter said there were only eleven Olympians so who was the twelfth? Mercury replied 'Yours truly!' He became the patron of trade, thieves and eloquence and served as Jupiter's messenger. His father provided him with a round helmet to protect him from the rain, winged sandals to speed him on his way, a cloak and the staff of an envoy to which white ribbons were attached; these later were mistaken for serpents and the staff became the *caduceus*. Porcelain models show him in traditional attire, sometimes holding the caduceus or a money-bag, with bales emblematic of 'Commerce', and often also a quill pen and ink-well.

After the war between the Giants and the Olympians had led to the defeat of the former, the gods implored Jupiter to enliven their feasts on Mount Olympus with the Arts. He coupled with the Titaness *Mnemosyne* and sired the nine Muses. They included *Calliope* (Epic Poetry), *Clio* (History), *Erato* (Love Poetry), *Euterpe* (Music and Lyric Poetry), *Melpomene* (Tragedy), *Polyhymnia* (Sacred Music), *Thalia* (Comedy), *Terpsichore* (Dance) and *Urania* (Astronomy). They resided on Mount Helicon but attended the feasts on Mount Olympus. Initially they were most chaste and when *King Daulis*, with whom they were staying, attempted to ravish them, they sprouted wings and flew away while the wretched monarch, who tried to follow them, fell to his death upon the rocks below. Later they took lovers selected from both gods and men. They were formidable creatures with whom it was folly to trifle for, when the *Pierides*, daughters of the Emathian king Pierus, challenged them to a musical contest, they were transformed forthwith into magpies for their presumption. Again, when the Thracian bard, *Thamyris*, boasted that he excelled their skill both in song and with the lute, he was struck deaf, dumb and blind for his temerity. Porcelain models show them seated or standing with accessories appropriate to their Arts.

This brief summary of the nature and deeds of the divinities of ancient Greece and Rome is designed to increase appreciation of the pantheon of porcelain gods and goddesses issued at Bow and accordingly omits a great deal that has no special application to this endeavour. Those wishing to delve more deeply into the myths and legends are referred to the work of Robert Graves.[10]

C BOW FIGURES AND HIGH FASHION

MANY BOW AND OTHER ENGLISH SOFT-PASTE FIGURES REFLECT, as it were in miniature, eighteenth-century *haute couture*, although when they are based on Meissen prototypes the styles may derive from Dresden or Paris rather than London. It may also be necessary to allow for the time elapsing between first issue of the original model, or its source, and the appearance of the Bow copy.

Nearly all eighteenth-century gentlemen wore wigs and those lower down the social scale grew their natural hair long and powdered it. The full-bottomed wig disappeared before 1720 and it was replaced by a bob-wig for the elder generation and members of the professions, and by the tie-wig for the younger fashionable set. Most Bow models of men show them, regardless of class, with natural hair although exceptions include a handful of portrait figures such as *Frederick the Great* (B119, Plate 162) and *Major-General James Wolfe* (B128, Plate 168) as well as a few *Gallants* (B118 and 122, Plates 161 and 164) who sport tie-wigs in which the hair was drawn back into a queue secured by a ribbon, or was contained within a wig-bag fashioned from ribbons.

Most of the shirt was concealed but openings at the neck and cuffs were generally frilled. About the neck was worn a cravat or a jabon (lace ruff) or perhaps a large decorative bow. Prior to 1720 the waistcoat had sleeves longer than those of the coat which were turned back over the coat cuffs. The coat was very long, extending almost to the knees, of which examples include those worn by *Henry Woodward as the Fine Gentleman* (A2, Plate 2), and the *Squire of Alsatia* (B121, Plate 163), the last mentioned after a sketch by Christophe Huet. The breeches, most of which lay behind the waistcoat, were loose-fitting with a prominent fly-opening. The waistcoat after 1740 progressively shortened until by c.1760 it conformed almost to the modern style. This left exposed the front of the breeches which became tighter-fitting and provided with a concealed fly-opening. The *Huntsman* (B110, Plate 153, Col. Plate IV) and seated male *Musician* (B104, Plate 148, Col. Plate XIII) with a drum and flageolet serve as examples. Also during the same period the style of the coat underwent major alteration. Sleeves became narrower when by c.1720 waistcoats were sleeveless. The coat skirt broadened, necessitating pleats both on either side of rear vent and at both sides. Also, the lower part of the coat was stiffened with buckram so that it flared out away from the thighs of the wearer, while pockets with closing flaps were obliquely placed. These features may be seen in the *Shepherd Bagpiper* (B117, Plate 160) and a male *Dancer* (B106, Plate 150), both of whom are intended to represent gentlemen in masquerade. Later, in the 1760s and after, a slimmer coat without any flared skirt was introduced which was cut away in front to slope downwards and outwards.

Stockings in the eighteenth century were made of wool, cotton or silk according to the occasion, and were sometimes secured by decorative garters. Shoes of stout leather had moderately high heels and buckles of metal or paste. Long boots, turned down just below the knees, were favoured for travelling or hunting. The wide-brimmed hat became *démodé* for the gentry but was still favoured by rustics as may be seen in the model of the *Piedmontese Bagpiper* (B79, Plate 135); usually either a cocked or tricorn hat was worn. Long, heavy greatcoats or long mantles with attached shoulder capes were normal outdoor winter wear. Many dandies carried a cane while a sword was almost the hallmark of a gentleman. Probably owing to technical problems making slender objects in soft paste, canes and swords are rare in Bow figures, although at least one version of the *Fine Gentleman* (A2, Plate 2) wears a sword and a *Midshipman* (B84, Plate 138) bears a gold-headed cane.

Ladies began to paint their faces from the age of fourteen and continued to do so until it was no longer possible to conceal the ravages of time. Beauty patches were worn in society, and quack remedies to preserve the complexion and abolish wrinkles abounded, many of them containing poisonous ingredients like mercury, lead or arsenic. Poor Maria Gunning probably succumbed to one of them and at twenty-eight died in a darkened room, mirror in hand, in a pathetic attempt to preserve her good looks. Until c.1765, natural hair was powdered, with the face framed in ringlets or curls or with the hair drawn back and secured with a ribbon. After about 1765, the crown was elevated upon a core of horsehair to which were attached false hair-pieces elaborately dressed with ribbons, lace, jewels and tall plumes. The overall effect was lampooned in contemporary engravings and in Continental hard-paste porcelain model groups portraying the hairdresser mounted upon a ladder to perform his task with a bystander regarding the result through a telescope! It was said that ladies attending an important function would arrive having sat upon the floor of their carriages to provide sufficient accommodation for their coiffure. However, before these excesses became evident, during the period of dishabille before noon, many ladies wore mob-caps, with nodular crowns and a frilled edge secured by a ribbon. Examples may be seen on models of *Kitty Clive as Mrs Riot* (A1, Plate 1) and the *Dancing Shepherdess* (B115, Plate 158, Col. Plate X) who wears hers beneath a brimmed hat.

The shift or blouse had elbow-length sleeves and an oval neck opening decorated with frills. It was worn beneath a boned bodice that served both to elevate the breasts and as a short corset. The front was usually covered with a decorative piece of material, called a stomacher, which was shaped like an inverted triangle with the point over the top of the skirt. This might simply be pinned into position or secured, either with criss-cross ribbons or a vertical line of small bows, *parfaits contentements*, which are evident in portraits of the Marquise de Pompadour both by La Tour and Boucher, and may be seen in models of the *Flower Seller* (B72, Plates 129–30) and *Lady playing a zither* (B104, Plate 148, Col. Plate XI). The farthingale, or hooped skirt, had been introduced into England from Spain in the sixteenth century but, by the commencement of the eighteenth, was flattened in front and became progressively narrower until, by c.1770, it was represented only by small half-hoops, or hip-pads. The model of *Kitty Clive* (A1, Plate 1) shows a fairly wide hooped skirt. By c.1745 a divided overskirt was added and often drawn upwards like curtains to frame the underskirt, revealing perhaps quilting that added fullness, warmth and decoration, or, after c.1755, flounces. Triple flounces may be seen upon the updated dress of the *Dancing Shepherdess* (B115, Plate 158, Col. Plate X), and upon the underskirt of two ladies, one comprising the *Blown Kiss* (C64, Plate 229) and the other the companion of a *Gallant* (B122, Plate 164).

An elegant garment called a mantua was introduced from France, consisting of a loose robe left open in front, usually with elbow length pagoda-sleeves that were turned back to reveal a triple funnel-shaped frill. This was modified over the space of some fifty years and had many variations, one of which may be seen on the *Sailor's Lass* (B82). Ladies' hats were usually wide-brimmed to protect their complexion, but when they accompanied their men hunting they seem to have preferred a tricorn or cocked hat, and wore either a jacket over their dress or a winter cloak with attached cape. Shoes for outdoor wear were leather with high platform soles and heels. These not only added to the stature of the person concerned, but elevated her above the garbage that littered the streets of most cities. Court shoes of coloured satin with rosettes or paste buckles were worn at formal functions and, here, one recalls the blue satin shoes that provided the badge of shame, or achievement, worn by ladies at the Würrtemberg Court! Aprons were decorative rather than protective and often expensive items, for when Nash once reprimanded a duchess for wearing one in the Assembly Rooms at Bath, she murmured as she removed it that it had cost her a hundred guineas. Gloves made of calf or suede were worn elbow-length, cloth purses suspended by a coloured cord or ribbons, while the fan was an essential means of communication in the silent language of flirtation. Chokers of velvet or silk with decorative bows in front were usually preferred to necklaces, which rarely amounted to more than a single short string or pearls or a gold cross and chain.

Very few Bow models issued after 1753 portray members of the lower orders: exceptions include the *Five Senses* (B44, Plates 98–102), the *Piedmontese Bagpiper* (B79, Plate 135), the *Tyrolean Dancers* (B86, Plate 139) and several of the *Cris de Paris* after Bouchardon. Models of children were, as was the practice in real life, dressed like small adults.

The failure of the Bow manufactory in 1774 came before the change that affected ladies' fashions when the wrist-length sleeve was introduced c.1780 and the hooped skirt yielded to a slimmer line with a high waist and *décolleté* emphasising the bust.

D REPRODUCTIONS, FORGERIES AND FAKES

REPLICAS OF ANTIQUE PORCELAIN made during the nineteenth or twentieth centuries and bearing the device adopted by their manufacturer are *reproductions*. However, unwanted enamelled marks may subsequently have been removed with hydrofluoric acid, although when the suspect area is viewed in an obliquely directed light the ghost outline and a patch of roughened glaze may be visible. When copies bear spurious marks they clearly comprise *forgeries*, but between these two extremes lie many replicas where the intention of the modeller remains in doubt. Often, for example, an unmarked copy was created from an original that is itself unmarked. These and other aspects of the subject have been discussed by Wallace Elliott[11] and by the present author.[12]

Reproductions of Continental hard-paste figures were made in profusion from the second half of the nineteenth century onwards. Some were cast from original moulds retained by their factory of origin, others were taken from fresh moulds at lesser manufactories such as Postchapel near Dresden, Rudolstadt and other establishments in Thuringia.[13] Especially dangerous forgeries were made by Weise of Dresden. Correct identification will usually require fine judgment relating to the colour and texture of the hard paste, the quality and thickness of the glaze, treatment of the bases and the spectrum of enamels used in decoration. An opaque chrome-green and maroon were not employed, for example, until c.1800, while the lifeless appearance of floral sprays may suggest a forgery. Some crudely modelled figures made after 1851 at Sitzendorf, in Thuringia, are unlikely to deceive because of the large red anchors that may be painted underneath their bases; the genuine Chelsea device is always small and inconspicuously sited behind the figure or its base.

The history and products of the Samson factory in Paris have been summarised by John Cushion.[14] Founded in 1848 by Edmé Samson in the Rue Vendôme (later renamed the Rue Béranger), the factory initially decorated porcelain blanks but, in 1871, under the influence of the proprietor's son, Émile, fresh kilns were built in the Montreuil-sous-Bois and production diversified to include hard-paste copies of faience and hard and soft-paste porcelain originating from both Europe and the Orient. Replicas of Bow figures were press-moulded in a Continental hard-paste body, often from moulds taken directly from prototypes and are, therefore, slightly smaller. Despite the excellence of many copies, they lack that semblance of animation which is characteristic of so many Bow models and instead call to mind people posing for a long exposure still photograph. Geoffrey Godden has pointed out that the clear, tight-fitting, transparent glaze is free from blemishes invariably present in eighteenth-century porcelain, such as pooling, crazing, sanding, pin-hole defects and smoke-staining.[15] Sprigging includes thin sharp-edged leaves and flowers resembling those of a strawberry plant that do not have the usual long, pointed Bow petals. The undersurfaces are too clean and any dirt present can readily be removed with a damp cloth. Ventilation holes are small and are sometimes sited behind the figure rather than in the central undersurface of the base.

The colours may deviate from the Bow factory palette and their even texture, brilliance and gloss are unlike the pale, uneven and blotching appearance of enamels that have sunk deeply into a thick lead glaze. Also, the thin, pale colloidal gold is dissimilar from the richness of Bow honey-gilding. Small impressed Arabic numerals may be found beneath the bases, sometimes also two letters L back to back, and upper case letter S, or a gilt swastika. These points that serve to distinguish Samson copies from originals are superfluous if the examiner can recognise the hard paste of which they are constructed. However not everyone possesses this skill and one curator of an important provincial museum, who was an author and acknowledged expert on Derby porcelain, erroneously identified Rockingham bone china models as Derby soft-paste biscuit!

Forgeries of eighteenth-century porcelain made of soft paste or a superficially similar chalky white earthenware are most likely to deceive. Shortly before the first World War Sigmund and Jessie Katz purchased a raised anchor Chelsea model of *Dottore Boloardo*, after Watteau, from Ernest Allman which had earlier passed through the hands of a well-known London restorer.[16] The figure was 11½in (29.2cm) high and, in the mid 1920s, a series of copies 9½in (24.1cm) high made of an opaque white earthenware appeared on the market. These had obviously been cast from a mould taken directly from the prototype. Mrs Katz commissioned George Savage to purchase a copy which she placed beside the genuine figure; Lady Ludlow, however, believing a copy to be authentic, included one in her collection at Luton Hoo.

The creation of convincing soft-paste forgeries requires skill, time and expense and those responsible confine their activities to the most rare and expensive items. Until fairly recently Bow figures did not command sufficiently high prices to become targeted but in the last decade all this has altered. The so called Creative Studios (Torquay) Ltd operated from Union Street between 1951 and the death of the proprietor, Reginald Newland, in 1971. He employed a chalky white earthenware which, to palpation, resembles soft-paste, for it is not, of course, practicable with a figure to demonstrate the presence or absence of translucency by transillumination. George Savage examined during the 1950s some primitively modelled *Birds* mounted upon 'chimney-pot' bases, some with funnel-shaped ventilation holes.[17] Initially these were, by exclusion, tentatively ascribed to Derby but when analysis revealed a phosphatic paste, reappraisal showed them to be modern forgeries. In 1971 Geoffrey Godden purchased what appeared to be a Longton Hall model of a youth, emblematic of *Spring*, from a London dealer.[18] The rather flat facial features, heavy jowels and unfamiliar enamel painting later suggested this also was a forgery. The present author has examined and illustrated modern copies of the dry-edge Derby *Florentine Boars*, and the *Stag and Doe* at lodge.[19] Most copyists work from photographs which rarely, if ever, reveal the form taken underneath the bases which, accordingly, have to be improvised. Usually they are ground flat but remain slightly uneven, and have ventilation holes with an irregular circumference from which radiate stress-cracks. Arthur Lane noted their weak modelling, dark brown discoloration of exposed paste, and often a glaze that both looks and feels greasy.[20] Colouring deviates from the normal palette and may include hesitant spidery brush strokes to indicate animal hide, while eyes may be outlined by a continuous ring of dark brown. Early examples of Torquay reproductions were often good but standards declined as the number produced multiplied. So far no Bow examples have been seen by the author.

David Battie has described the collection of reproductions and forgeries formed by James Kiddell in his 'Black Museum', for the instruction of trainees at Sotheby's.[21] It would also seem likely they were employed to deflate the ego of self-styled experts who appeared over-confident. Thieves broke into Mr Kiddell's home and removed many of these items so we must expect to see some reappearing in the years to come both in provincial auction rooms and in the premises of dealers and collectors!

A genuine antique that has been altered fraudulently to increase its market value is correctly termed a *fake*. Most examples relate to service wares and vases where, for example, a rare ground colour has been added, or a banal blue and white design has been removed and replaced by more important polychrome painting. Occasionally a rather plain piece has been embellished by gilding. When a soft lead glaze is reheated in a muffle kiln some months or years after its initial glost-firing, myriads of small bubbles form, some of which rupture to roughen the surface, and multiple black specks appear. When soft-paste is reheated it becomes discoloured a blue-black colour. The few attempts that have been made to enamel a soft-paste model issued white have proved disastrous, with debased enamel colour, sanded and roughened glaze and deep staining of areas of exposed paste. An example cited by Severne MacKenna involved the Chelsea head of the *Duke of Cumberland*.[22]

The addition of bogus marks must also be considered. It is, of course, impossible to reproduce the ploughed-up edges of an incised mark made before the biscuit firing, but impressed marks may be simulated with the aid of a dental drill. Usually the freshness of the furrow and its granular surface point towards the deception. It is quite easy to add marks painted overglaze and fixed by a brief passage through a muffle kiln and it is wise to ignore any enamelled marks that do not accord with other diagnostic criteria. Also consider the size, form and siting of any such devices that may be found.

E DAMAGE AND RESTORATION

ENGLISH EIGHTEENTH-CENTURY PORCELAINS are fragile substances and after over 200 years many examples have sustained damage. Today, even a millionaire would find it difficult to form an interesting collection of soft-paste models in mint condition and those who resolutely demand perfection run the risk that it may be created especially for them. Clearly the extent of damage and restoration deemed to be acceptable must always be a personal judgment, but it should be related to cost, the beauty or rarity of the item, available funds and to the theme portrayed by the collection. Needless to say, one should always seek to acquire quality in the finest condition available.

Restoration carried out many years ago may have incorporated rivets or, in the case of models, heads may have been re-attached by metal pillars. These have been rendered superfluous by the advent of epoxy resins and should be removed for, unless made of rustless material, they will eventually cause irreversible staining of soft paste. Fire-cracks, arising from unequal shrinkage of paste during the biscuit firing, may be partially filled with glaze and are widest in thickly potted areas. These traits distinguish them from cracks arising from physical damage. Provided they are small and do not impair the overall artistic effect and are reflected in a reduced price, they do not comprise an insuperable barrier to purchase. Old varnish may have become yellow and started to peel off and, in this state, should be removed with either alcohol or acetone to reveal the underlying extent of repair. Small chips to the edges of garments, bases, sprigged decoration or bocage may be regarded as almost a normal finding and are best left alone. It should be remembered that finials, spouts, knobs and parts of models were cast from individual moulds and subsequently luted into position. Accordingly, clean fractures through the junctions of such portions that have been restuck do not amount to a catastrophe. When, however, fragmentation of porcelain adjacent to the fracture has necessitated replacement with composition, unless the model is especially desirable it is best to reject it. The composition is usually painted with oil colours and sprayed with three coats of thin transparent varnish, each succeeding one covering a wider area. It is extremely difficult to match the colouring of the fired enamels and to reproduce the decoration in the same style. Accordingly, the restorer may be tempted to overpaint a wide zone that has not been damaged to render his work less conspicuous. Indeed, when added paint and varnish are stripped away the underlying restoration may be quite small.

Freshly applied varnish will retain its characteristic odour and remains slightly tacky to the touch. When the point of a pin is laid against an area that has been varnished, and the object is inclined towards the vertical, it continues to maintain its position whereas when laid upon a fired glaze it will slide away. It is unnecessary to scratch or perforate the surface. Light percussion of porcelain with the blunt edge of a knife or a coin will emit a sound quite different from the dull note when composition is struck. Transillumination, difficult to perform in a model, may show hair-cracks as lucencies or, if filled with cement, as opaque bands. The tinge of colour evident, tears or moons, may prove useful in establishing the date and factory of origin but cannot be usefully assessed with figures.

Occasionally, missing or severely damaged parts of figures or wares have been replaced with others pirated from discarded items. Here, the substitution may initially be betrayed by a knowledge of factory shapes, enamel decoration and gilding. Accessories attached to models, such as gardening tools, musical instruments and weapons, which have been taken from elsewhere, may be erroneous in scale or, even, totally absurd when, for example, a huntsman acquires a spade. Even heads have been transplanted, sometimes with comical results. Fragments of antique porcelain may be reshaped to supply a missing feature and in one example of this, the brim of a hat worn by a shepherdess was transformed into the peak of a huntsman's cap. Candle-holders, drip-pans, and sconces are especially prone to damage and may be replaced by nineteenth-century, or even quite modern, sources which are usually declared by their brilliant pale gilding. A clever restorer may expertly conceal major damage but leave, as a decoy, obvious restoration to a minor item. I once possessed a Chelsea-Derby *Gardener* (No. 3 in Haslem's List), emblematic of Earth. The handle of the spade was represented by a thin solid rod of uncoloured composition that stood out like a sore thumb. Under an ultraviolet lamp it was clear that the model had been broken in half and a wide area replaced with composition that had been most carefully and skilfully painted to hide the work.

The Ultraviolet Lamp (Mercury Lamp), now available in several inexpensive battery or mains models, requires no special skills to operate and poses no health hazard. There are two different lamps: one providing maximum radiation at 2,537 Å is most suitable for research; the other at 3,660 Å is best adapted for assessing restoration. The surface must first be cleaned and free from grease, dust and grime, and examination conducted in a darkened room. Soft-paste porcelain will appear under the lamp as a purplish-blue colour, whereas any foreign substance like varnish or paint will fluoresce a yellowish white.

Radiographic Examination should be performed only by a professionally qualified person owing to the known hazards of gamma irradiation. It will reveal metal pillars and rivets as areas of increased radio-density while composition replacements are usually less opaque than soft-paste porcelain. The presence or absence of a central cavity in a model cannot be demonstrated, however, owing to the high radio-density of the phosphatic Bow paste and the irregular contours of the figure. Elsewhere, radiographic tomography is described which will provide this information.[23]

Until the skills necessary to assess damage and restoration have been acquired, the collector is well advised to seek expert help prior to making a purchase. Condition reports are available at most auction rooms on request if the would-be purchaser is unable to attend a preview. Better still, he should buy only from a reputable dealer who will provide a written statement detailing the factory of origin, approximate date of manufacture, the extent of any damage and restoration, and the price. In the unlikely event of the item being proved to deviate from this there is usually no difficulty in obtaining a refund from the vendor if it is returned intact.

Adams and Redstone. Elizabeth Adams and David Redstone, *Bow Porcelain*, Faber & Faber, London, 1981.

Albert Amor Bow Ex. Cat. Catalogue of a Loan Exhibition of Bow Porcelain c.1747–75, in Memory of Geoffrey Freeman. Held at Albert Amor's, St James's, London, 4–24 June, 1982.

B. and T. Hughes. Brian Hughes and Therle Hughes, *English Porcelain and Bone China, 1743–1850*, Lutterworth Press, London, 1955.

Bow Special Ex. Cat. H. G. Tait, *Bow Porcelain 1744–1776. A Special Exhibition of Documentary Material to Commemorate the Bi-centenary of the Retirement of Thomas Frye*, London, 1959. Held at the British Museum October 1959 to April 1960.

Bradshaw. Peter Bradshaw, *18th Century English Porcelain Figures 1745–1795*, Antique Collectors' Club, Woodbridge, 1981.

Burl. Mag. Burlington Magazine.

Christie's. Christie Manson & Woods, London, Sale Catalogue.

Cushion. John Cushion, *English Porcelain*, Charles Letts & Co., London, 1974.

E.C.C. 1948 Ex. Cat. Catalogue of the Exhibition held by the English Ceramic Circle in 1948 at the Victoria & Albert Museum.

E.C.C. 1977 Ex. Cat. R. J. Charleston and Donald Towner, *English Ceramics 1580–1830*, London, 1977.

Egan Mew. Egan Mew, *Old Bow China*, London, 1909.

Freeman. Anton Gabszewicz, *Bow Porcelain – the Collection formed by Geoffrey Freeman*, Lund Humphries, London, 1982.

Godden. Collection of Mr G. Godden.

Godden Encyclopaedia. Geoffrey Godden, *An Illustrated Encyclopaedia of British Pottery and Porcelain*, Herbert Jenkins, London, 1960.

Harris. Nathaniel Harris, *Porcelain Figurines*, Sampson Low, London, 1975.

Herbert Allen. Bernard Rackham, *Catalogue of the Herbert Allen Collection of English Porcelain*, London, 1917.

Honey. W. B. Honey, *English Pottery and Porcelain*, A. & C. Black, London, 1964.

Hughes. Bernard Hughes, *English Pottery and Porcelain Figures*, Lutterworth Press, London, 1964.

Hurlbutt. Frank Hurlbutt, *Bow Porcelain*, Bell & Sons, London, 1926.

King. William King, *English Porcelain Figures of the Eighteenth Century*, Medici Society, London, 1925.

Lady Ludlow. Arthur Hayden, *Catalogue of the Lady Ludlow Collection*, London, 1932.

Lane. Arthur Lane, *English Porcelain Figures of the 18th Century*, Faber & Faber, London, 1961.

Morley-Fletcher. Hugo Morley-Fletcher, *Investing in Pottery and Porcelain*, Barrie & Jenkins, London, 1968.

Phillips. Phillips Ltd, London, Sale Catalogue.

Poole. Julia Poole, *Plagiarism Personified?*, Cambridge 1986. Catalogue of an Exhibition held at the Fitzwilliam Museum 15 July to 31 August 1986.

Savage. George Savage, *English 18th Century Porcelain*, Barrie & Rocklif, London, 1952.

Schmidt. Robert Schmidt, *Porcelain as an Art and a Mirror of Fashion*, London, English Edn, Harrap, 1932.

Schreiber. Bernard Rackham, *Catalogue of the Schreiber Collection*, Victoria & Albert Museum, London, 1915. Newly allocated nos in parentheses.

Scott and Scott. Cleo M. Scott and G. Ryland Scott, *Antique Porcelain Digest*, The Ceramic Book Co., Newport, 1961.

Sotheby's. Sotheby Parke Bernet, London, Sale Catalogue.

Stoner. Frank Stoner, *Chelsea, Bow and Derby Porcelain Figures*, R. H. Johns Ltd, Newport, 1955.

Trans. E.C.C. Transactions of the English Ceramic Circle.

Trans. E.P.C. Transactions of the English Porcelain Circle.

Untermyer. Yvonne Hackenbroch, *Chelsea and other English Porcelain, Pottery and Enamel in the Irwin Untermyer Collection*, Harvard University Press, Cambridge, Mass., 1957.

Upton House. John Mallet, *Bearsted Collection Catalogue: Porcelain*, The Curwen Press, Plaistow, 1964.

NOTES

CHAPTER 1

1   Elizabeth Adams, 'The Bow Insurances and Related Matters', 1973, *Trans. E.C.C.*, Vol. 9, pt. 1, 69–70.

2   Elizabeth Adams and David Redstone, *Bow Porcelain*, London, 1981, 35.

3   Court Book for 1744, Record Office, County Hall, London.

4   Samuel Richardson, Daniel Defoe's *A Tour of Great Britain*, 4th edn, London, 1748, Vol. 1, 2.

5   Adams and Redstone, op. cit., 65.

6   Hugh G. Tait, 'The Bow Factory under Alderman Arnold and Thomas Frye', 1963, *Trans. E.C.C.*, Vol. 5, pt. 4, 199.

7   Idem.

8   Geoffrey Willis, 'The Bow Factory of Edward Heylyn', 1954, *Connoisseur*, Vol. CXXXIII.

9   Michael Wynne, 'Thomas Frye 1710–1762', 1972, *Burlington Magazine*, Vol. CXIV, 79–84.

10   Bernard Watney, *English Blue and White Porcelain of the 18th Century*, London, 1973, 8.

11   Adams, op. cit., Sun Insurance Records, Guildhall MS 11936/173 240448, 18 December 1766.

12   Adams and Redstone, op. cit., 38.

13   Hugh G. Tait, 'Some Consequences of the Bow Porcelain Special Exhibition. Part IV, Thomas Frye and a Rival Factory in Bow', 1960, *Apollo*, Vol. 72, 111–14.

14   Adams and Redstone, op. cit., 27, cites a personal communication with Mr and Mrs Weatherby of Stoke-on-Trent.

15   Idem. Sun Insurance Records, Guildhall MS 11936/87 116972, 6 July 1749.

16   Arnold R. Mountford, 'Thomas Briand – A Stranger', 1967, *Trans. E.C.C.*, Vol. 7, pt. 2, 87–95.

17   Adams and Redstone, op. cit., 27. Sun Insurance Records, Guildhall MS 11936/152, 1 April 1764.

18   Idem. Sun Insurance Records, Guildhall MS 11936/128, 24 July 1759.

19   Watney, op. cit., 26.

20   J. E. Nightingale, *Contributions towards the History of Early English Porcelain*, Salisbury, 1881, 1. Reprinted Wakefield, 1973.

21   Nancy Valpy, 'Extracts from 18th Century London Newspapers and Additional Manuscripts, British Library', 1987, *Trans. E.C.C.*, Vol. 13, pt. 1, 82.

22   Idem.

23   Frank Hurlbutt, *Bow Porcelain*, London, 1926, 22.

CHAPTER 2

1   Hugh G. Tait, *Bow Porcelain 1744–1776. A Special Exhibition of Documentary Material to Commemorate the Bi-centenary of the Retirement of Thomas Frye* [British Museum, October 1959 to April 1960], London, 1959, 8.

2   Llewellynn Jewitt, *The Ceramic Art of Great Britain*, London, 1878, Vol. I, 320–1.

3   Hugh G. Tait, 'The Bow Factory under Alderman Arnold and Thomas Frye', 1963, *Trans. E.C.C.*, Vol. 5, pt. 4, 200.

4   William Chaffers, *Marks and Monograms on European and Oriental Pottery and Porcelain*, London, 1965, Vol. I, 270.

5   Tait, loc. cit., n. 3 above.

6   Chaffers, op. cit., 271.

CHAPTER 3

1   Elizabeth Adams, 'The Bow Insurances and Related Matters', 1973, *Trans. E.C.C.*, Vol. 9, pt. 1, 67–110: Sun Insurance Records, Guildhall MS 11936/87, 7 July 1749; Sun Insurance Records, Guildhall MS 11936/90 123709, 22 November 1750; Royal Exchange Company Records, Vol. III, No. 31533, 11 December 1755; Sun Insurance Records, Guildhall MS 11936/148, 28 July 1763; Sun Insurance Records, Guildhall MS 11936/152 207349, 9 March 1766.

2   Elizabeth Adams and David Redstone, *Bow Porcelain*, London, 1981, 57–60 summarises the above. See also revised edition, 1991.

CHAPTER 4

1   *Art Journal*, 1869, 203.

2   Frank Hurlbutt, *Bow Porcelain*, London, 1926, 145–7.

3   A. J. Toppin, 'Bow Porcelain – Recent Excavations of the Site', *Burlington Magazine*, 1922, Vol. XL, 88–91.

4   David Redstone, *St Mary's Gazette*, London University, 1969, Vol. LXXV, No. 4, 120.

5   Catalogue of an exhibition of Bow Porcelain, held 14 September–31 October 1981, at the Stoke-on-Trent Museum, Hanley, 37, pl. 159: biscuit sherd of the torso of a *Pugilist*.

CHAPTER 5

1   J. E. Nightingale, *Contributions towards the History of Early English Porcelain*, Salisbury, 1881, xlii–l.

2   A. J. B. Kiddell, 'An Early Advertisement of Bow Porcelain', 1928, *Trans. E.P.C.*, No. I, 30.

3   Nancy Valpy, 'Extracts from 18th Century London Newspapers', *Trans. E.C.C.* 1982, Vol. 11, pt. 2, 122–30; 1984, Vol. 12, pt. 1, 58–89; 1985, Vol. 12, pt. 2, 161–88; 1987, Vol. 13, pt. 1, 77–107.

4   *Gentleman's Magazine*, October 1762, Vol. XXXII.

5   Llewellynn Jewitt, *The Ceramic Art of Great Britain*, New York and London, 1883, 126.

6   William Chaffers, *Marks and Monograms on European and Oriental Pottery and Porcelain*, London, 1870, 691.

7   Peter Bradshaw, *Derby Porcelain Figures 1750–1848*, London, 1990.

8   Frank Stoner, 'Chelsea Moulds: An Important Discovery', 1924, *Connoisseur*, Vol. LXIX, 3–10.

9   Pamela Rowan, 'Figures and Moulds in Copelands', 1988, a lecture given in the Derby Museums and Art Gallery to the Derby Porcelain International Society.

CHAPTER 6

1   Bernard Watney, *English Blue and White Porcelain of the 18th Century*, London, 1973, 21, cites a letter among the Entwistle Papers, Liverpool Public Library, No. 6573/26.

2   Hugh G. Tait, *Bow Porcelain 1744–1776. A Special Exhibition of Documentary Material to Commemorate the Bi-centenary of the Retirement of Thomas Frye*, [British Museum, October 1959 to April 1960)], London, 1959. Items 149, 152, 153 and 154.

3   *Art Journal*, 1869, New Series, Vol. XCII, 239–43.

4   William Chaffers, *Marks and Monograms on European and Oriental Pottery and Porcelain*, 15th edn, London, 1965, Vol. II, 272–6.

5   Elizabeth Adams and David Redstone, *Bow Porcelain*, London, 1981, 89–90.

6   Tait, op. cit., item 125, the Bowcock Bowl; see also colour illustration on front cover.

7   Watney, op. cit., 21, n. 1.

CHAPTER 7

1   A. J. Toppin, 'Battersea: Ceramic and Kindred Associations', 1946, *Trans. E.C.C.*, Vol. 2, No. 9, 177.

2   Hugh G. Tait, *Bow Porcelain 1744–1776. A Special Exhibition of Documentary Material to Commemorate the Bi centenary of the Retirement of Thomas Frye* [British Museum, October 1959 to April 1960], London, 1959, item 111, the Craft Bowl; see also fig. 37.

3   Ibid., item 112, the cardboard box with the message written by Thomas Craft upon the undersurface of the lid.

4   A. J. Toppin, *William Hopkins' Craft, Enamel Painter*, 1959, *Trans. E.C.C.*, Vol. IV, pt. 4 cited by Tait, op. cit.

5   Elizabeth Adams and David Redstone, *Bow Porcelain*, London, 1981, 62; Sun Insurance Records, Guildhall MS 11936/280 423462, 12 January 1780.

6   Ibid., 45.

7   Ibid., Appendix VI.

CHAPTER 8

1   Elizabeth Adams and David Redstone, *Bow Porcelain*, London, 1981, 215, Appendix VI.

2   Geoffrey Godden, *Chamberlain-Worcester Porcelain, 1788–1852*, London, 1982, 208–9.

3   Henry Sandon, *Flight and Barr Worcester Porcelain 1783–1840*, Woodbridge, 1978, 208.

4   Adams and Redstone, op. cit., 140.

5   Eliza Meteyard, *The Life of Josiah Wedgwood*, London, 1865, Vol. II. See also for a summary of relevant letters Frank Hurlbutt, *Bow Porcelain*, London, 1926, 45–50.

6   J. T. Smith, *Nollekens and his Times*, London, 1829.

7   Mrs Donald MacAlister, 'Early Staffordshire China', 1933, *Trans. E.C.C.*, No. 1, 48.

8   Simeon Shaw, *The History of the Staffordshire Potteries*, Hanley, 1829, 167.

9   Adams and Redstone, op. cit., 215, Appendix VI.

CHAPTER 9

1   W. H. Tapp, 'Thomas Hughes. First Enameller of English China, of Clerkenwell', 1939, *Trans. E.C.C.*, Vol. 2, No. 6, 53–65.

2   Geoffrey Godden, *Eighteenth-century English Porcelain, a Selection from the Godden Reference Collection*, Granada Publishing, 1985, 100–3, pl. 80, showing an example of painting by T. Hughes.

3   Aubrey J. Toppin, 'Nicholas Crisp, Jeweller and Potter', 1933, *Trans. E.C.C.*, No. 1, 38–53.

4   Nancy Valpy, 'Nicholas Crisp: A Newly-found Benefactor', 1988, *Trans. E.C.C.*, Vol. 13, pt. 2, 158–60.

5   Bernard M. Watney, 'The Vauxhall China Works, 1751–1764', 1989, *Trans. E.C.C.*, Vol. 13, pt. 2, 212–22.

6   Aubrey J. Toppin, 'The Kentish Town Factory', 1933, *Trans. E.C.C.*, Vol. 1, 30–1.

7   Bernard M. Watney, 'The King, the Nun and Other Figures', 1968, *Trans. E.C.C.*, Vol. 7, pt. 1, 48–58.

8   Frank Hurlbutt, *Bow Porcelain*, London, 1926, 69–72.

9   Mrs Donald MacAlister, *William Duesbury's London Account Book, 1751–1753*, London, 1931, a special E.C.C. Publication.

10   A. J. Charleston, 'Decoration of Porcelain and Glass – James Giles in a New Light', 1967, *Trans. E.C.C.*, Vol. 6, pt. 3, 292–316.

11   W. B. Honey, 'The Work of Giles', 1937, *Trans. E.C.C.*, No. 5, 7–23, pls 11a–d, showing styles of decoration on the Grubb plates.

12   Watney, op. cit., n. 7, 55–8.

13   Honey, op. cit.

CHAPTER 10

1   Elizabeth Adams and David Redstone, *Bow Porcelain*, London, 1981, 236, Appendix XV.

2   F. Severne MacKenna, *Chelsea Porcelain, the Triangle and Raised Anchor Wares*, Leigh-on-Sea, 1948, 16.

3   Peter Bradshaw, *Derby Porcelain Figures, 1750–1848*, London, 1990, shows Derby models of same subjects as Bow.

4   Aubrey J. Toppin, 'Bow Porcelain – Recent Excavations of the Site', 1922, *Burlington Magazine*, Vol. XL, 86–91.

5   Bernard Watney, 'The King, the Nun and Other Figures', 1968, *Trans. E.C.C.*, Vol. 7, pt. 1, 48–58.

6   Peter Bradshaw and Ronald Grainger, 'Evidence that some Bow Figures were Solid Cast', 1972/3, *Journal of the Northern Ceramic Society*, Vol. I, 41–4.

7   Adams and Redstone, op. cit., 65.

8   British Museum, Franks Collection, biscuit model of *Kitty Clive as Mrs Riot*.

9   Museum of Fine Arts, Boston, USA, Sigmund and Jessie Katz Collection, biscuit model of *Henry Woodward as the Fine Gentleman*.

10 Private collection. *Trans. E.C.C.*, Vol. 7, pls 129b–c, biscuit pair of Bow *Huntsman and Lady*.

11 Bradshaw, op. cit., pl. 28, biscuit pair of Derby *Street Vendors*.

12 Frank Tilley, 'The Rare and the Curious', 1964, *Antique Collector*, June, 107–12, fig. 7, biscuit Longton Hall *Pheasant*.

CHAPTER 11

1   B. Rackham, *The Catalogue of the Collection of Lady Charlotte Schreiber*, London 1928.

2   A. Gabszewicz, *Bow Porcelain – the Collection formed by Geoffrey Freeman*, London, 1982.

3   A. Lane, *English Porcelain Figures of the Eighteenth Century*, London, 1961.

4   F. Stoner, *Chelsea, Bow and Derby Porcelain Figures*, Newport, 1955.

5   William Chaffers, *Marks and Monograms on European and Oriental Pottery and Porcelain*, 15th edn, London, 1965, Vol. II.

6   F. Hurlbutt, *Bow Porcelain*, London, 1926.

7   Yvonne Hackenbroch, *Chelsea and other English Porcelain, Pottery and Enamel in the Irwin Untermyer Collection*, Cambridge, Mass., 1957.

8   W. King, *English Porcelain Figures of the 18th Century*, London, 1925.

CHAPTER 12

1   Reginald Haggar, 1978, *Northern Ceramic Society Newsletter*, No. 29, 22, item 7.

2   Mrs Donald MacAlister, *William Duesbury's London Account Book, 1751–1753*, London, 1931.

3   J. V. G. Mallet, *Upton House – The Bearsted Collection: Porcelain*, Plaidstow, 1964, pl. 5.

4   Elizabeth Adams and David Redstone, *Bow Porcelain*, London, 1981, Col. Pl. H, enamelled model of *Kitty Clive* in the Godden collection.

5   H. G. Tait, 'Some Consequences of the Bow Special Exhibition. Part I, The Alderman Arnold Period', 1960, *Apollo*, Vol. LXXI, 40–4; fig. 1, Derby model of *Kitty Clive*.

6   Ibid., 42, fig. V, engraving of *Catherine Clive* as the *Fine Lady* (Mrs Riot) by Charles Mosley, after T. Worlidge.

7   Idem, fig. V, engraving of *Henry Woodward* as the *Fine Gentleman* by James McArdell, after Francis Hayman.

8   Yvonne Hackenbroch, *Chelsea and other English Porcelain, Pottery and Enamels in the Irwin Untermyer Collection*, Cambridge, Mass., 1957, pl. 77, fig. 241 and pl. 269, fig. 145, model of *Henry Woodward* incised 1750.

9   Fitzwilliam Museum, Cambridge, model of *Kitty Clive* incised 1750.

10 R. Mander and J. Mitcheson, 'China Statuettes of Quinn as Falstaff', 1958, *Theatre Notebook*, No. 2, 54–8, pls 8–10.

11   A. J. Toppin, 'The Origin of Some Ceramic Designs', 1948, *Trans. E.C.C.*, Vol. 2, No. 10, 266–76; pl. CIc, engraving of *James Quinn* as *Falstaff*, after Francis Hayman; pl. CId, Bow model.

12   Arthur Lane, (1961) *English Porcelain Figures of the 18th Century*, London, 1961, 86.

13   John Twitchett, *Derby Porcelain*, London, 1980, pl. 66, Derby model of *Quinn as Falstaff* in the Royal Crown Derby Museum.

14   H. G. Tait, 'Some Consequences of the Bow Special Exhibition. Part III, Alderman Arnold and Thomas Frye', 1960, *Apollo*, Vol. LXXI, 181–5; fig. III, p. 183, portrait of *Peg Woffington* by Arthur Pond, also Bow *Sphinxes*.

15   Jane Dunbar, *Peg Woffington and her World*, London, 1968.

16   Bernard Rackham, *Catalogue of English Porcelain, Earthenware, Enamels and Glass collected by Charles Schreiber Esq. M.P. & the Lady Charlotte Elizabeth Schreiber and presented to the* [Victoria & Albert] *Museum in 1884*, London, 1924, Vol. III, 20, nos 36–7, plaques of *Maria and Elizabeth Gunning*.

17   B. Watney and R. J. Charleston, 'Petitions for Patents concerning Porcelain, Glass and Enamels with Special Reference to Birmingham, The Great Toyshop of Europe', 1966, *Trans. E.C.C.*, Vol. 6, pt. 2, 57–123: pl. 65a, engraving of *Maria Gunning* by John Brooks; pl. 65b, enamel plaque of *Maria Gunning*; pl. 65c, engraving of *Elizabeth Gunning* by John Brooks; pl. 65d, enamel plaque of *Elizabeth Gunning*.

18   Yvonne Hackenbroch, *Meissen and other Continental Porcelain, Faience and Enamel in the Irwin Untermyer Collection*, Cambridge, Mass., 1956: p. 292, *Arlecchino scowling*, c.1738 by Kändler; p. 323, *Columbina dancing*, c.1743/4 by Kändler and Reinicke; p. 310, three models of *Pulcinella*, c.1748 by Kändler.

19   Ibid., 341, *Scapino*, c.1743/4 by Kändler and Reinicke.

20   Ibid., pl. 55, fig. 78, *The Indiscreet Arlecchino*, c.1740 by Kändler.

21   Toppin, op. cit., pl. CIIIc, 'Belles n'écoutez rien', engraved by C. N. Cochin, pl. CIIId, Bow group of *The Italian Lovers*. Pl. CIIIa, 'Pour garder l'honneur d'une belle', engraved by C. N. Cochin after Watteau, pl. CIIIb, Bow group of *The Italian Musicians*.

22   K. Berling, *Festive Publication to Commemorate the 200th Jubilee of the Oldest European China Factory, Meissen*, Meissen, 1910, English language reprint New York, 1972: table 9, fig. 6, Meissen group of *The Italian Musicians*.

23   Marianna-Roland Michel, *Watteau, an Artist of the Eighteenth Century*, London, 1984, pl. 76, chalk drawing of 'Le Conteur' by Watteau, pl. 77, transposed engraving by Cochin.

24   K. Berling, op. cit., table 16, fig. 12, *Apollo* by J. F. Eberlein.

25   A. J. Toppin, 'Some Early Bow Muses', 1929, *Burlington Magazine*, Vol. LIV, 190, pls Ia–c and 191, pls IIa–d: seven *Muses* omitting Thalia and Calliope.

26   Toppin, op. cit. n. 11 pl. CIa, *Clio* engraved by D. Coster as frontispiece in *The Works of L'Abbé de St Real*; pl. CIb, Bow model of *Clio*.

27   Adams and Redstone, op. cit., 142.

28   Lane, op. cit., 88, 89.

29   Berling, op. cit., table 15, no. 10, group representing *Charity*, c.1740 by J. F. Eberlein.

30   Ibid., table 15, no. 9, *Mercury*, c.1740 by J. F. Eberlein.

31   Toppin, op. cit. n. 11: pl. CIIa, *Ki Mao Sao*, engraved by Aubert, after Watteau; pl. CIIb, Bow model.

32   Marianna-Roland Michel, *Watteau, an Artist of the Eighteenth Century*, London, 1984, 279–80.

33   *Louvre Inventaire Général*, Vol. II, no. 1415, fig. 9, 'Décoration chinoise', an engraving after Watteau.

34 E. A. Jones, *The Old English Plate of the Emperor of Russia*, London, 1909, no. 1, silver kettle by N. Sprimont. See also *Trans. E.C.C.*, 1939, pl. 11c.

35 William Chaffers, *Marks and Monograms on European and Oriental Pottery and Porcelain*, 15th edn, London, 1965, Vol. II, 275, entry for 28 April 1756 in the Bow Memorandum Book.

36 Bellamy Gardner, 'An Early Allusion to English Porcelain, Gouyn's Will, and some Chelsea Models', 1929, *Trans. E.P.C.*, No. 2: pl. VIIa, pair of Bow busts of *Mongolian Prince and Princess*; pl. VIIb, carved wall-brackets with *Mongolian Heads*.

37 H. G. Tait, 'Some Consequences of the Bow Special Exhibition. Part III, Alderman Arnold and Thomas Frye', 1960, *Apollo*, Vol. LXXI, 181–5: 183, pair of Bow *Sphinxes* on rectangular wedge-shaped bases; 183, fig. IV, engraving of similar *Sphinxes* c.1738 by J. F. Blondel.

38 T. H. Clarke, 'The French Influence at Chelsea', 1954, *Trans. E.C.C.*, Vol. 4, 44–7, pl. 24c, Vincennes group of *Two Putti with a Dolphin*.

39 Sotheby's Sale Catalogue 13.11.73, lot 23, Longton Hall group of *Two Putti with a Dolphin*.

40 F. Severne MacKenna, *Chelsea Porcelain, the Red Anchor Wares*, Leigh-on-Sea, 1951, pl. 48, fig. 95, Chelsea group of *Two Putti playing with a Fish*.

41 Len Adams and Yvonne Adams, *Meissen Portrait Figures*, London, 1987, col. pl. XLVII, model of the Dresden court lace-maker *Barbara Uttman* by J. F. Eberlein.

42 *Trans. E.C.C.*, 1969, Vol. 7, pt. 2, pls 29b–c, Bow biscuit models of *Huntsman and Lady*.

43 H. G. Tait, 'Some Consequences of the Bow Porcelain Special Exhibition. Part II', 1960, *Apollo*, Vol. LXXI, 93–8: 95, fig. iv, Bow *Fortune Telling Group*; 95, fig. v, 'La Bonne Aventure', engraved by P. Aveline; 96, fig. vi, painting by François Boucher.

44 K. Berling, 'Das Meissner Porzellan und seine Geschichte', Leipzig, 1900, 131, fig. 195, Meissen models after Lancret of *Liberty and Matrimony*.

45 British Museum, Drawings and Prints Department. Sixty red chalk drawings of *Les cris de Paris* by Edmé Bouchardon, bound *en face* with engravings of the same by the Comte de Caylus.

46 Adams and Adams, op. cit.: col. pl. xxx, model of a *Map Seller* c.1740 by Kändler; p. 92, Bouchardon's drawing of the same.

47 Frank Hurlbutt, *Bow Porcelain*, London, 1926, pl. 35b, Bow model of a *Fruitress*, inset with Bouchardon's sketch.

48 Lane, op. cit., 99, cites a Meissen model of an *Absinthe Seller*.

49 Adams and Adams, op. cit., 116, Meissen model of a *Night Watchman*.

50 Lane, op. cit., pl. 61c, Derby *Absinthe Seller*.

51 Adams and Adams, op. cit., 186, a *Negress* by Kändler.

52 Berling, op. cit. n. 23, pl. 74, no. 771, kneeling *Turk*, c.1746 by Eberlein.

53 Catalogue of an exhibition of Early Derby Porcelain 1750–1770, held at 3 Bury Street, St James's, London by Robert Williams, 9–18 January 1973, fig. 58, Derby groups of *Ewe and Lamb* and *Goat and Kid*, c.1752.

54 S. Ducret, *Meissner Porzellan 1710–1810*, Berne, 1952, no. 116, *Ewe and Lamb*; no. 117, *Goat and Kid*.

55 Patrick Singe-Hutchinson, 'Some Rare White English Porcelain in the Dudley Deleringne Collection', 1970, *Connoisseur*, Vol. 175, No. 700, 102, pl. 9, Chelsea *Medici Lion*.

56 R. J. Charleston and John Ayres, *The James A. de Rothschild Collection at Waddesdon Manor: Meissen & Oriental Porcelain*, London, 1971, 169, no. 58, a seated *Lion* with one paw raised, one of a pair, c.1745 by Kändler.

57 Sotheby's Sale Catalogue 11.4.80, lot 171, a pair of prowling *Lions*, c.1745 by Kändler.

58 Office of Compline: 'Fratres: Sobrii estote et vigilate: quia adversarius diabolus tantum leo rugiens circuit, quaerens quem devoret.'

59 Berling, op. cit. n. 23, table 10, no. 7, Meissen model of Count Brühl's *Pug Dog*.

60 Margot Newman, 'A Synonymous Concept – Porcelain Animals and Kaendler', 1971, *Antique Dealer & Collector's Guide*, January, 74–80, pls 7–8, *Pug Dogs* by Kändler.

61 Charleston and Ayres, op. cit., 162, no. 55, a pair of Meissen *Roquets* with cropped ears.

62 Adams and Adams, op. cit., 20, *Masonic Group* incorporating a Dame of the Moporden, by Kändler.

63 *Seated Pug Dog*, Chelsea c.1755, in a private collection.

64 Sotheby's Sale Catalogue 22.5.86, lot 86, Derby *Seated Pug Dog*.

65 Bernard Watney, 'Snowman Figures from Longton Hall, Staffordshire', 1974, *Antiques*, August, 278–84, fig. 18, *Recumbent Pug Dog*.

66 Sheenah Smith, *Lowestoft Models in the Castle Museum at Norwich*, London, 1985, Vol. II: nos 103–4, *Seated Pug Dogs*; no. 106, *Standing Pug Dog*.

67 Christie's Sale Catalogue 23.2.87, lot 45, Staffordshire earthenware *Pug Dog*.

68 Hackenbroch, op. cit. n. 8, pl. 13, fig. 15, a Chelsea taperstick *Crane*.

69 P. J. Donnelly, *Blanc de Chine*, London, 1969, pl. 112b, *Chinese Crane* beside a taperstick.

70 *Trans. E.C.C.*, 1966, Vol. 6, pt. 2, pl. 56, a Bow *Owl*, with three claws on one foot and four on the other.

71 Lane, op. cit., 89, n. 3.

CHAPTER 13

1 Peter Bradshaw, 'Some 18th Century Porcelain Figures with Blue Eyes', 1975, *Northern Ceramic Society Journal*, Vol. II, 93–8.

2 P. L. Duchartre, *The Italian Comedy*, New York, 1966. Original French edn, Paris, 1929.

3 Howard Daniel, *Callot's Etchings*, New York, 1974,

4 Yvonne Hackenbroch, *Meissen and other Continental Porcelain, Faience and Enamel in the Irwin Untermyer Collection*, Cambridge, Mass., 1956, pl. 36, fig. 57, a *Scowling Harlequin*, c.1738–40, by J. J. Kändler.

5 Hugo Morley-Fletcher, *Meissen*, London, 1971, 84–5, seated *Harlequin* with bagpipes and *Columbine* with a hurdy-gurdy, c.1740, by Kändler.

6 Victoria & Albert Museum, no. A.59–1956, a bronze *Boy Shepherd Piper*, by Giovanni da Bologna.

7 Reginald Blunt, *The Cheyne Book of Chelsea China and Pottery*, London, 1924, pl. 11, no. 157, seated *Harlequin* with bagpipes, Chelsea c.1756.

8 Bernard Watney, *Longton Hall Porcelain*, London, 1957, pl. 40a, seated *Harlequin* with bagpipes and *Columbine* with a hurdy-gurdy, Longton Hall c.1756.

9 Bernard Rackham, *Catalogue of the Schreiber Collection . . .*, London, 1915, Vol. I, pl. 6, no. 41 (new no. 54a), pot-pourri vase with *Boy Piper* as finial, Bow c.1760.

10 Erica Pauls-Eisenbeiss, *German Porcelain of the 18th Century*, London, 1972, Vol. I, 319–41, Italian Comedy models of the Weissenfels series: 323, *Columbine* dancing; 324, *Pantaloon*; 327, *Mezzetin*; 329, the *Doctor*; 339, *Pierrot*; 337, *Narcissus*.

11 K. Berling, *Das Meissner Porzellan und seine Geschichte*, Leipzig, 1900, pl. xii, 5, a standing *Harlequin* c.1740 by Kändler.

12 F. Severne MacKenna, *Chelsea Porcelain, the Red Anchor Wares*, Leigh-on-Sea, 1951, 97 and fig. 135, the erroneous identification of *Narcissus* as 'The Captain'.

13 Len Adams and Yvonne Adams, *Meissen Portrait Figures*, London, 1986, 213, the *Captain*, by P. Reinicke c.1744.

14 Rupert Brooke, *The Complete Poems*, London, 1932, 68–9.

15 MacKenna, op. cit., 65, fig. 130, Chelsea models of *Mezetin*, *Narcissus* and the *Doctor*, c. 1756.

16 Marianna-Roland Michel, *Watteau, an Artist of the 18th Century*, London, 1987, pl. 218, *Heureux Age d'Or*, engraving after Watteau.

17 Adams and Adams, op. cit., 206, children attired as *Harlequin* and *Columbine*, c.1765, by Kändler.

18 Julia Poole, *Plagiarism Personified?*, Cambridge, 1986, 23–4. Catalogue of an exhibition held 15 June to 31 July 1986 at the Fitzwilliam Museum.

19 F. Severne MacKenna, *Chelsea Porcelain, the Gold Anchor Wares*, Leigh-on-Sea, 1952, pl. 57, fig. 110, the *Four Elements*, Chelsea, c.1759.

20 Jacques Girard, *Versailles Gardens, Sculpture and Mythology*, London, 1985, 28, *Air*, by Le Hongre.

21 Ibid., 31, *Earth*, by Massou.

22 Ibid., 30, *Water*, by Le Gros.

23 Ibid., 29, *Fire*, by Dossier.

24 Simon Thomassin, *Recueil des figures, groupes, thermes, fontaines, vases, statues, et autres ornamens de Versailles*, Amsterdam, 1695.

25 Bernard Rackham, 'Mr. Wallace Elliot's Collection of English Porcelain', 1927, *Connoisseur*, Vol. LXXVIII, 7–15, no. vi, *Neptune riding a Dolphin*, and *Jupiter astride an Eagle*, wrongly ascribed to Derby.

26 K. Berling, *Festive Publication to Commemorate the 200th Jubilee of the Oldest European China Factory*, Meissen, 1910, table 9, *Mercury* c.1742, by Eberlein.

27 Ibid., table 6, no. 12, *Apollo*, c.1740, by Eberlein.

28 J. Dixon, *English Porcelain of the 18th Century*, London, 1952, pl. 38, Derby model of *Diana*, c.1758.

29 John Warrack, *Greek Sculpture – One Hundred Illustrations*, London, c.1910, pl. 69, archaic Greek marble known as *Artemis Chasseuse*, Louvre.

30 K. Berling, *Königlich–Sächsische Porzellan Manufaktur Meissen, 1710–1910*, Dresden, 1911, pl. 9, fig. 4, *Mars* c.1747, by Kändler.

31 R. W. Symonds, *Thomas Tompion, His Life and Work*, London, 1951, fig. 33, clock with *Minerva* finial.

32 Hugh Tait, *Porcelain*, New York and London, 1962, pl. 34, the *Temple of Minerva*, c.1745–50, by Kändler.

33 R. J. Charleston and Geoffrey Willis, 'The Bow Flora and Michael Rysbrack', 1956, *Apollo*, Vol. LXIII, 125–7.

34 Arthur Lane, *English Porcelain Figures of the 18th Century*, London, 1961, 32.

35 Cecil Higgins Museum, Bedford, a Chelsea model emblematic of *Smelling*, c.1760, sometimes called 'Flora'.

36 Houghton Hall, a model by Eberlein c.1750, emblematic of *Smelling*.

37 Margaret Newton, 1978, *Northern Ceramic Society News Letter*, No. 31, item 17.

38 Peter Bradshaw, *18th Century English Porcelain Figures, 1745–1795*, Woodbridge, 1981, col. pl. C, group representing *Charity*, Chelsea c.1760.

39 George Savage, *18th Century German Porcelain*, London, 1958, pl. 43a, a *Prelate giving Benediction* c.1740, by Kändler.

40 Adams and Adams, op. cit., 65, *Nun of the Order of St John* c.1742, by Kändler.

41 Lane, op. cit., 51, n.: *Briefve Histoire de l'Institution des Ordres Religieux*, Paris, 1658, with illustrations by Odoardo Fialetti; *Courte et solide Histoire de la Fondation des Ordres Religieux*, Amsterdam, 1688, with engravings by Adrien Schooncbeck; Idem, Augsburg, 1692–3, with engravings by Daniel Steuder; *Ordinum Religiosarum in Ecclesia Militanti Catalogus*, Rome, 1706–10, engravings by Filippo Bonanni.

42 Andrew Dando, Late stock, sold in 1986.

43 Rainer Rückert, *Meissner Porzellan 1710–1810*, Munich, 1966, 237, pl. 976, seated *Nun with star-spangled veil*, c.1744 by Kändler.

44 Bernard Watney, 'The King, the Nun and Other Figures', 1968, *Trans. E.C.C.*, Vol. 7, pt. 1, pl. 56a, Chaffers's Liverpool *Nun* in a habit decorated with floral sprays.

45 Poole, op. cit., 23.

46 Girard, op. cit., 47, marble emblematic of *Africa*, by Jean Cornu.

47 Ibid., 48, marble by Leonard Roger of *Asia*.

48 Ibid., 47, marble by Giles Guérin of *America*.

49 Ibid., 46, marble by Pierre Mazeline of *Europe*.

50 Ibid., 52, marble by Jean Drouilly of *Epic Poetry*.

51 The names of four mistresses of Louis XV: 'It is the same here as it is at Court — made of stone, without heart or bowels!'

52 Frank Hurlbutt, *Bow Porcelain*, London, 1926, pl. 51b, the *Antique Seasons* c.1755, by F. E. Meyer.

53 Christie's Sale Catalogue, 28.3.1977, lot 106, the *Classical Seasons* c.1746, by Eberlein.

54 MacKenna, op. cit. n. 12, pl. 54, fig. 108, Chelsea bustos of *Pagan Gods*.

55 Pauls-Eisenbeiss, op. cit., 110–11, the *Chinese Magician and Family* c.1745, by Reinicke.

56 I. Smith, 'An 18th Century Turkish Delight', 1964, *Connoisseur*, Vol. CLVI, 215–19, no. 958.

57 C. H. Fischer, *Katalog der Sammlung. Alt Meissner Porzellan des Herrn Rentners C.H. Fischer im Dresden*, Cologne, 1906, 146, no. 958, standing *Turk and Levantine Lady* c.1746, by Eberlein.

58 Yvonne Hackenbroch, *Chelsea Porcelain, Pottery and Enamel in the Irwin Untermyer Collection*, Cambridge, Mass., 1957, pl. 21, fig. 36, Chelsea standing *Turk and Levantine Lady* c.1756.

59 R. J. Charleston and John Ayres, *The James A. de Rothschild Collection at Waddesdon Manor: Meissen & Oriental Porcelain*, London, 1971, 118–21, no. 34, seated *Turk and Levantine Lady* holding shells c.1746, by Eberlein.

60 F. A. Barrett and A. L. Thorpe, *Derby Porcelain*, London, 1971, pls 65–6, pair of Derby *Blackamoors*, c.1762.

61 John Twitchett, *Derby Porcelain*, London, 1980, pl. 39, pair of Derby *Turks*.

62 Adams and Adams, op. cit., 183, *Negress with basket of Fruit*; 184, *Negro Page*, c.1748 by Reinicke.

63 Pauls-Eisenbeiss, op. cit., 196–7, the *Hand Kiss*, by Kändler c.1737.

64 Hurlbutt, op. cit., pl. 35b, inset, drawing of a *Cook* by Edmé Bouchardon.

65 Adams and Adams, op. cit., 95; Bouchardon's drawing of the *Savoyard Drummer*; also model by Kändler c.1748.

66 Morley-Fletcher, op. cit., 86–7, a pair of *Woodmen*, by Kändler c.1745.

66a Adams and Adams, op. cit., 161, Bouchardon's drawing of a *Woodman with a saw*.

67 E. Dacier and A. Vuaflart, *Jean de Jullienne et les graveurs de Watteau*, Paris, 1929, Vol. I, no. 6, engraving by Laurent Cars, after Watteau, of 'La Diseuse d'Aventure'.

68 Adams and Adams, op. cit., 114, a *Street Cook* by P. Reinicke c.1757.

69   Ibid., col. pl. XXXII, *Peep-Showman* by P. Reinicke c.1757.

70   Ibid., 162, *Tinker* by Kändler c.1750.

71   R. Blunt, op. cit., pl. 9, no. 143, the *Rat Catcher*; pl. 9, no. 216, the *Salt Box Player*, both Chelsea c.1756.

72   Adams and Adams, op. cit., 123, drawing by F. Boucher of 'Two Flower Girls'; col. pl. XXXV, model of a *Flower Girl*, by Kändler and Reinicke c.1755.

73   Late Fitzhenry Collection, *Boy and Girl Fish Sellers*, by Eberlein c.1748.

74   Albert Amor Ltd, late stock, a boy *Fish Seller* wearing a soft cap.

75   Berling, op. cit. n. 26, table 8, no. 297, the *Piedmontese Bagpiper* c.1741, by Kändler; *Apollo*, 1925, 154, engraving by J. Daullé after J. Dumont le Romain of the *Piedmontese Bagpiper*.

76   Pauls-Eisenbeiss, op. cit., 81–2, *Tyrolean Dancers* c.1738, by Eberlein.

77   Frank Stoner, *Chelsea, Bow and Derby Porcelain Figures* Newport, 1955, pl. 54, Derby *Tyrolean Dancers*.

78   Hugo Morley-Fletcher, *Investing in Pottery and Porcelain*, London, 1968, col. pl. facing p. 55, Chelsea *Tyrolean Dancers*.

79   Fitzwilliam Museum, Chinese copy of *Tyrolean Dancers*.

80   MacKenna, op. cit. n. 12, pl. 65, fig. 129, Chelsea *Flower Girl* emblematic of 'Spring', c.1756.

81   T. Clarke, 1959, *Trans. E.C.C.*, Vol. 4, pl. 24, wood and bronze versions of a *Pilgrim*.

82   J. G. Mann, *Catalogue of Sculpture in the Wallace Collection*, London, 1931, S.244, replica of a *Pilgrim*, for which a Flemish source is suggested.

83   Adams and Adams, op. cit., col. pl. xxix, *Woman playing a Guitar* c.1750, by Eberlein.

84   MacKenna, op. cit. n. 12, pl. 74, fig. 147, Chelsea *Woman playing a Guitar* c.1757.

85   John Twitchett, *Derby Porcelain*, London, 1980, pl. 366, Bloor Derby *Woman playing a Guitar* and companion *Fiddler*.

86   David Wakefield, *French 18th Century Painting*, London, 1984, pl. 10, François Boucher's portrait of the *Marquise de Pompadour*.

87   Sotheby's Sale Catalogue, 14.6.1988, lot 539, seated male *Cellist* and *Hurdy-gurdy Girl* c.1765, Chelsea.

88   Adams and Adams, op. cit., col. pl. lv, *Columbine Dancing* c.1748, by Kändler.

89   Christie's Sale Catalogue, 23.2.1987, lot 247, *Columbine Dancing* wearing a hat c.1756, Chelsea.

90   Sotheby's Sale Catalogue, 22.5.1984, lot 134, small Longton Hall models of *New Dancers* c.1754.

91   Robert Williams, *Early Derby Porcelain, 1750–1770*, London, 1977, catalogue of an exhibition held at 3 Bury Street, St James's, fig. 20, early Derby models of *New Dancers* c.1754.

92   Adams and Adams, op. cit., col. pl. v, *Huntsman and Lady*, each with a gun; col. pl. vi, a pair of *Falconers*. Both c.1745–6, by Eberlein.

93   Bradshaw, op. cit. n. 38, pl. 89, *Boy Shepherd Piper and Dancing Shepherdess*, dry-edge Derby.

94   Christie's Sale Catalogue, 18.6.1984, lot 291, Bow *Boy Shepherd Piper* in Scottish dress; D. G. Rice, *Derby Porcelain, the Golden Years 1750–1770*, London, 1983, col. pl. L, Derby versions of *Boy Shepherd Piper* and *Dancing Shepherdess*, in Scottish dress.

95   Adams and Adams, op. cit., 47, *Shepherd playing a Recorder* and *Shepherdess with Flowers* c.1750, by Kändler and Reinicke.

96   T. H. Clarke, 'Sir Charles Hanbury Williams and the Chelsea Factory', 1988, *Trans. E.C.C.*, Vol. 13, pt. 2, 110–20, pl. 78a, *Shepherd Bagpiper*; pl. 78b, companion *Shepherdess*. Both c.1748, by Eberlein.

97   Hugh G. Tait, *Bow Porcelain 1744–1776. A Special Exhibition of Documentary Material to Commemorate the Bi centenary of the Retirement of Thomas Frye* [British Museum, October 1959 to April 1960], London, 1959, cat. no. 101, figs 31–2, *Shepherd Bagpiper* inscribed IB 1757.

98   Rice, op. cit., col. pl. K, late Derby versions of *Liberty and Matrimony*.

99   *Antique Dealer & Collector's Guide*, May 1989, 23, portrait of the Marquess of Granby, by Sir Joshua Reynolds, National Army Museum, Chelsea.

100   Adams and Adams, op. cit., 133, engraving of a *Pimp* and *Courtesan* by Pierce Tempest, after M. Laroon, 132, models of the *Marquis and a Coquette* c.1750, by Reinicke; 116, water-colour sketch of the *Marquis*, by Christophe Huet; 115, models of a *Gallant and Lady*, c.1756, by Reinicke.

101   Robert Schmidt, *Das Porzellan als Kunstwerk und Kulturspiegel*, Munich, 1925. English edn by W. A. Thorpe, *Porcelain as an Art and Mirror of Fashion*, London, 1932, 308–9, engraving by Filloeul, after Pater, of 'Le Baiser Rendu'; fig. 208, Höchst group by J. F. Lück based on the engraving.

102   Hackenbroch, op. cit. n. 4, pl. 20, fig. 27, models comprising the *Blown Kiss* c.1755, by Kändler.

103   Adams and Adams, op. cit., 42, miniature *Equestrian Hussar* c.1742, by Kändler.

104   Sotheby's Sale Catalogue, 16.10.1990, lot 67, *Infant Bacchus* feeding grapes to a leopard c.1760, by Kändler.

105   Pamela Klaber, *Oriental Influence on European Porcelain, or Comparative Collecting* [Exhibition held at 2B Hans Road, Kensington, 10–23 April], London, 1978, pl. 72, *Naked Putto* with vase, c.1740, by Kändler; pl. 72b, Bow copy.

106   Some have suggested a baroque bronze as the source of the two porcelain groups but they are more likely by reason both of subject and treatment to follow rococo painting.

107   J. Guelard, *Singeries ou Différentes Actions de la Vie Humaine représentées par des Didiées au Public. Gravées sur les desseins de C. Huet*, c.1740.

108   Adams and Adams, op. cit., 194–5, ten models of the *Affenkapelle* c.1752, by Kändler.

109   John Austin, *Chelsea Porcelain at Williamsburg*, Virginia, 1977, 121–9, Chelsea *Monkey Musicians* c.1756.

110   Rückert, op. cit., nos 115–16, *Bullfinches*, c.1740 by Kändler.

111   Charleston and Ayres, op. cit., 154–5, no. 52, *Goldfinches*, by Kändler, c.1740–5, on a decorative clock.

112   Hackenbroch, op. cit. n. 4, fig. 10, *Parrot*; fig. 8, pair of *Parrots eating nuts*, c.1738 by Kändler.

113   S. Ducret, *Meissner Porzellan*, Bern, 1952, nos 1137–8, *Cockerel and Hen* c.1738, by Kändler.

114   Sotheby's Sale Catalogue, 11.4.1980, lot 170, *Cats seated with Prey* c.1736, by Kändler.

115   S. Ducret, *Meissner Porzellan 1710–1810. Ausstellung im Bayerischen Nationalmuseum München. Katalog Gearbeitet von Rainer Rückert*, Munich 1966: nos 1160, 1161, 1162 and 1166, Meissen *Sheep*; nos 1156, 1157 and 1172, Meissen *Cattle*.

116   Christie's Sale Catalogue, 20.10.1986, lot 169, Chelsea recumbent *Ewe and Ram*; standing examples in a private collection. Ibid., lot 171, Chelsea recumbent *Cow and Bull*; lot 172, Chelsea standing *Cow*.

117   Bradshaw, op. cit. n. 38, pl. 85, dry-edge Derby standing *Ewe and Ram*; F. Brayshaw Gilhespy, *Derby Porcelain*, London, 1961, pl. 151, Derby recumbent *Ewe*: Sotheby's Sale Catalogue, 25.3.1974, lot 193, Derby *Bull* and *Cow suckling a Calf*, both standing.

118   Berling, op. cit. n. 26, fig. 73, seated *Fox* c.1738, by Kändler.

119   Ducret, op. cit., nos 1153–4, Meissen *Goats*.

120   Charleston and Ayres, op. cit., 174–5, no. 60, pair of seated *Hares* c.1750, by Reinicke.

121   Sotheby's Sale Catalogue, 16.10.1990, lot 146, a seated *Hound Bitch* c.1752, Girl-in-a-Swing; Museum of Fine Arts, Boston, Sigmund Katz Collection, seated *Hound Dog*, companion model.

122   Peter Bradshaw, *Derby Porcelain Figures, 1750–1848*, London, 1990, pl. 10, dry-edged Derby *Wild Boars*.

123   Charleston and Ayres, op. cit., 171, no. 59, pair of recumbent *Lion and Lioness* c.1750, by Kändler.

124   Sotheby's Sale Catalogue, 11.3.1980, lots 168–9, a pair of *Monkeys*, c.1748, by Kändler.

125   Ducret, op. cit., nos 1150–1, *Stag and Doe* c.1740, by Kändler.

126   Charleston and Ayres, op. cit., 164, no. 56, pair of *Red Squirrels* with metal collars and chains c.1745, by Kändler.

127   Bradshaw, op. cit. n. 38, pl. 41, pair of *Squirrels*, red-anchor Chelsea.

128   Bradshaw, op. cit. n. 122, pl. 110, Derby seated *Red Squirrels*.

CHAPTER 14

1   F. Severne MacKenna, *Chelsea Porcelain, the Gold Anchor Wares*, Leigh-on-Sea, 1952, pl. 53, fig. 103, gold-anchor Chelsea models of *Apollo and the nine Muses*.

2   Margaret Legg, *Flowers and Fables. A Survey of Chelsea Porcelain 1745–1769*, National Gallery of Victoria, Australia, 1984, 65, pair of gold-anchor Chelsea groups known as the *Allegorical Seasons*.

3   Christie's Sale Catalogue 10.10.88, lot 275, gold-anchor Chelsea pair of *Harvesters*, $6\frac{3}{4}$in (17.5cm).

4   Frank Stoner, *Chelsea, Bow and Derby Porcelain Figures*, Newport, 1955, pl. 30, Chelsea group of the *Fortune Teller*.

5   H. W. Hughes, 'Authorship of some Designs on Porcelain and Enamel and Robert Hancock's Connection with Battersea and Bow', 1935, *Trans. E.C.C.*, No. 3, 85–96, pls XXXVIIa–b, engravings by Hancock after Boitard.

6   Bernard Watney, 'The Origins of some Ceramic Designs', 1975, *Trans. E.C.C.*, Vol. 9, pt. 3, 267–75, pair of Bow *Musicians*; pl. 180b, decorative brass fender. Originally discovered by Major Tapp.

7   Timothy Clifford, 'Derby Biscuit', 1969, *Trans. E.C.C.*, Vol. 7, pt. 2, 108–17, pl. 127c, Derby biscuit group of *Winged Time*; source suggested (p. 115) to be a transposed adaptation of the marble *Venus* by Giovanni da Bologna.

8   Len Adams and Yvonne Adams, *Meissen Portrait Figures*, London, 1983, 78, Meissen model of Cronus.

9   F. Severne MacKenna, *Chelsea Porcelain, the Triangle and Raised Anchor Wares*, Leigh-on-Sea, 1948, pl. 50, fig. 100, Girl-in-a-Swing group of *Fox and Stork*.

APPENDICES

1   P. L. Duchatre, *The Italian Comedy*, New York, 1966, 83–5.

2   Ibid., 315–45.

3   Howard Daniel, *Callot's Etchings*, New York, 1974: pl 86, Pantalone; pl. 87, Il Capitano; pl. 88, Scapino; pls 104–27, small etchings in the Mannerist style.

4   Marianna-Roland Michel, *Watteau, an Artist of the Eighteenth Century*, London, 1984. Paintings by Watteau: no. 144, 'Mezzetin'; no. 146, 'Mezzetin le donner de serenade'; no. 173, 'Pierrot content'; no. 175, 'La Partie quarre'. Engravings after Watteau: no. 172, 'Belles, n'écoutez rien', by C. N. Cochin; no. 173, 'Pour garder l'honneur d'une belle', by C. N. Cochin; no. 176, 'Les Jaloux', by G. Scotin; no. 177, 'Harlequin jaloux', by Chedel.

5   E. Dacier and A. Vualflart, *Jean de Jullienne et les graveurs de Watteau au XVIII siècle*, Paris, 1929.

6   R. M. A. Stevenson, *Rubens's Paintings and Drawings*, London, 1939, pl. 94, 'Saturn devouring one of his Children'.

7   F. Severne MacKenna, *Chelsea Porcelain, the Red Anchor Wares*, Leigh-on-Sea, 1951, pl. 57, fig. 114.

8   Peter Bradshaw, *Derby Porcelain Figures 1750–1848*, London, 1989, col. pl. VI.

9   F. Severne MacKenna, *Champion's Bristol Porcelain*, Leigh-on-Sea, 1946, figs 100–3, *The Four Classical Elements*, including *Vulcan* representing *Fire*, beside an anvil, Bristol, c.1772.

10 Robert Graves, *The Greek Myths*, Penguin Books, revised edn, 1960, Vols I and II.

11 Wallace Elliott, 'Reproductions and Fakes of English 18th Century Ceramics', 1939, *Trans. E.C.C.*, Vol. 2, No. 7, 67–82.

12 Peter Bradshaw, *18th Century English Porcelain Figures, 1745–1795*, Woodbridge, 1981, 270–88.

13 W. B. Honey, *German Porcelain*, London, 1947, 47.

14 John Cushion, 'Fakes of Collectors' Pieces', 1975, *Antique Collecting*, Vol. 10, No. 3, 22–5.

15 Geoffrey Godden, *Eighteenth-century English Porcelain. A Selection from the Godden Reference Collection*, London, 1985, 343–6.

16 George Savage, *Forgeries, Fakes and Reproductions*, London, 1963, chap. V, Ceramics.

17 George Savage, personal communication.

18 Godden, op. cit., pl. 293.

19 Bradshaw, op. cit., pls 172–4.

20 Arthur Lane, *English Porcelain Figures of the Eighteenth Century*, London, 1961, 62, n. 4; 74; 98, n. 2.

21 David Battie, 'The Black Arts', 1980, *Ceramics*, Vol. II, 81–6.

22 F. Severne MacKenna, *Chelsea Porcelain, the Triangle and Raised Anchor Wares*, London, 1948, 71.

23 Peter Bradshaw and Ronald Grainger, 'Evidence that a Few Bow Figures were Cast Solid', 1973, *Northern Ceramic Society Journal*, Vol. I, 41–4.

PICTURE CREDITS

Figures refer to Plate numbers

Peter Bradshaw: 16, 25, 27, 69, 71, 74, 75, 92, 94, 95, 98, 99, 100, 101, 105, 106, 117, 123, 127, 128, 136, 148, 152, 153, 158, 169; Colour Plates I–VII, IX–XIV. British Museum: 37, 41, 50, 114, 230. Castle Howard (Hon. Simon Howard): 22. Cecil Higgins Art Gallery: 4, 7, 49. Christies: 5, 29, 32, 33, 34, 35, 42, 48, 51, 55, 56, 57, 59, 62, 66, 126, 127, 131, 137, 144, 147, 148, 151, 158, 160, 170, 171, 177, 178, 179, 183 (Manson & Woods), 189, 193, 194, 199, 207, 211, 212, 217, 218, 222, 227, 231, 233, 234, 237. Dudley Delevinge Collection: 58. Fitzwilliam Museum, Cambridge: 11, 28, 120, 137, 139. George R. Gardiner, Museum of Ceramic Art, Ontario: 9. Grosvenor Antiques: 72, 112, 136, 177, 213, 236. Hoff Antiques: 125. Frank Hurlbutt: 111. Louvre, Paris: Fig. 16. Metropolitan Museum, New York: 12, 209, 210. Museum of Fine Arts, Boston, Massachusetts: 13, 14, 26, 43, 52, 64, 78 (Gift of Mrs Sigmund J. Katz). National Museum of Ireland: 1, 2, 40. Pallant House Gallery, Chichester (Geoffrey Freeman Collection): 8, 115, 175, 180, 196. Phillips: 19, 147, 167. Private Collections: 18, 46, 70, 73, 78, 79, 83, 102, 124, 131, 132, 134, 138, 143, 144, 146, 162, 164, 172, 195, 197, 198, 201, 202, 203, 204, 208, 214, 220, 228, 229, 235. George Savage: 30, 90, 91, 141, 145, 157; Colour Plate VIII. Sotheby's: 17, 20, 61, 67, 76, 77, 82, 84, 85, 87, 89 (Parke Bernet), 93, 103, 107, 121, 135, 149, 150, 156, 163, 165, 166, 173, 181, 185, 186, 190, 191, 200, 205, 206, 216, 219, 223, 232. Simon Spero: 10. Temple Newsam House, Leeds: 15, 44, 104. David Thorn Collection: 24, 36, 53, 54, 81, 160, 184, 187, 188, 192. Tullie House, Carlisle: 176, 224 (W. H. Williamson bequest). Upton House, National Trust: 96, 97, 154, 155. Victoria and Albert Museum: Plates 3, 6, 21, 23, 31, 45, 47, 63, 65, 68, 80, 86, 88, 110, 116, 122, 151, 161, 168, 182, 215. Dr B. Watney: 38, 39. Williams College Museum of Art, Williamstown, Massachusetts, gift of Judge Irwin Untermyer: 221 (54. 25).